I0321490

The Sorrowful Muslim's Guide

Based at the Aga Khan Centre in London, the Aga Khan University Institute for the Study of Muslim Civilisations is a higher education institution with a focus on research, publications, graduate studies and outreach. It promotes scholarship that opens up new perspectives on Muslim heritage, modernity, religion, culture, and society. The Institute aims to create opportunities for interaction among academics and other professionals in an effort to deepen the understanding of pressing issues affecting Muslim societies today.

In Translation: Modern Muslim Thinkers

Series Editor: Abdou Filali-Ansary

This series aims to broaden current debates about Muslim realities which often overlook seminal works produced in languages other than English. By identifying and translating critical and innovative thinking that has engendered important debates within its own settings, the series seeks to introduce new perspectives to the discussions about Muslim civilisations taking place on the world stage.

Available titles:

Islam: Between Message and History
Abdelmadjid Charfi

Islam and the Foundations of Political Power
Ali Abdel Razek

The Sorrowful Muslim's Guide
Hussein Ahmad Amin
Translated by Yasmin Amin and Nesrin Amin

Forthcoming titles:

Secularism in the Arab World: Contexts, Ideas and Consequences
Aziz al-Azmeh
Translated by David Bond

Islam and Human Rights
Mohsen Kadivar
Translated by Niki Akhavan

edinburghuniversitypress.com /series/tmmt

The Sorrowful Muslim's Guide

HUSSEIN AHMAD AMIN

Translated by
Yasmin Amin and Nesrin Amin

EDINBURGH
University Press
IN ASSOCIATION WITH

THE AGA KHAN UNIVERSITY
INSTITUTE FOR THE STUDY OF MUSLIM CIVILISATIONS

The opinions expressed in this volume are those of the authors and do not necessarily reflect those of the Aga Khan University, Institute for the Study of Muslim Civilisations.

Edinburgh University Press is one of the leading university presses in the UK. We publish academic books and journals in our selected subject areas across the humanities and social sciences, combining cutting-edge scholarship with high editorial and production values to produce academic works of lasting importance. For more information visit our website: edinburghuniversitypress.com

© Hussein Ahmad Amin, *Dalīl al-Muslim al-ḥazīn ilā muqtaḍā al-sulūk fī al-qarn al-ʿishrīn: wa-dirāsāt islāmīyah ukhrā*, 1983
English Translation © Nesrin Amin and Yasmin Amin, 2018, 2020

Edinburgh University Press Ltd
The Tun – Holyrood Road
12 (2f) Jackson's Entry
Edinburgh EH8 8PJ

First published in hardback by Edinburgh University Press 2018

Typeset in 10.5/13 Adobe Garamond Pro by
IDSUK (DataConnection) Ltd

A CIP record for this book is available from the British Library

ISBN 978 1 4744 3707 3 (hardback)
ISBN 978 1 4744 3708 0 (paperback)
ISBN 978 1 4744 3709 7 (webready PDF)
ISBN 978 1 4744 3710 3 (epub)

The right of Hussein Ahmad Amin to be identified as author of this work has been asserted in accordance with the Copyright, Designs and Patents Act 1988 and the Copyright and Related Rights Regulations 2003 (SI No. 2498).

Contents

A Tribute to Hussein Ahmad Amin by his Brother, Galal Amin vii

Introduction – Hussein Amin: A Courageous Voice Calling for Reform 1

Foreword to the Tenth Edition 13

1 The Sorrowful Muslim's Guide 23

2 Reflections on the Evolution of the Prophet's Biographies in the East and West 41

3 Reflections on the Truth about Abū Lahab (the Judas of Banū Hāshim) 61

4 The Role of *Aḥādīth* (Traditions) Ascribed to the Prophet in the History of Islamic Societies 73

5 Is Sufism Islamic? 99

6 Reflections on the Status of the *Awliyā*ʾ 125

7 Political and Social Roots of Islamic Sects 145

8 The Decline in the Position of the Clergy in the Eyes of Muslims 159

9 The Chances of Successfully Establishing a Society Based on Islamic Principles 177

10 The Awaited Mahdi in Contemporary Times 189

11 A Plea for Religious Reform 199

Index 209

A Tribute to Hussein Ahmad Amin by his Brother, Galal Amin

Of my seven siblings, my brother Hussein was always closest to me, not only in terms of age (I am the youngest, he was the second youngest), but also in our love for reading and writing, and our intellectual pursuits in general. From a very young age, Hussein was driven by a thirst for knowledge and a desire to accumulate as much of it as possible. He was highly intelligent, and possessed a brilliant memory. From the time when he first started writing, his style was beautiful and fluent, becoming more forceful and eloquent as he got older.

At the age of eight, Hussein embarked on writing a book on Umar Ibn Al-Khattab, whom he considered to be his role model at the time. His intention, he said, was to turn it into a three-volume masterpiece, only to find that his material had run out after the first thirty pages! This failed first attempt was followed by two historical novellas written at the age of ten, and a story, of which I still have a copy, titled *The Joy of Old Age*, written at the age of twelve, that I still find a delight to read. However, he was most proud of a novel he wrote soon after, titled *The Punishment*. My father, Ahmad Amin, wanted to encourage him to continue in his footsteps, and so he arranged for the Authorship, Translation and Publication Committee Press to print 200 copies of the book at his expense.

Hussein had a highly developed sense for beauty in literature, and would tirelessly roam the bookshops of Cairo and beyond for the next book on his reading list, and follow the news of the latest publications of authors he admired or believed to be significant.

His interests did not go unnoticed by our father, and so he asked the publisher of his books (the owner of the Al-Nahda Al-Misriyya bookshop in downtown Cairo) to allow Hussein to buy any books he wanted from the bookshop at a discount, to be deducted from my father's royalty payments. He only protested when he found that Hussein had purchased several volumes of André Gide's journals, a writer who my father believed to be immoral.

He read in English as much as he did in Arabic, and so quickly mastered both languages. I do not believe that I have met, or indeed heard of, anyone who succeeded as much as did Hussein in combining knowledge of Arab and Western literature at such a profound level, and in developing such a keen awareness of their aesthetic value, understanding their development and unlocking their secrets. Hussein was enthralled with Russian literature, but he was equally well versed on the minute details of the life and work of the likes of Goethe, Shakespeare, George Bernard Shaw and Henry James, as he was on the life and work of Al-Jahiz or Abu Hayan Al-Tawhidi, on Muḥammad's biographies and biographers, as well as contemporary Arab writers.

This wonderful, eclectic combination of Arab and Western literary influences shines through in his wide range of masterfully written works, including his play *The Imam* (on the life of Ali Ibn Abi Talib), his autobiography *Fī bayt Aḥmad Amīn* (*In the House of Ahmad Amin*), and his series of books on Islamic history and reform, starting with the widely acclaimed *The Sorrowful Muslim's Guide*.

Although reading and writing were his true passion, it was only in his late forties that Hussein finally found a publisher for his writings. I had introduced him to Ragaa Al-Naqqash, the Egyptian editor-in-chief of the popular Qatari *Al-Doha* magazine, who was hoping to turn the magazine into a platform for enlightened thought, and was therefore thrilled when Hussein sent him a series of articles which tackled various contentious issues on Islamic history and Islam in the modern world. The articles certainly elicited as much acclaim as they did outrage, and they ultimately led to the expulsion of Al-Naqqash from the magazine, and from Qatar. These and other articles were eventually collected and published in his book, *The Sorrowful Muslim's Guide*, in 1983.

As a result of the book's success, Hussein quickly became known as an "Islamic thinker", and this reputation was cemented with the publication of his subsequent works on similar issues. In his introduction to the fourth edition of *The Sorrowful Muslim's Guide*, Hussein confesses that he often perceived this label as a nuisance – not because he resented being thought of as an expert on Islamic affairs, but because he was frequently rebuked whenever he wrote in non-essay genres, or on non-Islamic topics: "Would the son of Sheikh Muhammad Abduh, for example, write romantic songs as you did"? He preferred to think of himself as a storyteller, a playwright, a poet and an essay writer, and argued that his versatility, and his varied interests, contributed to making his writing style more multidimensional, profound and compelling, regardless of the genre adopted.

And, indeed, it was, among other things, the great force and beautiful style of his writing that caused *The Sorrowful Muslim's Guide* to be received with enthusiasm and admiration among a large section of Arab readers. I am confident that a long time will pass before such issues are treated with equal force and depth.

Introduction
Hussein Amin: A Courageous Voice Calling for Reform

Paolo L. Branca, Catholic University of Milan

Hussein Ahmad Amin was born in Cairo in June 1932, where he also passed away in April 2014. He was educated at schools in Egypt before graduating from the Faculty of Law at Cairo University. Following his legal training he studied English literature in London, and subsequently practised law and worked as a broadcaster for Egyptian radio as well as the BBC Arabic World Service. He went on to a career in the Diplomatic Service of the Egyptian Ministry of Foreign Affairs. Following this, while he was Deputy Director of the Diplomatic Institute in Cairo, Hussein Amin produced some of his major works, namely, *Dalīl al-Muslim al-ḥazīn ilā muqtada-l-sulūk fi'l-qarn al-ᶜishrīn* (*A Guide for the Sad and Perplexed Muslim Concerning the Sort of Behaviour Required by and in the Twentieth Century*; translated here as *The Sorrowful Muslim's Guide*),[1] and *Ḥawla al-daᶜwa ᵓilā taṭbīq al-sharīᶜa* (*On the Implementation of Sharia*).[2] Both books elicited severe reactions from the official religious establishment and generated intense debate not only in Egypt, but around the Arab world more widely.

Hussein's father, Ahmad Amin (1886–1954), was the first teacher of the young Hussein. Ahmad had studied the classical Islamic disciplines at al-Azhar, where he came into contact with Muhammad Abduh, whose reformist views deeply influenced him. Ahmad subsequently became a teacher, after which he studied law at the newly established (1907) Islamic Judicial School (Madrassat al-qaḍāᵓ al-sharᶜī'), which also profoundly affected him.[3] After

---

1 Amīn, H. A., *Dalīl al-muslim al-hazīn ila muqtada al-sulūk fi-l-qarn al-ᶜishrīn*, Cairo: Dār al-Shurūq, 1983.

2 Amīn, H. A., *Ḥawla al-daᶜwa ᵓilā taṭbīq al-sharīᶜa*, Beirut: Dar al-Nahdah al-ᵓArabiyah, 1985.

3 For more on the effects of the Judicial School on contemporary Muslim thought, see, for example, Ghānim, D. A-W., *Athār madrassat al-qaḍāᵓ al-sharᶜī ᶜala al-fikr al-Islāmī al-muᶜāṣir*, Istanbul: Dār al-Maqāṣid, 2017.

working as a judge, he became a professor at Cairo University, eventually becoming the Dean of the Faculty of Literature at the same university.

In later years, Ahmad Amin conceived of a combined work with Taha Husayn to chart the history of Islamic culture. Taha Husayn published the first book in the series in 1926,[4] while Ahmad Amin published his well-known works on the intellectual history of Islamic culture between 1933 and 1952.[5] With respect to traditional production, these works stand out due to their subject, style and the sources used. In short, they are some of the most mature fruits of the Nahda, or Renaissance, that distinguished the Arab world at the end of the nineteenth century and beginning of the twentieth century. Soon the struggle for independence from colonialism and the nationalist and revolutionary regimes that followed would see a prevalence of apologetic and polemical works instead.

Ahmad Amin's unapologetic works and his critical view of certain historical developments greatly influenced Hussein. Indeed, Hussein took them a step further. For example, in his famous *Fajr al-Islam* (*Dawn of Islam*), Ahmad Amin wrote a few highly critical paragraphs on the way in which the *aḥādīth* (prophetic traditions) were collected and how several of the Prophet's Companions had accused one another of putting traditions in the Prophet's mouth. However, while Ahmad did not go on to say that these traditions were fabricated or forged, nor analyse the need and reasons for forging traditions at that time, Hussein did. He devotes an entire chapter (Chapter 4, "The Role of *Aḥādīth* (traditions) Ascribed to the Prophet in the History of Islamic Societies") in *The Sorrowful Muslim's Guide* to a discussion of the forged and fabricated traditions, the reasons for their fabrication and their continued use. While Ahmad Amin was a product of al-Azhar and a reformist, he was still conservative. Hussein did not have this loyalty to al-Azhar and went further in his criticism than his father.

Although Hussein was not a religious scholar like his father, he clearly benefited from his father's legacy and the surroundings in which he grew up. Indeed, such was his father's influence that Hussein wrote a book of memoirs entitled *Fī bayt Aḥmad Amīn* (*In the House of Ahmad Amin*).[6] In his later

---

4 *Fī al-shiʿr al-jāhilī* (*Pre-Islamic Poetry*), Cairo: Maṭbaʿat Dār al-Kutub al-Miṣrīyah, 1926.

5 *Fajr al-Islām* (*The Dawn of Islam*), Cairo: Maṭbaʿat al-Iʿtimād, 1938; *Duḥā al-Islām* (*The Aurora of Islam*), 3 vols., Cairo: Lagnit al-taʾlīf wa-l-targama, 1938; and *Zuhr al-Islām* (*The Noon of Islam*), 4 vols., Cairo: Maktabat al-Nahḍa al-Miṣrīya, 1952, which were then condensed into *Yawm al-Islām* (*The Day of Islam*), Cairo: Maktabat al-Nahdah al-Miṣriyah, 1952.

6 Amīn, H. A., *Fi bayt Aḥmad Amīn*, Cairo: Maktabah Madhbuli, 1989.

years, Ahmad Amin suffered from blindness. It was Hussein who read to him from the original sources his father had amassed in his library and who took down the thoughts that he dictated. This gave Hussein Amin an almost intimate familiarity with the ancient sources. In addition, thanks to Hussein's diplomatic appointments which had allowed him to travel around the world, he was able to tangibly experience the results of the intellectual stagnation his father had identified in his works. Furthermore, Hussein's diplomatic career exposed him to various schools of thought, especially modern Western ones, which affirmed the liberal and secular positions that he already held. From this awareness and his resulting sense of responsibility, came the intense pages of *The Sorrowful Muslim's Guide*, published here in English translation for the first time.[7]

As a 'Guide', it references the famous *Guide for the Perplexed* (*dalālat al-ḥāʾirīn*) by Mōsheh ben Maymōn, Mūsā ibn Maymūn ibn ʿAbd Allāh al-Qurṭubī al-Isrāʾīlī in Arabic, more commonly known as Maimonides (1135–1204). Without wishing to make improper comparisons between the great medieval philosopher and a modern Egyptian writer, the spirit of the former, which appears in his famous saying: "Do not consider it proof because it is written in books, for the liar who will deceive with his tongue will not hesitate to do the same with his pen," is also found in Chapter 4 of *The Sorrowful Muslim's Guide*:

> the jurists and scholars resorted to supporting any view which they saw as viable and desirable by a *ḥadīth* (prophetic tradition) that they ascribed to the Prophet, much like those who wrote the Book of Deuteronomy and then attributed it to Moses to give it an authoritative and trustworthy character. This practice became relatively easy after the death of the Companions' generation, who had alone been able to deny that the Prophet had uttered such and such *ḥadīth* (prophetic tradition). The jurists and scholars were reassured and their conscience rested easy, as they believed that putting words and sayings into the Prophet's mouth would serve the religion of Islam and stand against the worldly rule of the Umayyads.

7 It was previously translated into French as Amīn, H. A., *Le livre du musulman désemparé: pour entrer dans le troisième millénaire*, trans. R. Jacquemond, Paris: Editions la Découverte, 1992. However, the French translation omitted two complete chapters and several paragraphs in other chapters. The English translation is therefore the first complete translation in a European language.

A quotation from another book by Hussein Amin, published in 1985 and also written in the same spirit of critical enquiry, echoes a similar viewpoint:

> The number of legal provisions laid down explicitly by the Qur'an and in the traditions universally deemed valid is extremely low if compared to those contained in books of law. In the Qur'an, there are only about eighty verses with a juridical subject, such as those on the penalties for theft and adultery or concerning wills and inheritance. Most of these lines, moreover, are limited to stating general principles which allow different interpretations and applications, which can then be adapted to the requirements of different periods and different circumstances.[8]

Despite winning the prize for best work published in the previous year at the Cairo Book Fair in 1984, *The Sorrowful Muslim's Guide* was not received positively everywhere. Initially, most of the ideas explored in each chapter were published as articles in the Kuwaiti magazine *al-Arabi* and the Qatari magazine *al-Doha*. These articles generated heated discussions in several daily and weekly publications not only in Cairo, but around the Arab world. His writings met with fierce criticism from some quarters, including, for example, Ahmed Bahgat in *al-Ahram*, Ismail al-Kilani in Abu Dhabi's *Manar al-Islam*, and George Tarabishi in Bahrain's *al-Magalla al-Thaqafiyya*. Hussein was called a fame-hungry atheist and accused of disseminating evil, and worse. However, his work was also praised by other leading journalists of the time, such as Anis Mansur of *October*, who was the first to publish Hussein Amin's articles in Egypt. Fathi Radwan of *al-Hilal* called him the most important religious writer of the year, and Yusry Hussein of *al-Arab* described him as a writer who shakes the silence and reopens the doors of *ijtihād* (independent legal reasoning).

These discussions prompted Amin to expand his articles and collect them in *The Sorrowful Muslim's Guide* in order to provide them with more depth and substance. He also wanted the articles to incorporate a running theme, namely, that of refuting the misconception that the Prophet and his

8 Amīn, H. A., *Hawla al-daʾwah ila tatbiq al-shariʾah al-Islamiyah wa-dirasat Islamiyah ukhra*, Cairo: Dar al-Nahdah al-ʿArabiyah, 1985, p. 26.

Companions were infallible, and that Islam as a religion was not influenced by political and economic factors.

Like Muhammad Abduh and his own father before him, Hussein agreed that since Islamic law had been established in the past, it was changeable. He went a step further, arguing that many of its rules and regulations were not applicable to contemporary social problems. The publication of *The Sorrowful Muslim's Guide* reopened this debate. Whilst leading intellectuals in Egypt and the Arab world more widely commended Hussein Amin for his courage, knowledge and meticulous research, describing him as a voice of reform in a period of stagnation,[9] the book also generated much criticism from Muslim clerics, such as Mohamed al-Ghazali, for example. Several journalists, authors and public figures with a variety of Islamist leanings also attacked the book.[10] They were most critical of Amin's description of political Islam and his accusation that Islamists who, in his opinion, despite not knowing much about Islamic history, *Sharīᶜa* and *fiqh* (jurisprudence), demanded the application of *Sharīᶜa* in contemporary life. Amin argued extensively that political Islam developed as a result of social and economic decline as well as corruption in government circles. Islamists refuted this vehemently, arguing along the lines of the Muslim Brotherhood slogan that "Islam is the solution". These intense debates clearly illustrate that *The Sorrowful Muslim's Guide* addresses several subjects of great contemporary importance that are relevant to current global affairs and the challenges that face Muslim societies today. Indeed, at the time of its publication in 1983,

9 These included, for example, Sayyid Hegazy, Fathi Radwan, Ahmed al-Daᵓig and Salah Eissa.

10 These included Mohamed Said Ramadan Al-Bouti, known as the Shaykh of the Levant; Shaykh Adel Jalil Shalabi, who published a very critical review of the book in the *Middle Eastern Times*; as did Shaykh Abdel Moneim Selim in *al-Arabi*. Other critics were Mohamed Galal Kishk, Egyptian Islamist journalist and writer in *October*; Fahmy Howeidi in *al-Ahram*; and Saudi writer Mundhir al-Asᶜad, who wrote three highly polemical books refuting *The Sorrowful Muslim's Guide*. In 1990, he published the short book *Islām ākhir zaman: qirāᵓah fi ārāᵓ Ḥusayn Aḥmad Amīn* (*What has Islam Come To? A Reading of Husayn Ahmad Amin's Views*), Riyadh: Dār al-Miᶜrāj lil-Nashr wa-al-Tawzīᶜ, which was followed four years later by *Al-Kādhib al-ḥazīn wa-ḥabīb al-mulḥidīn wa-al-munaṣṣarīn, Ḥusayn Aḥmad Amīn* (*The Sorrowful Liar, Lover and Supporter of Atheists: Husayn Ahmad Amin*), Cairo: Dār al-Ṣaḥwah lil-Nash, 1994. Finally, in 1997, he published an expanded version of his first book titled *Islām ākhir zaman: tafnīd ᶜilmī shāmil li-abāṭīl al-mustashriqīn wa-al-mutagharribīn allatī saraqahā Ḥusayn Aḥmad Amīn* (*What has Islam Come To? A Complete Scientific Refutation of the False Claims of Orientalists and Westernised Writers stolen by Husayn Ahmad Amin*), Riyadh: Maktabat al-ᵓAbīkān, 1997.

Hussein Amin already foresaw the dangers of political Islam and the terrorist movements associated with it.

Moving now to the specific subject of the book. While it is not the intention here to summarise it or to offer a detailed description or commentary, its basic idea is strong and compelling. It recounts that today's Muslims are sorrowful because they cannot reconcile what they believe in and what their religion imposes on them, with what contemporary life demands from them. The sorrowful Muslims are torn, because if they follow the dictates of their religion, they will be forced to deny what has become familiar and prevalent among their contemporaries, and if they adopt what is commonplace and prevalent among their contemporaries, they will find themselves obliged to deviate from the principles of their religion and its teachings.

The book raises questions regarding issues about which many other Muslim intellectuals and thinkers have been silent; questions still considered taboo by many in the Muslim world. These include – among others – current religious practice versus the Islamic ideal; the many additions to the original revelation; the veracity of the Prophet's biography and his sayings; the development of Sufism; and the many historical and ideological influences on Islamic thought.

To illustrate the originality of Amin's arguments and how he developed them, I will discuss his analysis of the biographies of the Prophet; an apparently rather technical subject, but with a far wider scope. Indeed, the way in which the narrative of the founder of a religion is explored is revealing about the way in which the sense and the mission of a community are conceived.

The first of these biographies, *al-Maghāzī*, is an obvious example of this. In it, Muḥammad is mainly presented as a political and military leader. Yet in the first twelve years of his preaching, he was the representative of a few dozen monotheists in a pagan city which was largely hostile towards him. However, he had no armed clashes in this city. It was only in the following ten years, after the *Hijra* (migration of Muḥammad to Medina in 621) and until his death, that armed battles and skirmishes erupted. Since Muḥammad was clearly much more than a military leader during his first twelve years of preaching, it is clear that this type of literary genre was used more to support the needs of the Islamic conquests – in full swing at this time – than to faithfully reconstruct Muḥammad's life.

The subsequent *al-Sīra al-nabawiya* (Prophet's biographies), the more recent and far more 'politically correct' biographies, tend to paint Muḥammad as a precursor of, for example, ecological or feminist movements. For this reason, they are no less problematic in the eyes of serious scholars. Indeed, the continual risk is that current circumstances and fashions are followed, thereby fatally moving away from historical context and falling into the trap of apologetics and ideology. In *The Sorrowful Muslim's Guide*, Hussein Amin therefore highlights the need for a new and unapologetic biography of Muḥammad.

A similar discourse applies to the material known as the Sunna, or Prophetic Tradition, the collected deeds and words of the Prophet and his Companions. However, in this case the topic is much more sensitive and delicate, as these *aḥādīth* (sing. *ḥadīth*; or deeds, acts and words of the Prophet) are one of the main sources of Islamic law – as commonly understood – or the *Sharīᶜa*.

Hussein Amin was very critical of the idea that Islamic law could be applied in today's world. His chapter on *ḥadīth* is not only a critique of their various different historical abuses, but also of the claim by contemporary violent and militant groups engaged in *takfīr* (accusing someone of *kufr*, i.e., heresy or disbelief) and terrorism who claim their ideologies are based on *ḥadīth* – a very topical issue with regard to the so-called Islamic State and before that al-Qaeda.

However scrupulously and diligently Muslim scholars collected the traditions, they were collected over a long period of time characterised by violent oppositions between different sects and divergent interest groups in the *umma* (community of believers in the world). To this day, the effects of this can be felt. For example, the way in which the different and opposing creeds that evolved, and which are discussed in Chapter 7 ("Political and Social Roots of Islamic Sects") of the book, can be explained by their different contexts (historical, ideological, political, cultural and even economic). These creeds did not evolve alone, but rather in response to one another. These contexts and currents include Sufism, for example, which concentrated on the founding spiritual aspects of an authentic religious experience, just as other sects became the mouthpieces of the concerns of ethnic groups and communities that feared losing their voice in the structure of the nascent universal caliphate. In these cases, religion was employed as an instrument rather than as a genuinely theological application of the doctrinal aspects.

The Arabisation and perhaps also the sudden secularisation of Muslim societies promoted by new nation-states, paradoxically allowed anyone to approach the sources without the mediation of a category of specialists and scholars. The simple and even at times layman application of Islamic law is revealed in this context as window-dressing. It practically marginalises fundamental aspects of long years of dedication to responsible training and education. Even the eschatological visions of very early Islam, presented at the onset of the Prophet's mission as imminent, have been relegated to sometime in the future. This has very little influence on the present, except to re-emerge in caricatured and deviated form in the worst subversive and nihilist movements, the expression of a superficial and contradictory Westernisation and falsely linked with a celestial perspective worthy of this name.

In tackling these subjects, Hussein Amin's work is more courageous and explicit than most, since he addresses controversial subjects and muffles his explosive criticality with wisdom, wit and temperate satire. At the same time, as a faithful continuer of the reformist spirit of his father and his father's teachers, his work reflects the views of earlier reformist modernists, especially Muhammad Abduh.

His work can therefore be considered as the reconciliation between authenticity and modernity, or the reconciliation of Islam with modernity and the contemporary world. However, it is more representative of modern Islamic humanism in the tradition of historical Islamic humanism as practised by the Mu^{c}tazila (theological school founded on reason and rational thought that flourished under the ^{c}Abbāsid caliphate from the eighth to the eleventh centuries) and as apparent in the writings of many of their eminent scholars, most notably al-Jāḥiz (159/776–255/868 or 869). Hussein Amin can definitely be viewed as a member of this humanitarian tradition. His knowledge of classical Islamic culture and sources, as well as his equally thorough grounding in Western culture, allowed him to distinguish between the essentially original and the superfluous additions in religious belief. This enabled him to suggest reform of corrupted beliefs, and adjustment of religious feelings, local values and culture in order to adhere to the principles of humanism. He read the religious heritage inherited from his ancestors whilst wearing the glasses of humanism. After re-reading and interpreting it according to human values, he recognised that the past holds the present hostage by stifling it through fundamentalist Islamic thought.

The Sorrowful Muslim's Guide also echoes Hussein Amin's previous calls for reinstating *ijtihād* and to which he devoted a whole book.[11] This resulted in many heated discussions about whether or not the *Sharīʿa*, or rather Islamic law, could be applied in today's world. Some of these discussions became violent and he was accused of heresy. However, Hussein Amin stayed true to his convictions and reiterated his beliefs in his subsequent books. For example in *Ḥawla al-daʿwah ila taṭbīq al-sharīʿah al-Islāmiyah* (*Regarding the Call for the Application of Islamic Shari'a*) mentioned above, he included a chapter titled "Defending Dogs in Islam". This was because his daughter, being part of a family that kept dogs at home, had become upset after her religious studies teacher told her class that dogs were unclean and that angels do not enter a house where dogs are kept. For the sake of reason, rather than *taqlīd* – or blind following – Amin mined the pages of Islamic heritage for information and evidence for the source of this opinion, which he did not find.

Fundamentalists are accused of usually following blindly, unless the matter is in their own best interests. This brings to mind a well-known anecdote of a peasant meeting his neighbour, a religious cleric, to whom he says: "What do I do now that a dog has urinated on one of the walls of my house?" The cleric replies: "Nothing will help other than the demolition of this wall that was defiled!" The poor peasant replies: "But this is the wall separating your house and mine, so will you pay half the cost?" The cleric replies: "In this case a little water will purify the wall."

Hussein is a man to whom we must be grateful, since he is one of the many who, from Morocco to Indonesia, but also in the Diaspora, struggled and continue to struggle to make their voices heard. A deafening silence, complicit with too many interests that cannot be confessed but which are evident in their tragic consequences, is at long last broken in *The Sorrowful Muslim's Guide* in favour of listening more attentively to the voices of an Islam that wants to be modern, while remaining faithful to its origins.

These two intentions are opposed only in appearance, and are in actual fact complementary for all those who intend to save ancient traditions from the sad destiny of ending up in the display cases of a museum. Indeed, in

11 Amīn, H. A., *al-Ijtihād fi al-Islām Ḥaqq huwā amm wājib?* Cairo: al-Hay'ah al-Miṣrīyah al-'Āmmah lil-Kitāb, 1993.

addition to *The Sorrowful Muslim's Guide*, Hussein Amin also devoted books to discussing the state of Islam in a changing world,[12] to exploring renewed religiosity and Islamic revival, which he felt promoted rituals at the expense of core Islamic values and spirituality.[13]

The challenge facing reformers and followers of Islamic humanism, such as Hussein Amin, is that their attempts to apply humanity and reason to Islamic heritage, and their extraordinary efforts to free the original texts from previous interpretations and to offer a modern humane one instead, are not easily acceptable to the wider public. As radicalisation reaches new heights – thanks in part to certain interpretations of Islam – calls for reform have occasionally lacked direction and have suffered from an absence of public support. In Egypt, calls by the authorities for a "renewal of religious discourse" have been concurrent with the jailing of outspoken writers and scholars on charges of contempt for religion. In 2015, for example, Islam El-Behairy received a one-year prison sentence for criticising al-Bukhari and other scholars, such as Ibn Taymiyyah and the four founders of the Islamic Legal Schools. In 2016, writer Fatima Naoot received a three-year prison sentence for criticising the practice of ritual sacrifice during Eid al-Adha (the feast of the sacrifice). In February 2017, preacher Mohamed Abdullah Nasr was sentenced to five years in prison for criticising al-Bukhari and declaring he was the "awaited Mahdi". More than ever, perplexed and sorrowful Muslims need a voice that reconciles religious teachings and the demands of contemporary life.

Hussein Amin's message is therefore still as relevant and timely today as it was when it was first published. Eleven editions of the book have already been published in Arabic with a twelfth under way, indicating its popularity in Egypt and the wider Arab world. The value of its translation into English is not only to make an important work of liberal thought in modern Egypt available to the Anglophone world, but also to highlight antiquated religious thought and particular inherited customs that were subsumed into Islamic heritage and that urgently require radical disentangling and reinterpretation.

---

12 Amīn, H. A., *al-Islām fī 'ālam mutaghayir wa maqalat Islamiyyat ukhra*, Cairo: Maktabat Madbuli, 1988.

13 Amīn, H. A., *al-Mawqif al-ḥaḍārī min al-naza'āt al-dīnīyah wa-dirāsāt ukhrā*, Cairo: Sīnā lil-Nashr, 1994.

The Sorrowful Muslim's Guide

Foreword to the Tenth Edition

The Book The Sorrowful Muslim's Guide *in a Changing World*[1]

I recently re-read my book *The Sorrowful Muslim's Guide* in preparation for this edition (more than twenty-three years after the first edition). I did not find a single phrase or paragraph that necessitated deletion or change in the light of the events of the past twenty-three years.

However, some issues have become worthy additions after gaining in significance, for Muslims and non-Muslims alike, even being at the centre of their concerns. At the top of these concerns are two issues: terrorism and democratisation.

Terrorism

1. In the last chapter of his book about the history of the twentieth century *The Age of Extremes*, Eric Hobsbawm[2] predicted that terrorism would become a major feature of the twentieth century due to fundamental changes in the world order. Following the collapse of the Soviet Union and socialism in Eastern Europe, the United States dominated the world's resources and controlled the economies of recipient countries through aid packages as well as via International Monetary Fund and World Bank loans. This increased US capacity to pressure foreign governments or even overthrow them, and to destabilise them should they pursue policies that did not serve American interests, insisting on their right to independently take decisions. In view of the increasing difficulty for the opponents of US policy to escape, even if it was to distant caves in remote countries, there will be an increase in the number of disillusioned people, rebelling against

---

1 All footnotes are translators' footnotes, unless it is explicitly stated that they are the author's own footnotes.

2 Eric John Ernest Hobsbawm (1917–2012), British Marxist historian. Eric Hobsbawm, *The Age of Extremes: 1914–1991*, London: Michael Joseph, 1994.

such policies. They will resort to terrorism and acts of violence rather than pursuing normal channels of opposition and disobedience. They will resort to the dissemination of hostile ideas and attempt all possible scenarios – doomed to fail – to eliminate the injustice.

This situation is reminiscent of al-Nābighah al-Dhubiyānī[3] when he incurred the wrath of al-Nuᶜmān b. al-Mundhir[4] and chanted the following verse:

> You are like the night that will catch up with me
> Even if I think that my distance from you is large

It is also reminiscent of those who rebelled against the Roman emperors during the first and second centuries AD, when the vast Roman Empire was governed by one man. It was impossible for the opponents to find a safe haven to turn to and seek refuge in, so they increasingly resorted to the assassination of emperor after emperor, and to acts of sabotage that culminated in burning down Rome itself.

2. Contemporary international law considers acts of violence against civilians in peacetime as "terrorist acts". Many non-Muslims and non-Arabs (and perhaps also Muslims and Arabs themselves) denounced the recourse to such acts outside the battlefield. However, those seeking liberation are often unable to engage in a military confrontation with their enemy in combat. They are confident that they will face defeat in such a confrontation, because of the obvious superiority of the enemy's arms and numbers. Hence, the only options for them are hit-and-run tactics, guerrilla warfare or suicide attacks, even if they claim innocent lives. These attacks are used to heighten their enemies' panic, to force them to respond to their demands, to draw the attention of the international community to their cause, forcing it to rethink whether this cause is fair and deserves support.

3. Killing, vandalism and violence are therefore not in themselves the ultimate goal of those called terrorists by their opponents, and martyrs by their

3 Al-Nābighah al-Dhubiyānī – this is the name given to Ziyād b. Muᶜāwiyah (*c.* 535–604 AD), one of the last Arabian pre-Islamic poets.

4 Al-Nuᶜmān b. al-Mundhir, Nuᶜmān III, also known as Abū Qābūs, the last Lakhmid king of al-Ḥīrāh (r. 582–602 AD).

sympathisers. The goal – as I mentioned – is to make the international community aware of their demands and grievances, which they believe were inflicted on them. They also want to let the authorities in charge know that there are some who are determined to continue their defiance, and that safety and stability are but an illusion. Publicisation of their cause is therefore a focal point for "terrorism". Failure to arouse the interest of the international community, or to scare the society in which the killings and violence takes place, or force the authorities to abandon their policies or to address certain grievances, will result in terrorism no longer being a viable weapon in the ongoing conflict.

However, for the individuals and groups who resort to terrorism, terrorism is not always used to accomplish a purpose. It is also likely that these persons resort to terrorism after despairing of attaining their demands or achieving their aims. Some of these terrorist acts are merely an expression of anger and despondency or useless acts of vengeance, akin to Samson's actions in bringing down the temple on himself and on his enemies.[5] It is interesting to note here that the exegetes commenting on the Old Testament unanimously agree that Samson's actions are not to be considered suicidal, but are a return to his judiciary activity. He sentenced his enemies to death after they imprisoned and tortured him, resulting in the loss of his eyesight. They conclude that he did not seek his own death, but his deliverance and the destruction of his enemies.

4. In the New Testament we find Jesus, upon seeing one of his supporters drawing his sword against one of his enemies, exclaiming: "Put your sword back in its place, for all who draw the sword will die by the sword."[6]

These are the exact words I would like to say to all parties involved in the current international situation, which will not be resolved unless the individuals, states, regimes and international organisations realise the need to work together, shoulder to shoulder, in order to show the helpless, the desperate and the disenfranchised that terrorism – whether domestic or international – is not the only way available to them to bring about change and have their grievances addressed.

5 Judges 16:28 and 16:30 quotes Samson's cry before the destruction of the temple as: "O Lord God, remember me, and restore to me now my former strength, O my God, that I may revenge myself on my enemies" and "Let me die with the Philistines!"

6 Matthew 26:52.

Undoubtedly, there are effective ways to confront terrorism and the terrorists, other than security measures or the use of force. The most effective way to face domestic terrorism is to establish a strong foundation for democracy (which will be elaborated on in the next section). This means free transparent elections, respect for the popular will, encouraging the establishment of strong trade unions which defend the rights of its members, freedom of expression, freedom of the press and allowing strikes and protests in order for people to express their grievances or legitimate demands. In doing so, every terrorist action will be seen as an attempt to defy the will of the nation and to impose the will of a small rogue group on the majority.

As for the most successful way to combat international terrorism, it is for the powerful rich countries to abandon their traditional pursuit of their own interests and objectives. They should commit to greater objectivity in dealing with regional conflicts, and to concepts of social, political and economic justice around the world. They should aim at eradicating the causes of poverty and discontent, as well as the roots of racial and religious hostilities.

Democratisation

In spite of the strict adherence to the Sunna[7] by Muslim religious scholars, they did not always ignore the changing needs and new circumstances that arose in their community over time. Even in the early decades of Islamic history, there was a need to develop political and economic systems, unknown to Islam at its inception. The majority did not obstinately refuse to take new circumstances and developments into consideration, nor did they feel that such considerations are inconsistent with the spirit of the Sunna.

The founder of one of the four Islamic schools of jurisprudence, Mālik b. Anas,[8] opined that the interests of the majority must be the guide when applying the law. That is to say, that one is entitled not to follow the path set out by *Sharīʿa* if it is proven that the best interests of the majority is not

7 Sunna is the traditional part of Muslim law based on Prophet Muḥammad's words or deeds, accepted (after the Qur'an) as authoritative by Muslims.

8 Mālik b. Anas b. Mālik (93 AH/711 AD–179 AH /795 AD), also known as "Imām Mālik", one of the most highly respected scholars of *fiqh* in Sunni Islam and founder of the Mālikī Madhhab (one of the four schools of jurisprudence).

served by following its rules. This was permission to follow rules and laws other than *Sharīᶜa*.

This opinion was ratified by one of the greatest Muslim jurists, al-Zarqānī,[9] who declared, clearly and unambiguously, that new circumstances and conditions allow Muslims to adopt new laws and provisions. He added that laws must keep pace with the developing circumstances. The door of renewal, innovation and reform is therefore not closed in Islam. Islamic societies over time are entitled to adopt new systems and methodologies borrowed from Western civilisation and approved by *fatwa*s issued by leading revered scholars in these societies.

If we move to the field of constitutional law, we find that many of the scholars of the twentieth century welcomed the principle of adopting the constitutional system of government. They cited verses from the Qur'an itself to prove that only the parliamentary form of government is consistent with Islamic law. They exerted great effort in order to extract the relevant *aḥādīth* (Prophetic traditions) that meet the needs of contemporary political life and are consistent with the principles of democracy. They argued that the most important verse in the Qur'an in this regard is verse 42.38[10] ". . . and their rule is to take counsel among themselves . . .",[11] and verse 3.159 ". . . and take counsel with them in the affair . . ."[12]

However, these two Qur'anic verses referring to consultation between believers in the processes of governance are both rather ambiguous. There is no consensus among the exegetes and Qur'an commentators on their exact meaning. Ottoman Sultan Mehmed V[13] initiated his speech opening the new parliament session in 1909 by reading verse 42.38, and stating that "Islamic law requires the establishment of parliamentary governments".

---

9 Muḥammad b. ᶜAbd al-Bāqī al-Zarqānī, Mālikī jurist, died in Cairo in 1122 AH/1710 AD.

10 Unless otherwise noted, all translations of the Holy Qur'an are taken from the electronic version, translated by M. H. Shakir and published by Tahrike Tarsile Qur'an in 1983.

11 Q. 42.38: "*And those who respond to their Lord and keep up prayer, and their rule is to take counsel among themselves, and who spend out of what We have given them.*"

12 Q. 3.159: "*Thus it is due to mercy from Allah that you deal with them gently, and had you been rough, hard hearted, they would certainly have dispersed from around you; pardon them therefore and ask pardon for them, and take counsel with them in the affair; so when you have decided, then place your trust in Allah; surely Allah loves those who trust.*"

13 Sultan Mehmed V (1844–1918), reigned as a constitutional monarch between 1909 and 1918, surrendering all authority to the Committee of Union and Progress, the liberal–nationalist organisation of the Young Turk movement.

In addition, many contemporary scholars assert that verse 42.38 contains a divine command to commit to democratic consultation among Muslims in all matters. While the majority espouse this view, a minority of scholars opine that the consultation in the verse is related to tribal or family matters, social or economic problems affecting the interests of the community, its prosperity and order, as evidenced by the verses directly following verse 42.38, which deal with revenge, the need to avoid great wrongdoing and the preference for amnesty and forgiveness over vengeance. This, according to these scholars, is a clear indication that the verse does not refer to a parliamentary system of government.

The author believes the second view to be more correct. This is supported by the fact that neither the Qur'an, nor the Sunna of the Prophet, nor the conduct of the Rightfully Guided Caliphs, refer in any detail to how such consultation is to be managed, who would be in charge of it and who would have the authority to enforce the decisions agreed upon in that consultation. Not one single answer is found within the pages of books to the question of the status or number of those whom Muslim authorities are enjoined to consult. Neither are there answers on what form this consultation should take or the nature of issues to be forwarded to such a *Majlis al-Shūra* (Consultative Council), or – more importantly – whether those in authority are bound to follow the opinion of the majority and implement what they advised. On the contrary, what is evident is that no majority of any size – even if it is a consensus – has the right to supersede provisions decided on by the divine *Sharīᶜa*.

Looking at the regular mundane affairs of the nation, we ask ourselves: did Abū Bakr[14] consult the nation before appointing ᶜUmar b. al-Khaṭṭāb[15] as his successor? Did ᶜUmar b. al-Khaṭṭāb consult anyone before deciding to conquer Egypt or when he dismissed Khālid b. al-Walīd[16] from commanding

14 Abū Bakr ʿAbd Allāh b. Abī Quḥāfah, known as Abū Bakr al-Ṣiddīq (*c.* 50 AH/573 AD–13 AH/634 AD), father-in-law of the Prophet and his successor as the first of the Rightfully Guided Caliphs (r. 11 AH/632 AD–13 AH/634 AD).

15 ᶜUmar b. al-Khaṭṭāb, known as al-Fārūq ᶜUmar (*c.* 40 AH/583 AD–23 AH/644 AD), father-in-law of the Prophet and the second of the Rightfully Guided Caliphs (r. 13 AH/634 AD–23 AH/644 AD).

16 Abū Sulaymān, Khālid b. al-Walīd b. al-Mughīrah of the Banū Makhzūmī clan (c. 42 AH/585 AD–21 AH/642 AD), also known as Sayf Allāh al-Maslūl (Drawn Sword of God), one of the Companions of the Prophet, noted for his military tactics and, hence, commanded the Muslim forces in Medina at the time of the Prophet and later also the forces of his immediate successors, the Rightfully Guided Caliphs.

the Muslim army in the Levant? No answer to such questions is to be found in the books by Muslim historians, suggesting that consultations before any such important decisions did not happen.

Nevertheless, we notice in the writings of most of the scholars of the nineteenth and early twentieth centuries (including Abul A'la Maududi)[17] that they believed the Qur'anic concept of *Shūra* to be equivalent to the modern concept of democratic rule. They deserve praise for that, as it was a serious attempt to adapt to the new circumstances and the needs of modern times. However, it really was a reaction based on the consensus among Muslim scholars – after initially opposing new ideas and foreign behavioural manifestations, which they considered a *bid*ᶜ*a* (innovation) – to end their resistance and defiance.

However, there has always been a minority within Muslim communities that was less willing to reconcile and compromise with respect to Sunna and *bid*ᶜ*a*. They adhered to a literal reading of religious texts, not adding anything to or omitting anything from these texts. They did their best to keep Islam pure from any additions or innovations, rejecting the idea of Islam's flexibility and any sort of appeasement, even if this rejection led them to resort to violence and – terrorism.

With the intensification of fundamentalism in recent times, fundamentalists busied themselves with trying to confirm the differences between Islamic values and concepts and their Western counterparts, such as Western democracy and Islamic *Shūra*.

Sayyid Qutb[18] sent a letter to Major General Muhammad Naguib,[19] "Leader of the Revolution", in July 1952, two weeks after the outbreak of the revolution. In his letter he called for the establishment of a "fair benevolent dictatorship granting political freedoms exclusively to the righteous and virtuous". In his book *In the Shade of the Qur'an*, he writes that *Shūra* should be imposed on the authority governing the Muslims and that this

---

17 Abul A'la Maududi (1903–1979) Indian–Pakistani *ḥādīth* scholar, jurist, journalist, Islamist and founder of the Jamaat-e-Islami, an Islamist political party with the objective of making Pakistan an Islamic state, governed by *Sharī*ᶜ*a* law.

18 Sayyid Qutb (1906–1966), Egyptian author, educator, Islamic theorist, poet and a leading member of the Egyptian Muslim Brotherhood in the 1950s and 1960s. He was executed in 1966 after being convicted of plotting the assassination of Egyptian president Gamal Abdel Nasser.

19 Muhammad Naguib (1901–1984), primary leader of the Egyptian Revolution of 1952 and first president of Egypt, serving from the declaration of the Republic on 16 June 1953 to 14 November 1954.

authority must consult even if only with some of the ruled (usually from the elite) within the framework of the provisions of *Sharīᶜa* law, which is irrevocably binding. However, in his book, Qutb did not refer at all to elections of any kind as a means of choosing the ruler, nor did he indicate whether the ruler was obliged to take the advice of those he consulted (whether an elite group or others).

Initially, Qutb refused to describe Islam as democratic. However, in the 1950s this refusal turned to an outright contempt for democracy. He described it as one of the failed forms of governance that has proven its deficiency and complete bankruptcy in the West, and that it has therefore become pointless to try to import it.

The Syrian Islamic thinker Sa'id Hawwa[20] followed in Qutb's footsteps, denying that Islamic *Shūra* is in any way similar to Western democracy. He even went as far as stating that, in some cases, democracy is the antithesis of Islamic *Shūra*. He writes that: "The modernists who want to dress Islam in the garb of democracy have seriously deviated from the true meaning of the concept of *Shūra* in the Islamic system of governance." He noted that democracy was derived from the Greek for "government by the people", who then become the source of law, which is used to legislate and govern. *Shūra*, however, means that the ruler consults one or several persons about the interpretation of a certain aspect of Islamic law. In Islam, the people do not rule themselves by laws that they formulate and implement (as in the democratic systems of governance), but they are ruled by laws imposed upon them by God. They have no right to change or alter these divine laws in any way. Therefore, the concept of majority rule cannot be recognised by the system of Islamic rule. Islam does not attribute any authority to the majority.

Sa'id Hawwa's ideas were echoed in the writings of the fundamentalists after him, asserting that the state in Islam should follow divine *Sharīᶜa* and not the people. Shaykh Muhammad Metwali al-Sha'rawi[21] declared, in an interview in 1982, that Islam and democracy cannot be reconciled. He added that *Shūra* does not mean having to ingratiate oneself with the majority or

20 Sa'id Hawwa (1935–1989), leading member and prominent ideologue of the Muslim Brotherhood in Syria.

21 Muhammad Metwali al-Shaʾrawi (1911–1998), Islamic scholar, former Egyptian Minister of Endowments (1976–1978) and Muslim jurist and host of a very popular Friday afternoon TV programme preaching Islam.

gain their approval or sympathy. King Fahd[22] repeated the same argument, speaking to his people about the contradiction between Western democracy and the Islamic concept of *Shūra* and the incompatibility between Western democracy and the needs and traditions of the people of the Gulf region.

These clear words about democracy express the real position of the fundamentalists. This must be taken into account whenever one of their political parties (such as the Islamic Salvation Front in Algeria),[23] especially on the eve of the general election, claim that they are ready to accept the principles and rules of the democratic game, or to implement the concept of political pluralism, or that they would allow other political parties to engage in governance activities under Islamic rule. This sort of rhetoric was voiced by Islamic Salvation Front leader Abassi Madani[24] in his election campaign in 1990, in contradiction to previously made statements, which were consistent with the position of Sayyid Qutb, Sa'id Hawwa, Shaykh Muhammad Metwali al-Sha'rawi and many others of their ilk.

Therefore, this is merely a means to justify the end or a ploy designed to appease the liberals, dispel their fears and dissipate the concerns of democracy devotees in their communities, until the Islamists win the elections and impose their authority. There is no other position with regard to the principles of democracy that can be expected from those who call their party the "Party of God" and refer to all other parties as "Parties of the Devil".

This had been the overall situation in the Islamic world until the events of 11 September 2001, followed by the American administration's declaration of what it named "the war on terror", which was launched in alliance with Britain and a large number of Western countries. It was clear that the accusatory finger pointed at Islam and Muslims. Nevertheless, the vast majority in the West avoided naming Islam openly as responsible, for fear of provoking the feelings of their own local Muslim minorities or communities, or exposing their own material interests in the Muslim world to any risk. However, Western leaders were not embarrassed to emphasise one particular issue as

22 Fahd b. ʿAbd al-ʿAzīz Āl Saʿūd, Custodian of the Two Holy Mosques (1921–2005), King of Saudi Arabia, 1982–2005.

23 The Islamic Salvation Front is a Sunni Islamist political party in Algeria. The party had two major leaders representing its two support bases: Abbassi Madani, who appealed to pious small businessmen; and Ali Belhadj, who appealed to the angry, often unemployed, youth of Algeria.

24 Abbassi Madani (b. 1931), president of the Islamic Salvation Front, Algeria.

the main cause of the phenomenon of terrorism, and the involvement of many Muslims and Arabs in terrorist acts, namely, the lack of a democratic system, liberalism and freedom of expression in Muslim countries. George W. Bush[25] and Tony Blair[26] expressed their determination to pressure the leaders of those countries to refrain from their oppressive and tyrannical policies, to initiate democratisation in ways that would ultimately ensure the eradication of terrorism from its roots, and thus dispel Western fears.

None of the regimes in the Muslim and Arab world dared to resist this Western pressure, fearing that it could quickly turn into an explicit attempt to overthrow the resisting regimes. Everyone demonstrated their approval, and pretended to comply. Some even went as far as to claim that this was precisely what they were about to implement before the West embarked on exerting pressure on them.

Western and Eastern rhetoric about democracy only meant the Western democratic concept. It neither meant *Shūra*, nor any other concept that may be applied. If Muslims insist on describing Islam as democratic, they should add that this democracy is the one defined and applied by the West.

Hence, global acceptance of the idea that Muslims are responsible for breeding terrorism, is a worry that drives Muslims – albeit temporarily – to abandon their insistence that Islamic *Shūra* is very different from Western democracy and that "*You shall have your religion and I shall have mine*".[27] This is a kind of *taqiyya* (dissimulation),[28] which by definition is only temporary in nature, and contains the meaning of "wait and see" what unexpected developments will happen.

Hussein Ahmed Amin
Heliopolis
27 September 2006

25 George W. Bush (b. 1946), 43rd president of the United States (2001–2009).

26 Anthony Charles Lynton Blair (Tony Blair) (b.1953) British prime minister (1997–2007) and leader of the Labour Party (1994–2007).

27 Based on Q. 109.6: "*You shall have your religion and I shall have my religion.*"

28 *Taqiyya*, mainly a Shi'ite concept, is an Islamic juridical term allowing a Muslim, under *Sharīʿa* law, to lie or omit parts of the truth when under duress or fearing for his life.

1
The Sorrowful Muslim's Guide

> *It is very easy to beget in a people a contempt of ancient observances; never any man undertook it but he did it; but to establish a better regimen in the stead of that which a man has overthrown, many who have attempted it have foundered.*
>
> Michel de Montaigne, *Essays*, II, 17

1

Muslims always regarded the victories of the armies of Islam – even during the Prophet's life – as one of the strongest proofs of the truth of Prophet Muḥammad's message. Their remarkable political success bolstered their confidence, and filled them with a sense of superiority over followers of other faiths. There was a long and violent confrontation, lasting nearly a thousand years, between the Islamic and Christian worlds. Generally speaking, we can say that Islam emerged victorious, for even if Spain and other territories were lost by the Muslims during that confrontation, vast areas and entire countries were seized from the Christians by the Ottoman armies, who stood threatening at the gates of Vienna in the late seventeenth century.

This ebb was followed by a tide, the effects of which we still suffer from to this very day. The eighteenth and nineteenth centuries were brutally cruel to Islam and Muslims. The Muslim world was subjected to many attacks by European Christians and most nations fell into the clutches of Western colonialisation. These endless defeats at the hands of their religious opponents upset the Muslims: "... and the people of Bulaq[1] returned to the city weeping and wailing, bashing their faces and saying: 'woe on us, we have become slaves after falling into the hands of the Franks!'"[2] Their self-confidence was shaken, even though for some time they kept their dignity in the face of the colonisers, finding support in their conviction that they are the people of the true religion, and that the coloniser is, in their view, a despicable infidel worthy of contempt.

Al-Jabartī,[3] who condemned the French for their disbelief, their propensity to drink wine, and their uncovered and immodest women, could no longer openly refer to the Franks as cattle as Prince Usama b. Munqidh[4] did during the Crusades. When he saw a good quality Egyptian-made good or commodity, he observed that whoever saw it would have no doubt that it was manufactured by the Franks, and he wrote that the morals of whoever went to their country "improved with what he saw of their country's civilisation, good governance, welfare and craftsmanship, as well as the probity of their rulers to their subjects, in spite of their disbelief".

However, for many, this religious pride quickly dissipated. Their view of their religion was shaken as they saw the superiority of Western Christians in the fields of armaments and civilisation, which continued even after the Islamic countries gained their independence. Some did not understand the meaning of defeat in the mundane sense, but wondered about their humiliation and downfall, as the Qur'an says, "*and to Allah belongs the might and to His Apostle and to the believers*",[5] and "... *helping the believers is ever incumbent on Us*".[6] Had they read ᶜUmar b. al-Khaṭṭāb's missive to Saᶜd b. Abī Waqqās[7] as he prepared to fight the Persians, they would have seen that he wrote:

---

1 Bulaq is a district of Cairo, Egypt.

2 As described by Niqula b. Yusuf al-Turk (1763–1828), scholar, historian and poet.

3 ᶜAbd al-Raḥmān al-Jabartī (1753–1825), an Egyptian scholar, historian and chronicler.

4 Usāma b. Munqidh (488 AH/1095 AD–584 AH /1188 AD), also known as al-Muᵓayyad, was a medieval Syrian Muslim prince, poet, author, diplomat and knight of Ṣalāḥ al-Dīn al-Ayyūbī (532 AH/1138 AD–589 AH/1193 AD).

5 Q. 63.8: "*They say: If we return to Medina, the mighty will surely drive out the meaner therefrom; and to Allah belongs the might and to His Apostle and to the believers, but the hypocrites do not know.*"

6 Q. 30.47: "*And certainly We sent before you apostles to their people, so they came to them with clear arguments, then We gave the punishment to those who were guilty; and helping the believers is ever incumbent on Us.*"

7 Saᶜd b. Abī Waqqās (23 AH/595 AD–55 AH/674 AD), a famous Muslim commander.

> I command you and all those fighting with you to be most cautious of sins, more so than your enemy, for the army's sins are graver than the enemy. Muslims become victorious through their enemy's disobedience of God. Without it, we would not defeat them, for our numbers are not like theirs, and our equipment is not like theirs. However, if we are equal in sin and disobedience they surpass us in force . . . Do not say that our enemy is more evil than us and hence will not overpower us even if we sin. For some folks may be overpowered by those worse than them, as Banū Isrāʾīl[8] were overpowered by the infidel Majūs[9] for the evil they committed against God, "and they *jāsū* (probed) into the homes, and it was a promise fulfilled".[10]

Hence, God would not grant victory to the Muslims without the slightest advantage inherent in them except that they declare themselves Muslims. Nor should they wonder about being abandoned by God, as they lost their ancestors' resolution and did not attempt to change their own condition.[11] So, indeed, it would be more surprising if God did not change their situation from splendour and greatness to humiliation and indignity.

Be that as it may, it was inevitable that the strength and powers of the Christian West and the superiority of their material civilisation allowed doubts to creep into the hearts of many Muslims about their faith.

But during the attacks on the Muslim countries, was the West truly Christian?

2

In the fifteenth century, Western civilisation was very similar to other civilisations existing at the time in various parts of the ancient world, such as

8 Qur'anic term to denote "Children of Israel", the Israelites of the time of Moses

9 Term originally used for the Zoroastrians of pre-Islamic Iran, in Qur'anic usage it is used for all followers of that religion.

10 Q. 17.5: "*So when the [time of] promise came for the first of them, We sent against you servants of Ours – those of great military might, and they probed [even] into the homes, and it was a promise fulfilled.*"

11 This alludes to the Q. 13.11: "*For his sake there are angels following one another, before him and behind him, who guard him by Allah's commandment; surely Allah does not change the condition of a people until they change their own condition; and when Allah intends evil to a people, there is no averting it, and besides Him they have no protector.*"

Eastern Orthodox Christian, the Arab-Islamic, the Turkish and Persian Islamic civilisations, the Hindu and the East Asian civilisations. Each of these civilisations existed within a religious framework. However, during the seventeenth century a revolution occurred in the Christian world, which is the most important event in its history to date: the West broke out of the traditional Christian framework, opting for a worldly secular framework where technical knowledge (or technology) replaced religion as the most important area of human activity.

Western civilisation today is, in fact, simply a reaction that lasted about three centuries; a reaction to the evils resulting from religious intolerance in the Middle Ages. On the one hand, enlightened Europeans felt deep disgust with the bitter religious differences that invoked hatred in the souls and wreaked havoc on their continent. On the other hand, intellectuals found it very difficult to accept the old religious interpretation of the world, which was founded on the Biblical text. When people turned their attention away from religion and towards technical knowledge, the spiritual vacuum left by the collapse of their confidence in Christianity was filled by a drive to experiment, aimed at subduing nature to human control. Technical knowledge was a beneficial activity over which humans could not fight or kill each other. Hence, people redirected their creative mental energy away from fighting over futile religious differences and instead towards attempts to create a heaven on earth, and to increase wealth and prosperity by means of focusing on the sciences.

Thus, the most prominent hallmark of this modern Western civilisation became the great trust of man in himself and in his abilities. This was accompanied by a Western trend to designate non-Western civilisations as semi- or pseudo-civilisations, and to refer to its own former religious civilisation as the "Dark Ages". Ever since Western civilisation adopted a purely worldly, or secular, framework, the barrier that precluded its reception by other non-Western civilisations, namely religion, was removed. By the middle of the twentieth century, most – if not all – of the non-Western world had adopted the secular model of Western civilisation in a historically unprecedented manner. So much so, that some believe that humanity is on its way now towards a global social unity.

Initially, the leaders of these non-European societies only wanted to take advantage of the military know-how of Western civilisation in order to defend themselves against Western aggression. However, it soon became clear that if they wanted to emulate the European military systems, they had to accept Western civilisation as a whole. Civilisation is indivisible, as each part is closely linked to its other parts. European military superiority arose from the superiority of Western weapons in the hands of disciplined soldiers. Military order is a fruit of the prevailing law and order in civil life, good health care and the regular payment of wages to the soldiers. The soldiers' good health depends on the general well-being of the population as a whole and on the availability of physicians who are versed in advanced medical practices. The regularity of wage expenditure requires an accurate budget, which is, in turn, one of the results of a sound production economy that requires the development of industry, agriculture and trade, all at the same time.

Although most non-Western countries reluctantly acquiesced to various manifestations of Western civilisation and were forced to accept it, two things facilitated that. First, the colonialists' disinterest in religion, so that it did not seem that certain adherents of one religion enslaved the followers of another religion. The second was the acceptance by the majority in the various colonised countries of Western claims that their civilisation is an enduring and perfect civilisation, and that its secular liberation from the yoke of religion is the final and most mature evolution of civilisation at large, one that cannot deteriorate or be corrupted.

3

The close contact between Muslims and Western civilisation, as well as the invasion by this civilisation of their countries, had a profound impact on the class of enlightened Muslims. It also affected the relationship of its members with their inherited customs and religious theories and traditions. They felt a very urgent need to adapt and reconcile these theories and traditions with the new conditions in which they suddenly found themselves.

It was highly unfortunate that these efforts to reconcile Muslim life and thought with the demands of Western civilisation came at a time when their confidence in their heritage – and even their religion – was shaken, and they looked to the colonialists as being a sort of demigods.

Hence, it was not surprising, then, that their attempts were coloured by a form of rationalism which was a purely European trend. Their thoughts were affected by the prevailing currents in Western civilisation, and they adopted all, or most, of the values of their Western colonisers. Even though these thinkers rushed to defend Islam and to fight the campaigns launched by Christians to discredit it so that it would not halt the invasion of their civilisation (and their goods); their defence focused on removing the stigma that Islamic teachings are contradictory to and incompatible with civilisation, and to demonstrate the flexibility of Islamic rulings, and the ease of adaptation to the needs of mankind in all times and places. Some of them denied the necessity of *jihad* in our time and dropped it from being one of the mandatory teachings, while others called for peace and tolerance and condemned intolerance and fanaticism. Yet others focused on the development of science and culture, improving education, and called for women's liberation and improved health care. The most intelligent of them called for the separation and distinction between the original teachings of Islam and the superfluous historical increments, which were added by consensus, and could easily be sacrificed for the needs of modern civilisation and progress.

Thus, the so-called reformers adopted a similar call in every Islamic country. They called for the populace to take from Western civilisation what suited them, and to retain from Islamic civilisation what was appropriate. This was done by Midḥat Pasha in Turkey,[12] Sir Ahmad Khan in India,[13] al-Afghanī in Persia and Egypt,[14] and Khayr al-Dīn al-Tunisī in Morocco,[15] as if they had all derived their ideas from the same source and built their methodologies using the same mould. The core of their teachings was as follows:

The "Gordian Knot",[16] the main dilemma facing Muslims today is how to reconcile Western civilisation with Islamic principles. Fortunately, Muslims

---

12 Aḥmad Shafīq Midḥat Pasha (1822–1883), Ottoman statesman, most famous for introducing the First Constitutional Era (1876–1878), and a leading reformist in the educational and provincial administrations.

13 Syed Ahmad Khan (1817–1898), Indian Muslim modernist, philosopher and social activist and one of the founders of the Aligarh Muslim University.

14 Sayyid Jamāl al-Dīn al-Afghānī, known as al-Afghānī (1838/9–1897), political activist and Islamic ideologist, advocate of pan-Islamic unity and one of the founders of Islamic Modernism.

15 Khayr al-Dīn al-Tunsī (*c.*1820–1890), Grand Vizier of the Ottoman Empire (1878–1879), Ottoman–Tunisian political reformer.

16 The "Gordian Knot" is a metaphor meaning an intractable problem, based on a legend about Alexander the Great.

are not forced to choose between adhering to their religion and converting to Western civilisation, for the latter is not founded on religion, but on science and experimentation, in addition to being limited by materialism. Therefore, there is nothing to prevent Muslims from adopting material aspects of Western civilisation and enriching them with Islamic spirituality. In fact, the two are not inherently antagonistic to one another, but the idea of their adversity is the result of a mutual misunderstanding. It is possible to strengthen the bond between them and for each to benefit from the other. It is better for the Muslim world today to adopt Western civilisational knowledge and experience in industry, agriculture, commerce, medicine, engineering and all other sciences unconditionally, while infusing them with their spirituality, and directing them towards the good of humanity and the general good, rather than towards excessive money-making, increased materialism and power abuses. This principle is the one to light the way for Muslims, dispel their bewilderment, and to solve many of their problems. Islam does not prevent any of that; on the contrary, Islam urged Muslims "to seek knowledge even in China",[17] and nothing prevents them from doing so other than their strict adherence to inherited customs and traditions. Religion is guiltless in that regard.

This was the call of these reformers; a call that was endorsed and approved of by the colonisers, especially where espoused by prominent clerics like Shaykh Muḥammad ᶜAbdūh.[18]

The results of this call were expected: it opened the door for the unconditional and uninhibited replication of Western civilisational aspects. However, the second half of the original call was omitted, as if it was just a form of hypocrisy, used by the preachers to camouflage and facilitate the adoption of Western values. What was observed by everyone at home and abroad was that the populations of the Islamic countries – unlike the Japanese, for example – did not adopt Western efficiency, effectiveness and their enthusiasm in learning or

---

17 This is part of a famous *ḥadīth* (prophetic narration) which translates to "Seek knowledge even in China, for seeking knowledge is an obligation for every Muslim." The tradition was deemed forged by Muḥammad Nāṣir al-Dīn al-Albānī, who discussed it in his *Ḍa'īf al-Jāmi' al-ṣaghīr wa-Ziyādatih (al-Fatḥ al-Kabīr)*, arguing that only the part "Seeking knowledge is an obligation for every Muslim" which is found in *Ṣaḥīḥ Sunan Ibn Mājah* is to be considered as being a *ṣaḥīḥ* (authentic) narration.

18 Muḥammad ᶜAbdūh (1849–1905), Egyptian Islamic cleric, jurist, religious scholar and liberal reformer, regarded as one of the key founding figures of Islamic Modernism.

in construction. Instead, they embraced their consumption habits, their attire and their leisure habits. Sir Richard Burton[19] wrote: "The land of the Pharaohs is becoming civilised, and unpleasantly so: nothing can be more uncomfortable than its present middle state, between barbarism and the reverse."[20] While Clot Bey[21] commented: "This is because Easterners, when imitating others, mostly display callow, unpolished behaviour and stupidity . . . Whenever they mingle with us – they only adopt the most repugnant of customs."[22]

4

As mentioned, the worldly or secular character of Western civilisation was a reaction to the horrors of religious conflicts in the Middle Ages. However, it was inevitable that sooner or later counter-movements would emerge in the West. Religion is an essential element in human life that cannot be ignored or suppressed for a long time. This counter-movement began to clandestinely crystallise at a time when the rest of the world was drawing extensively from Western civilisation, abandoning their own cultural heritage, traditions and religion. The tragi-comic situation was that at the time non-Western populations were adopting secular Western civilisation, these populations found themselves caught in the net of the grave spiritual crisis of the West that suddenly emerged in the twentieth century, which resonated in various parts of the world. Since the outbreak of the First World War in 1914, the West itself realised that their modern secular civilisation is not at all as perfect as originally perceived, and that it is far from being immune against collapse or violent crises. This jump-started a return to thinking about matters such as good and evil, after neglecting them for more than three hundred years.

This spiritual crisis had become extremely dangerous as a result of the spread of Western civilisation to the entire world, making it a significant crisis

19 Sir Richard Francis Burton (1821–1890), famous British explorer, geographer, translator, writer, orientalist, cartographer, ethnologist, linguist, poet and diplomat.

20 Burton, Sir Richard F., *Personal Narrative of a Pilgrimage to Al Madinah and Meccah*, ed. Isabel Burton, London: G. Bell, 1898.

21 Antoine Barthélemy Clot (1793–1868), French physician known as Clot Bey during his time as chief surgeon to Muhammad Ali Pasha, Viceroy of Egypt.

22 Clot, Antoine Barthélemy, *Aperçu Général sur l'Egypte*, Paris: Masson, 1840.

of non-Western countries as well. In this way, the West may have unintentionally cheated other civilisations to whom it "sold" their civilisation. Both the "buyer" and "seller" realised that the qualities they thought were there at the time of the sale were actually deceptive. The image that secular Western civilisation was immune from spiritual crises was the ultimate deception. This crisis has now been eating away at Western civilisation's vitality. In fact, this has been even more unfortunate for the people of non-Western countries than to the Westerners. They found themselves lost between a heritage, a religion and traditions they had left to decay and lost all confidence in, and a Western civilisation they had not mastered as yet. No sooner had they stretched out their hands to taste the fruit, than they realised that this fruit was defective and unhealthy. This resulted in an acute sense of bitterness towards the West, and a kind of schizophrenia, both on a societal and individual level, that has not healed. They became like the ostrich that went looking for two horns, and returned without ears.[23] Or the crow that wanted to learn how to walk like the peacock, but ended up not learning that and forgetting its own way of walking.[24]

5

The Western spiritual crisis reverberated among all those who adopted it. "Those in authority"[25] paid lip service to Islam, while adopting the Western systems of rule. The position of Islamic "scholars" was outwardly characterised by sincerity, yet inwardly characterised by mere hypocrisy. The youth had lost their religion and had developed contempt for their heritage, which did not fill their spiritual vacuum. Most were greedily accumulating as much money as possible, yet for non-beneficial purposes, focusing on consumption without the slightest desire to produce anything. Most of the clergy acquiesced to an authority that abused this same acquiescence to discredit

---

23 This is based on a proverb mentioned in *al-Mustaqṣā fī amthāl al-ᶜArab* by Maḥmūd ibn ᶜUmar al-Zamakhsharī, see section 737.

24 A tale from Arab folklore.

25 The term "those in authority" comes from Q. 4.59: "*O you who believe! Obey Allah and obey the Apostle and those in authority from among you; then if you quarrel about anything, refer it to Allah and the Apostle, if you believe in Allah and the last day; this is better and very good in the end.*" It has been used to denote the clergy, the rulers or those in power.

them among the general public. The governments of the armies defeated at the hands of the West – or their allies – rushed to supply Western sexually explicit movies to the cinemas to distract their populations from that defeat. Women did not find an appropriate means to balance their consumption lust with honourable behaviour. The law of the jungle prevailed to the extent that everyone who was still holding on to decency and appropriate behaviour seemed to be an idiot, naive or helpless. Morals on the streets, in homes or at work made it impossible to identify Muslims or non-Muslims. And to top it all off, the problems of daily life weighed heavily upon the shoulders of the majority, leaving them unable to devote any energy to learning or gathering knowledge or perfecting morals and good behaviour.

The despondent sorrowful Muslim, who – despite of all this – has still adhered to a remainder of his religion wonders: "What to do now?" His continued efforts to rationalise and think about this problem only results in the discovery of one major fact, namely, the difficulty of practising one's religion in the society in which he finds himself. In addition, he also realises the difficulty of protecting his family and progeny. The secular youth preferred the idea of immigrating along with their degrees, experience and contempt for the community in which they grew up. The religious and pious among them also decided to "migrate" to their religion and beliefs, describing the society they lived in as "heretical". Muslims then started parroting traditions ascribed to the Prophet, such as "There will come a time when those still adhering to religion will be as if they are clutching hot coals,"[26] and "Islam began as something strange and will return to being as strange as it was at its onset, blessed are the strangers."[27]

"Blessed are the strangers!" Today this has become the motto for both religious and secular people! It is known that, in societies undergoing violent tremors or huge successive developments, often isolationist religious groups emerge, who tend to shut the doors on themselves to remain in a world of their own. They minimise connections with the rest of the world as much as possible. Such groups emerged among Jews, Christians and Muslims, and perhaps among the followers of other religions. Among the most prominent historical examples of such groups rejecting any adjustment to

---

26 Aḥmad b. Ḥanbal quotes this tradition from Abū Hurayrah in his *Musnad.*

27 Muslim al-Ḥajjāj quotes this tradition from Abu Hurayrah in his *Ṣaḥīḥ Muslim.*

new conditions are the Pharisees.[28] They imposed strict exhaustive rules to ensure that any association with non-Jews was avoided. This attitude may have been justified in the second century BC, when Hellenism (or Hellenisation)[29] was threatening to engulf Judaism and eradicate it from existence. However, the situation changed over the next century, when a disdain for the beliefs of paganism spread in the Roman Empire, and thousands in the Empire's cities began to search for a strong coherent doctrine, like the Jewish religion. Therefore, the Pharisees' extreme intolerance was no longer justified. The Christian religion made it easier for people to accept the new conditions, and its ethics became the best way to ensure a peaceful coexistence between the Palestinian population and its Roman rulers, while the Pharisees' ethics impeded such harmony.

In many parts of the Christian world – especially in the mid-nineteenth century – many such groups also appeared (most notably Jehovah's Witnesses[30]), whose members were devout Christians who found it difficult to reconcile the recent scientific discoveries in astronomy, biology, chemistry and new theories of the history of Earth and the emergence of life with their traditional conceptions based on the Bible. Hence, their biggest concern became avoiding contact with all scientific and intellectual currents that prevailed in their community. In order to protect their faith, they imposed a strict isolation from a society whose culture and belief patterns would lead them to disbelief or heresy. The result was that such groups accepted a position of minorities in a society whose members adhere – in appearance at least – to the same religion.

This phenomenon also occurred in Islam. One of the examples is the militant group called *al-Takfir wa-l-Hijra* in Egypt, which appeared as an offshoot of the Muslim Brotherhood.[31] However, there is one huge difference between this group and the Muslim Brotherhood, though Qur'an 5:44 "... *whoever did not judge by what Allah revealed, those are they that are the*

---

28 The Pharisees are an ancient Jewish sect, distinguished by strict observance of traditional written law, and commonly held to have pretensions to superior sanctity.

29 Hellenism is the ancient Greek culture, while Hellenisation is the spread of Hellenism in places conquered by the Greeks.

30 Jehovah's Witnesses, founded in the late 1870s by Charles Taze Russell, is a millenarian restorationist Christian denomination with non-Trinitarian beliefs distinct from mainstream Christianity establishing all their doctrines based on their interpretations of the Bible.

31 *Takfir wa-l-Hijra*, "Excommunication and Exodus", is a radical Islamist group founded by Shukri Mustafa in Egypt in the 1960s as an offshoot of Muslim Brotherhood.

unbelievers . . ."[32] is a cornerstone for both of them. The difference is that the Muslim Brotherhood is not an isolationist group, nor was it the one choosing to close its doors on society. In fact, it strives to spread its doctrines as widely as possible among all social and intellectual circles and classes. This is not to say that the *Takfir wa-l-Hijra* group was not pleased to see new members swell its ranks, but the difference between the two positions is substantial and meaningful. The former strives actively to enforce their vision until it prevails over society as a whole, hence, it does not hesitate to engage in any arguments to persuade others or prove them wrong. To increase their numbers, the latter group mainly depended on the spontaneous "migration" of individuals from the community at large into their closed isolationist group. Many who joined them did so because of similarities in their personality traits, or an agreement with their attitudes towards contemporary life. The Muslim Brotherhood extends a hand to attract supporters, while the *Takfir wa-l-Hijra* supporters were attracted to it without any effort on behalf of its members.

It is noticeable that in all isolationist groups, the members perceive an excellence and superiority over their opponents, both those who chose to remain silent about it and those who chose to express it in the form of *takfir*[33] of the community in which they live. This is very similar to the principle known in Christianity as "*extra Ecclesiam nulla salus*".[34] These groups are also characterised by taking their rigid doctrinal positions in the face of changing circumstances, leading many others to call for flexibility in interpretation and application. It must also be mentioned that such a conservative attitude also has some advantages, as it ensures continuity in religious matters. Moreover, any conservative direction in any field is credited with protecting all that remains of the "old", which can be made to fit with the existing society.

---

32 Q. 5.44: "*Surely We revealed the Taurat in which was guidance and light; with it the prophets who submitted themselves (to Allah) judged (matters) for those who were Jews, and the masters of Divine knowledge and the doctors, because they were required to guard (part) of the Book of Allah, and they were witnesses thereof; therefore fear not the people and fear Me, and do not take a small price for My communications; and whoever did not judge by what Allah revealed, those are they that are the unbelievers.*"

33 *Takfir* is the practice of "excommunication", meaning that one Muslim declares another Muslim as *kāfir* (non-believer).

34 Meaning: "there is no salvation outside the church".

However, one has to be alerted to two facts. First, not everyone who leans towards such groups or joins them does so to protect a religion he reveres or wants to protect. It is clear that many people have taken religion as a cover to mask what they feel with regard to their inability to prevail or to defend themselves in the daily battles of life. They may also join the ranks of these groups to satisfy their natural desire to belong, or their desire for superiority over a society that marginalised them or treated them with contempt. Second, at certain times, some fundamental changes may occur and sweep over society as a whole, which are impossible for any human effort to oppose. In such situations, individuals – for their own sanity, and even survival – hold on to a continuing original religious vision, yet feel forced to arrive at a compromise or an individual formula for their own behaviour in such times and developments. They are compelled to display some kind of flexibility to enable themselves to live with what they can neither resist nor stop.

Is there a way forward to offer to the sorrowful Muslim?

6

In contemplating the word "sorrowful" itself, a part of the solution may be found!

It is the opinion of the author that sorrow shows the misery and helplessness of the Muslim feeling it. The sorrowful Muslim is one who feels despondent about the oppression around him. He is oppressed thinking of an Islam he perceives inside himself. This in itself is an irreconcilable contradiction. It is the author's opinion that the pious Muslim believes – beyond a shadow of a doubt – that Islam is a religion that is suitable for every time and place, and that Islam could provide for his community (and others) the most effective solutions to the problems facing it. In clinging to its threads, the Muslim believes he will find happiness in this world and the hereafter. It is assumed that the Muslim believes that non-Muslims, though they are numerous, are people deserving of his pity and commiseration, for they have gone astray and failed to accept God's guidance to find the right path and ultimately deliverance. Sorrow is the best evidence that his confidence has been shaken, and that he no longer believes in his religion being the key to solve all dilemmas. He no longer finds in his teachings the serenity he desires. This is also evidence that can be used by his opponents to prove his impotence and feebleness, to demonstrate that Islam alone is no longer sufficient to ensure his happiness and contentment.

It is known that St Francis of Assisi[35] always exhorted his followers to display their joy about their faith, and to show delight and happiness in all of their conduct and in life generally. He believed that this was the best way to attract people to religion, for surely they will ask what has filled their hearts with glee and certainty. Satisfaction and peace of mind, once known, would create a will to experience it again.

If the Muslim is a true believer, why does he not follow that same method?

If he claims that he is unable to do so, because he feels alone in his community, or alone-like, a stranger, or stranger-like, the best answer is a half-line from one of al-Mutanabbī's[36] verses: "The Noble is always a stranger wherever he is", and that he is not the only one suffering from loneliness or alienation. Do our intellectuals not feel alienated when they crave intellectual stimulation in their communities? Do our scientists in their laboratories not feel alienated when they are deprived of the tools that enable them to continue their research? Do our artists not feel alienated when all they encounter is a lack of appreciation and an inability to sense beauty?

Hence, the Muslim must contemplate his religion, for perhaps then he will find that which reinforces his belief in its ability to comfort and satisfy him, even if he feels alone or if he is the only Muslim in his surroundings. Does not every pious person from any religion feel alone within the secular Western civilisation that has stretched out to include our entire world?

However, rethinking religion itself, we believe, is a point open to questions!

7

How do we rethink religion?

In other words: we do know that much of what we believe is religion was added and forced on to it over centuries and centuries of struggles with

---

35 Saint Francis of Assisi (San Francesco d'Assisi, 1181/1182–1226 AD) was born Giovanni di Pietro di Bernardone in Italy. He was an Italian Roman Catholic friar and preacher who founded several Franciscan Orders: the men's Order of Friars Minor, the women's Order of Saint Clare, the Third Order of Saint Francis and the Custody of the Holy Land. He was canonised as a saint just two years after his death, by Pope Gregory IX.

36 Abū-l-Ṭayyib ʾAḥmad b. al-Ḥusayn al-Mutanabbī (915–965 AD), was one of the greatest poets in the Arabic language, known for his wit and sharp intelligence and megalomania.

various passions and different sects. The prevalence of ignorance and superstition, a desire to satisfy the rulers and sultans, and false interpretations of the Qur'an by members of different doctrines or schools of thought were contributing factors, as were the reinterpretations of the Qur'an away from its manifest and apparent meanings to accommodate and serve new issues, and the forging of *ḥadīth* (Prophetic traditions) and putting statements into the Prophet's mouth to impose certain opinions. Add to this the exaggerated reverence and sanctification of the Prophet in order to pave the way for the sanctification of *awliyāʾ*, the writing of the Prophet's biography in a manner consistent with the vanishing values of certain eras, and the proliferation of lies that were thought to serve the faith. All of these issues formed a heavy "religious" legacy that led the believer astray and into a labyrinth. A believer may embrace some of these matters, even though they are not part of the religion, which in turn would become the reason of his misery, and the barrier between him and the ability to keep up with progress. They might be his motive to condemn that which should not be condemned and lead to his isolation and useless solitude, for which there is no place in today's society.

Is it not more rational for the dejected sorrowful Muslims to redirect their efforts in an attempt to break through to the truth of religion, and purify it from the superfluous impurities that have infected it? Is it not more constructive to uncover religion's precious essence and display it to a society that may have abandoned religion to other concerns, precisely because of the foreign elements that crept into it?

We are in desperate need of a biography of the Prophet that does not blur or fabricate facts. We need to exclude the forged *aḥādīth* (prophetic traditions), even if *ḥadīth* as a whole should suffer as a result. We need to return to a manifest unambiguous interpretation of the Qur'an that is influenced by neither the mystical, nor socialism or capitalism, nor attempts to see in it the achievements of modern science. We need to rewrite Muslim history on a new basis, and to closely investigate the different sects and Islamic doctrines that called themselves religious to mask purely economic and socio-political motives. We need to re-adjust our view of religion and heritage, and cease to see them as a way to run from our problems by escaping to the past, thereby creating a false sense of security, but use it as a means to address the problems of the present and the future. We need to instil faith in the emerging generations and the youth; a faith based on established facts not the lies that when exposed and refuted will do away with faith in its entirety. We need to purge the faith of the myths and superstitions that have always been and still remain the biggest cause of perplexity to all those who were fortunate enough to get some form of education.

Perhaps then we can achieve some certainty and faith, the faith of the joyous and strong, not the faith of the powerless, the grieving and the oppressed. Possibly then can we face Western civilisation from a position that is not governed by inferiority, and devoid of humiliation or shameful arrogance. Then, and only then, will we be able to borrow from their system and realise that it came naturally, just like our ancestors borrowed from civilisations around them, without any sense of shame or servitude, perhaps even without feeling that we are emulating them. If we reject some of their methods and values that do not conform to our habits, then this rejection will happen without arrogance or intolerance, maybe even without consciously realising that we are rejecting these.

8

It is not far-fetched to believe that at some point in time Muslim countries can become a bloc like the great powers of the day and have clout, prominence and the ability to influence international affairs. However, it is an illusion to imagine that such an "Islamic bloc" may enjoy all of this based only on the extent of the piety of its individuals and the ordinary man's sense that Islam fulfils all the needs of his daily life. The eighteenth and nineteenth centuries brought about momentous changes and developments in people's lives which require Muslims to redouble their efforts in the areas of intellectual thought, to prove that Islam could contribute to meeting their needs in modern times.

They will have to acknowledge that the world has become one unit, and that there is no way to avoid contact with the followers of other religions and adverse cultures. They will have to recognise that they are bound to accept the scientific consensus and then put it in its proper place, so as not to be forced into isolation or to engage in *takfir*. They will have to accept that the old doctrinal formulations to which they are attached are not related to the original vision of the religion and may not represent more than a flaw or a contamination in a person's existential outlook. Then

Muslims can bring their spiritual treasures to the world and to the common global civilisation, as a contribution to the religious heritage, especially given that in the last three centuries the West has, much like the Romans at the advent of Christianity, been looking into what other religions may have to offer to guide them to the truth.

2
Reflections on the Evolution of the Prophet's Biographies in the East and West

Do not [over] extol me as the Christians have [over] extolled Jesus Son of Mary, for I am a servant, so say servant of Allah and His messenger.

Ḥadīth (Prophetic tradition)

The writing of history and biographies has a history of its own. This is not only due to the evolution of methodologies and research methods, but also due to the predominance of particular theories, and the writers' reflection of the spirit of their age and of certain prevalent intellectual "fashions" or trends. The impact of such trends on historical and biographical writings (interesting and revealing though it may be) would have been enough to belittle both genres and call their value into question were it not for the ignorance of the majority, or their deliberate choice to ignore such effects, as well as the philosophical acceptance on the part of the minority of the inevitable subjectivity that characterises both these branches of knowledge.

It is noticeable that the greater the amount and diversity of information available on a certain historical era, event or prominent historical figure, the more likely it is for the writing about them to be subjective and for a variety of theories to be formulated about them. The historian or biographer then has a bigger pool of data to choose from, to pick the events that agree with his inclinations or that confirm his opinion. In his book *What is History?*,

E. H. Carr[1] likened the position of the historian with regard to the information available to him to that of a fisherman setting out to catch a certain kind of fish, choosing certain tools and utensils and steering his boat to the place where this type of fish is known to be plentiful. He then forays into the sea until he reaches the distance that he deems appropriate. Some of the fish that come out in his net or attach to his fishing rod may be of the type he does not want, so he returns them to the sea, keeping only those he set out to catch!

The Early Muslim Historians' Concept of History

Some have criticised the early Muslim historians who wrote the history of the Islamic world after the death of the Prophet for simply listing the events without commentary, and for producing a mere record without any preconceived perspective. The reason behind this method of historical writing, and this astonishing objectivity in their works, was their belief that history was the external manifestation of God's will in our world. They believed that it was possible to extrapolate the meaning of God's will by interpreting its manifestations. Hence, they saw it as their duty to record these manifestations accurately and to refrain from allowing whims or passions to rule their selection. They were therefore similar to investigators in a certain affair, collecting all evidence and facts without knowing beforehand which of them will prove to be relevant to what they want to detect. This does not mean that they were not selective (for who can record every single fact about any topic?), nor does it mean that none of them conceded to the whims of their rulers or the creeds they followed. However, Muslim historians of the Middle Ages committed themselves to a measure of objectivity that is rarely found in others, and that was foremost due to their piety. Many of them – like al-Ṭabarī – began their careers by writing exegetical works or collecting and writing about *ḥadīth* (Prophetic traditions). When they turned to writing history, they continued to commit to the same methodology, accuracy, piety and standards. If piety drove other historians to record lies and fabricate materials in good faith, the Muslim historians' concept of piety meant adhering to truth and honesty as much as possible, which may be what is known today as the "scientific spirit".

---

1 Edward Hallett Carr (1892–1982), English historian, diplomat, journalist and international relations theorist. E. H. Carr, *What is History?* Cambridge: Cambridge University Press, 1961.

The Attitude of the Early Muslims towards the Biography of the Prophet

Where the writing of the *Sīra* (Life of Muḥammad) was concerned, matters were somewhat different, especially as the gap between the author's time and the time of the Prophet widened. The early *Sīra* works, such as those by ᶜUrwa b. al-Zubayr b. al-Awwām (22–93 AH/642–712 AD),[2] Ābān b. ᶜUthmān b. ᶜAffān (22–104 AH /642–723 AD)[3] and Mūsa b. ᶜUqba al-Asadī (d. 141 AH/758 AD),[4] were more authentic and honest, with few accounts of miracles. Unfortunately, these works were lost and did not reach us, except for short passages which are reported in the works of Ibn Isḥāq (84–150 AH/704–768 AD), al-Wāqidī (130–207 AH/748–822 AD), Ibn Saᶜd (167–230 AH/784–845 AD), al-Ṭabarī (224–310 AH/839–922 AD) and others.

The openness and honesty that characterised the early writings were due to several reasons. Most importantly, the values, standards and customs of their time had not changed much from the time of the Prophet. Furthermore, the sayings of the Prophet's Companions and his contemporaries about the events of their time and the actions of the Prophet and his words were still fresh in the minds of the *tabiᶜūn* (followers).[5] Moreover, their intense admiration for the character of the Prophet and their determination to gain comprehensive knowledge of his entire life, all his sayings and deeds in order to lay the foundations of theology and jurisprudence and to establish the religious rules regarding the minutest details of daily life, drove them to record everything they heard about him. They were not selective, nor did they feel any embarrassment about recording any incident or other. Everything the Prophet said or did was worthy of reverence and study, and if some of the underlying motives for some of his deeds were difficult to understand or were no longer consistent with the common practice, they

---

2 Nephew of ᶜAʾisha bint Abū Bakr (one of the Prophet's wives), one of the seven *fuqahāʾ* (jurists) who formulated the Medinan *fiqh* (jurisprudence of Medina) and one of the early Muslim historians.

3 Son of ᶜUthmān b. ᶜAffān, the third of the Rightfully Guided Caliphs, a traditionist and governor of Medina during the rule of ᶜAbd al-Malik b. Marwān.

4 Student of al-Zuhrī, who wrote one of the first *Kitāb al-Maghāzī*, no longer extant except in quotations in later works.

5 The generation of Muslims who were born after the passing of the Prophet Muḥammad but who were contemporaries of the *Ṣaḥāba* (Companions).

believed this to be due to their limited understanding of the significance and wisdom behind these motives, which may become evident to subsequent generations. This was done without the slightest inclination on their part to sanctify their prophet along the lines of what the Christians did, and without losing sight of the fact that Muḥammad was a human being like them, who received divine revelations. Their attitude towards the Prophet's biography was therefore in line with how the Muslim historians who came after them viewed history as a science. They saw it as their duty to record the manifestations of God's will as they were (or as they appeared to them), and then to reflect upon them in order to derive lessons, or to allow subsequent generations to reflect upon them to detect the essence of God's will.

How the Evolution of Customs and Values affected Sīra *Writing*

With the passage of centuries, the change in customs and values, and the contact with and influences from the conquered territories and followers of other religions, the writing of the *Sīra* deviated from its quintessentially Arab standard. This deviation continued to increase, reaching its peak in modern times, particularly as later biographies were written by the *mawālī* (non-Arab Muslims),[6] whose standards, concepts and perceptions differed from those of the Arabs. While the Arabs had become preoccupied with managing the affairs of the state and the tides of war, the *mawālī* embarked on learning and studying various sciences, particularly the religious sciences, until they excelled in them.

This deviation in *Sīra* writing began with the Islamic conquests, and the attempts to spread Islam in the conquered territories. These led to religious polemics between the conquerors and the natives, especially the Christians and Jews, who in defence of the superiority of their religion pointed to the supernatural miracles of the prophets of the Old Testament, or to Christ's rejection of worldly pleasures and purposes. The Muslims responded by ascribing an increasing number of miracles to the Prophet, similar to or

6 *Mawālī* is the Arabic term which gained prominence during the Umayyad caliphate (*c.* 41–132 AH/661–750 AD), and was used for non-Arab Muslims, meaning people all over the Islamic empire who were not Arab, but had converted to Islam.

different from the miracles of Christ and the Jewish prophets. They further attributed political or other motives to the acts which their opponents attacked, such as the multiple wives of the Prophet, his treatment of the Medinan Jews or how he sent his Companions to kill the poets who insulted him. These miracles and motivations were not found in the early *Sīra* works.

This increased need to "defend" the Prophet (a defence that was, in fact, neither necessary nor justified) ties in with the previously mentioned evolution of morals, values and customs. One thing may be denounced in a particular era, which in an earlier era was not, and vice versa. One example is the ruling to cut the throats of all male prisoners of war of the Banū Qurayza[7] tribe. Later biographers saw an urgent need to justify this ruling, while they simply accepted the Prophet's command to cut down and burn all the palm trees of the Banū al-Naḍīr[8] tribe during the siege by the Muslims, considering this merely as an act of cutting off vital supplies to the enemy. This command had shocked the Prophet's Companions, as in *Jahiliyya* the cutting down of palm trees was completely disapproved of, even in wartime. They were not appeased until a Qur'anic verse was revealed in this regard, namely Q. 59:5.[9] The changing customs are also what prompted Ibn Hishām (d. 217 AH/833 AD) to write in the introduction to his abridged version of Ibn Isḥāq's *Sīra*: "I am, God willing, going to leave out some of what Ibn Isḥāq mentioned in his book . . . some of the things which are reviled and which would upset people if mentioned and some which al-Bakkāʾī[10] has not permitted us to narrate."

The Trend towards Blurring Facts and Inventing Stories

This is when biographers began to mess with the *Sīra*, to blur some facts or to invent stories in order to alleviate a certain effect or to remove it altogether, or to produce another effect or reinforce it. Facilitating the misrepresentation and distortion of some aspects of the *Sīra* – though more apparent in the

7 A Jewish tribe which lived in northern Arabia, at the oasis of Yathrib (now known as Medina), until the seventh century AD.

8 Another Jewish tribe which lived at the oasis of Yathrib until the seventh century AD.

9 Q. 59:5: "*Whatever palm-tree you cut down or leave standing upon its roots, It is by Allah's command, and that He may abase the transgressors.*"

10 Abū Muḥammad Ziyād b. ʿAbd Allah b. al-Ṭufayl al-ʿĀmirī al-Bakkāʾī al-Kūfī, one of the main narrators of Ibn Isḥāq's *Sīra* (d. 183 AH).

ḥadīth – was the fact that the writers adhered to differing religious or political doctrines. The *mutashayiᶜūn* (those following the Shīᶜa doctrine) added stories about ᶜAli b. Abū Ṭālib's heroics, while the *mawālī* of Persian origins added stories about Salmān al-Fārisī.[11] The writers of the ᶜAbbāsid courts added stories that glorified al-ᶜAbbās'[12] and confirmed his early conversion to Islam, while introducing stories that disgraced the Umayyads and magnified Abū Sufyān's[13] enmity of the Prophet.

All this resulted in a significant deterioration in the biographical literature following the works of Ibn Isḥāq, al-Wāqidī, Ibn Saᶜd and al-Ṭabarī. In our opinion, al-Wāqidī's biographical writings, be it his book *al-Maghāzī* or his accounts narrated by Ibn Saᶜd in his book *al-Ṭabaqāt al-Kubra*, are the most comprehensive and most reliable biographical accounts, although *al-Maghāzī* only addressed the Medinan period of the Prophet's life and his military conquests and invasions. Ibn Isḥāq's *Sīra* only reached us in the form of an abridged and edited version by Ibn Hishām. Its major value – compared with al-Wāqidī's *al-Maghāzī* – is that it reported the life of the Prophet before the start of the military excursions, his private life and non-military events until his death.

Sīra *Books*

The four books (the *Sīra* of Ibn Isḥāq, *al-Maghāzī* of al-Wāqidī, *al-Ṭabaqāt al-Kubra* of Ibn Saᶜd and *Tārīkh* of al-Ṭabarī) are – together with the Qur'an – the most important sources of the *Sīra*. The subsequent literature is almost

11 Salmān's original name was Rouzbeh. He was born and raised a Zoroastrian and was attracted to Christianity later, and then converted to Islam after meeting Muḥammad in the city of Yathrib, which later became Medina. He was a Companion of the Prophet and the first Persian to convert to Islam. He is credited with the suggestion of digging a trench around Medina when it was attacked by the Meccans during the Battle of the Trench. He is said to have translated part of the Qur'an into Persian, thus becoming the first person to interpret and translate the Qur'an into a foreign language. His death is said to have occurred in (35 AH/655 or 656 AD).

12 Al-ᶜAbbās b. ᶜAbd al-Muṭṭalib (b. *c.* 56 before *Hijra*/568 AD; d. *c.* 32 AH/653 AD). He was the paternal uncle and a *Ṣaḥābī* (Companion) of Prophet Muḥammad. The ᶜAbbāsid dynasty was founded in 132 AH/750 AD by Abū-l-ᶜAbbās ᶜAbd Allah al-Saffāḥ who claimed the title of caliph through his descent from ᶜAbbās' son, ᶜAbd Allah.

13 Sakhr b. Ḥarb (b. *c.* 66 before *Hijra*/560 AD; d. 29 AH /650 AD), was the leader of the Quraysh tribe of Mecca and a staunch opponent of Muḥammad. He accepted Islam later in his life and fought during the early Muslim conquests. His cousin Maymūna bint al-Ḥārith was one of the Prophet's wives.

devoid of historical value unless supplemented by narrative quotes from earlier books that are lost to us (even though these quotes are minimal).

This applies to *ᶜUyūn al-athār* by Ibn Sayyid al-Nās (671–734 AH/1272–1334 AD), *al-Mawāhib al-laduniyya bi-l-minaḥ al-Muḥammadiyya* by al-Qasṭallānī (851–923 AH/1448–1517 AD), *al-Sīra al-Shāmiyya* by Shams al-Dīn al-Shāmī (d. 942 AH/1536 AD), *al-Sīra al-Ḥalabiyya* by Nūr al-Dīn al-Ḥalabī (975–1044 AH/1567–1635 AD), as well as the biographical works by Ibn Khayyāṭ (160–240 AH/777–854 AD), Ibn Ḥazm (384–456 AH/994–1064 AD), Ibn al-Jawzī (510–597 AH/1116–1201 AD), Abū-l-Fida (672–732 AH/1273–1331 AD), al-Nuwayrī (667–733 AH/1279–1333 AD), al-Dhahabī (673–748 AH/1274–1348 AD), Ibn Kathīr (701–774 AH/1301–1373 AD), Ibn Khaldūn (732–808 AH/1332–1406 AD), al-Maqrizī (764–845 AH/1364–1442 AD), Ibn al-ᶜImād al-Ḥanbalī (1032–1089 AH/1623–1379 AD), al-Diyār Bakrī (d. 966 AH/1559 AD) and Ibn al-Athīr (555–630 AH/1160–1233 AD).

Nevertheless, one could find valuable material on the Prophet's biography scattered in various other books, such as *Kitāb al-aṣnām* by Ibn al-Kalbī (110–204 AH/737–819 AD) or *Akhbār Makkah* by al-Azraqī (d. 250 AH/837 AD), as well as the *ḥadīth* collections by Ibn Ḥanbal (164–241 AH/780–855 AD), al-Bukhārī (194–256 AH/810–870 AD), Muslim (206–261 AH/821-875 AD) and others. Other books of value are *Futūḥ al-Buldān* and *Ansāb al-Ashrāf* by al-Balādhurī (d. 279 AH/892 AD), *Tarīkh* by al-Yaᶜqūbī (284 AH/897 AD) and the exegetical works, especially *Tafsīr* al-Ṭabarī and *Murūj al-Dhahab* by al-Mas'ūdī (283–346 AH/896-957 AD), *Akhbār al-Madīna* by al-Samhūdī (844–911 AH/1440-1504 AD) and *Ḥayāt al-ḥayawān* by al-Damīrī (742–808 AH/1344–1405 AD), as well as the biographical dictionaries about the Companions' lives such as *Usd al-ghāba fī maᶜrifat al-ṣaḥāba* by Ibn al-Athīr and *al-Iṣāba fī tamyīz al-ṣaḥāba* by Ibn Ḥajar al-ᶜAsqalānī (773–852 AH/1372-1449 AD), and books on literature and linguistics such as *al-Aghānī* by Abū-l-Faraj al-Isfahānī (284–356 AH/897–967 AD), *al-Ishtiqāq* by Ibn Durayd (223–321 AH/837–933 AD) and *al-Kāmil* by al-Mubarrad (210–286 AH/826–898 AD).

Generally speaking, the *Sīra* books which followed the four seminal works referred to above tended to either summarise or extract from previous books, or to direct their attention to the proofs of prophethood and the Prophet's merits. Hence, these later books are closer to the genre of "hagiography"[14]

14 A biography whose author sanctifies his subject or presents them as perfect.

than to a biography in the conventional sense. The purpose was to write about a role model to be emulated rather than record the truth for its own sake. This reflected an attitude of scepticism towards the truth where it did not serve a moral or religious purpose. It is a position that is still acceptable and legitimate to some, even to this day. Some of these authors did not hesitate to fabricate *Sīra* and *ḥadīth* content if they thought it would strengthen the faith. Over time, the realistic and vivid image of a human prophet of flesh and blood diminished in the books and in the minds, making way for irrational myths and stories of miracles. The Prophet himself had not attributed such miracles to himself, nor had his Companions attributed them to him. These miracles were also not mentioned in the Qur'an, which did not omit any signs of Muḥammad's prophethood in order to persuade his religious opponents of his sincerity. However, it appears that these books were well received among the readers and found greater acceptance than those written by Ibn Isḥāq or al-Wāqidī, particularly as intellectual life degenerated under Ottoman rule. Until the late nineteenth century it was difficult (and sometimes impossible) to find a copy of the *Sīra* by Ibn Hishām or al-Waqidī's *al-Maghāzī* or Ibn Saᶜd's *Ṭabaqāt*.

The Effect of Contact with the West on Sīra *Writing*

However, *Sīra* writing reached its low point in the phase that followed, starting with the first contacts between the Muslim world and the Western world, followed by the European colonisation of India and various Arab countries, and lasting until the present day. As Muslim intellectuals became acquainted with the colonisers' views of Muḥammad and Islam, expressed in their books and conversations, and as a result of the Muslims' conscious or subconscious belief in the superiority of the Christian colonisers' civilisation, *Sīra* writing experienced a serious and troublesome shift towards becoming apologetic. This apology stemmed from a sense of danger, and – notwithstanding the severity of the authors' attacks against the Orientalists – revealed an inferiority complex towards the Europeans. Worse still, their defence of Muḥammad and Islam was always undertaken on the basis of purely Western values, as if these were not subject to any debate. The only purpose, it seemed, was to demonstrate the compatibility of Islam and the Prophet's virtues with these values. Hence, these authors were keen to clarify, for example, how Islam raised the status of women and improved their position within the family and in society, or how it alleviated the impact of slavery by urging the manumission and good treatment of slaves, or how it encouraged interest in science, literacy, health care and hospital-building. They argued that Islam fought racial discrimination and laid the foundations of social justice ("socialists, you are their Imam!"),[15] and that polygamy was a political and social necessity which the Qur'an actually aimed at reducing, as it recommended equity and equality between the wives while adding "*you will not be able to do justice*".[16] They further claimed that numerous modern scientific discoveries were hinted at or prophesied in the Qur'an. Some even felt the need to explain the verse pertaining to the cutting off of thieves' hands[17] as a plea to provide work and an honest means of making a living to enable the thief to cease stealing, in the same way as in Arabic we say "cut off so-and-so's leg from the house", in the sense of preventing him from visiting. There are dozens of examples whose truth or error will not be discussed here, but we are only pointing out the extent of our compliance – albeit inadvertent – to the standards of Western civilisation.

The Sīra *in the Twentieth Century*

Syed Ameer Ali (1849–1928)[18] in India was the first to fall into the trap set by the Westerners, perhaps unintentionally, for Islam and Muslims. Hundreds of Arabs, Muslims and others, Qur'an interpreters and exegetes, biographers

15 Ahmed Shawqi (1868–1932), famous Egyptian poet, known as *Amīr al-Shuʿarāʾ* (Prince of Poets), wrote a poem in praise of the Prophet Muḥammad titled "*nahj al-burda*" ("The way of the *burda*", i.e., the mantle of the Prophet). The lines pertaining to this quote are as follows: "God alone is above all creation / and the people are equal under His banner / Religion is ease and the caliphate is by allegiance / and matters are by consultation and rights are the law / Socialists, you are their *imām*! / if it were not for the allegations of the radical people."

16 The two verses meant here are Q. 4:3 and 4:129, which read as follows: Q. 4:3: "*And if you fear that you cannot act equitably towards orphans, then marry such women as seem good to you, two and three and four; but if you fear that you will not do justice (between them), then (marry) only one or what your right hands possess; this is more proper, that you may not deviate from the right course*"; Q. 4.129: "*And you have it not in your power to do justice between wives, even though you may wish (it), but be not disinclined (from one) with total disinclination, so that you leave her as it were in suspense; and if you effect a reconciliation and guard (against evil), then surely Allah is Forgiving, Merciful.*"

17 Q. 5:38: "*And (as for) the man who steals and the woman who steals, cut off their hands as a punishment for what they have earned, an exemplary punishment from Allah; and Allah is Mighty, Wise.*"

18 Prominent Indian political leader, author of a number of influential books on Muslim history and the modern development of Islam, and a jurist who is credited for his contributions to Indian Law, particularly Muslim personal law.

and leaders of religious "reform" and other advocates of Islam's compatibility with the modern *Zeitgeist*[19] followed his direction and methodology.

It is our belief that, due to the reasons mentioned above, the worst works of *Sīra*, those which pose the greatest threat to Islam, were the books written by Muslims in the twentieth century. Furthermore, of all the *Sīra* works, they were furthest from religious as well as scientific logic, despite the relative paucity of miracles and myths found in them. Compare, for example, al-Wāqidī's position on the Banū Qurayza military campaign (and we find it most surprising how little the Muslim biographers rely on al-Wāqidī's book as a primary source and consider it untrustworthy) with the position of any of the modern writers. Rather than trying to apologise for or justify the killing of the prisoners of war, al-Wāqidī merely wrote that Muḥammad followed God's command to fight Banū Qurayza. This reference to God's command to wage war is a position that is defensible and even required by religious logic, given that the Prophet described the ruling of Saᶜd b. Muᶜādh[20] as the judgement of God and His Messenger. The modern account, which tries to find a justification or motive for that judgement, and the wisdom behind it can be considered – from a certain perspective – as a weakness in one's faith. The mere act of justifying any specific action implies that a believer's faith may be shaken if no justification could be found for that particular action.

The first half of the twentieth century saw more works of *Sīra* written than were written since the death of the Prophet. The most famous of these in the Arab world was Muhammad Husayn Haykal's[21] *The Life of Muhammad* (published in 1935). Haykal described it as just the first, wise step in the call to a progressive Islam in the modern era. Much like William Muir,[22] the pious Christian, was dismayed – despite his preference for Islam over

19 *Zeitgeist* is the defining spirit or mood of a particular period of history as shown by the ideas and beliefs of the time.

20 Saᶜd b. Muᶜādh (32 before *Hijra*–5 AH/590–626 AD) was the chief of the Aws tribe in Medina and one of the prominent Companions of the Prophet. Some of the Jews of Banū Qurayza agreed to accept his verdict as an arbitrator to pronounce judgement upon them. Saᶜd, who would later die of his wounds from the Battle of the Trench, decreed the sentence according to the Torah (Deuteronomy 20:10–14), in which the men shall be killed and women and children enslaved.

21 Dr Muhammad Husayn Haykal (1888–1956), prominent Egyptian writer, journalist, politician and Minister of Education in Egypt.

22 Sir William Muir (1819–1905), Scottish Orientalist, scholar of Islam, and colonial administrator as a financial member of the Viceroy's Council and later a member of the Council of India in London.

paganism – to see Islam establish a barrier to the spread of Christianity among the pagan tribes in Africa, we, too, despite our preference for Haykal's book over other works of *Sīra* penned in the ten centuries after al-Ṭabarī, are dismayed to see Haykal's book stand as a barrier between modern readers and the original primary sources of the *Sīra*. These readers tend to believe that a book written in the twentieth century by one of the most prominent Arab intellectuals would surely allow them to dispense with ancient, yellowing books that use convoluted language, lack a coherent methodology and abound in chains of narrations and myths. They could not be more mistaken. The consequences of this position may be as grave as the consequences of the position of the Church, which stood between the masses and the New Testament until Luther's time. Haykal dealt with the original primary sources of the *Sīra* in the same way that Ibn Hishām dealt with the *Sīra* by Ibn Isḥāq, by leaving out "some of the things which are reviled and which would upset people if mentioned". It is not surprising, therefore, to find many people in this day and age who think of themselves as deeply familiar with the Prophet's biography and then are stunned to read for the first time some of the stories mentioned in the *Sīra* by Ibn Isḥāq, *al-Maghāzī* by al-Wāqidī and the *Ṭabaqāt*"of Ibn Saᶜd.

The Prophet's Biographies in Europe in the Middle Ages

The Prophet's biographies written in the Western Christian world are not less interesting or troubling. The image of Muḥammad and Islam first took shape in the West in the times of fierce religious wars: the wars of the Islamic conquests, followed by the Arab–Byzantine wars and the Crusades, in an era in which ignorance and superstition were prevalent in Europe. In reaction to Islam's political and religious threat, and driven by a desire to enhance the self-confidence of Christians, the Church and its clerics spearheaded a raging, malicious and defamatory campaign against the Prophet and his "new religion". The depiction of Muḥammad as a renegade cardinal was not even the most outrageous of the lies fabricated against him. Islam, for them, was nothing but a distorted image of Christianity, a pagan religion built on violence and with a sword as its pillar, which, in order to spread, allows its followers to satisfy their sexual desires in this world and in the Hereafter. Muḥammad was portrayed as nothing but a false, lustful prophet whose sole purpose in proclaiming this religion was the pursuit of his personal aspirations. This position was reflected in Dante's *Divine Comedy*,[23] which placed the Prophet of Islam in one of the lowest, darkest circles of Hell, in a paragraph ignored completely by the translators into Arabic in order not to offend their Arab readers!

As long as wars were the only opportunity for contact between Europeans and Muslims, it was easy for the Europeans to accept this image. However, in the aftermath of the Crusades, as Europeans established their kingdoms in the Levant, entered into commercial and cultural relations and debates with the Muslims, and were exposed to their culture, science and literature, some of them even learning their language, they became less susceptible to the slanders of the clerics against Islam. These clerics, in turn, were dismayed to see those returning from the East conveying to their acquaintances and relatives their admiration for some aspects of the Islamic civilisation, sciences, culture and ethics, and speaking of what they learned of the Prophet's life from the books of Muslims and through conversations with them. Now that the Europeans had become less ignorant about Muslims and Islam, it was necessary for the clerics to pursue another approach, one that was more "scientific" and more committed to facts, in order to preserve the enmity of Christians to Islam and the Prophet.

Thus began a new trend in the second quarter of the twelfth century, when Petrus Venerabilis,[24] the distinguished head of France's famous Cluny Monastery, formed a committee to publish a series of judicious "scientific" works of literature about Islam in order to counter Islam's intellectual challenges and claims. It proceeded to translate the Qur'an and the *Sīra*, as well as other books about the teachings of Islam and the history of Muslim nations. These books were based, not on fiction or hatred, but on Muslim sources. Nevertheless, one could sense a strong spirit of hostility, a mixture of admiration and fear, and a desire to distort the image of the Prophet and Islam in the minds of the intellectuals in particular. This European interest in Islam received another strong impetus with the emergence of the

23 Dante Alighieri (*c.* 1265–1321 AD), a major Italian poet of the late Middle Ages. His *Divine Comedy*, originally called *Commedia* and later christened *Divina* by Boccaccio (1313–1375 AD), is considered to be the greatest literary work composed in the Italian language and a masterpiece of world literature.

24 Petrus Venerabilis (1092–1156 AD), also known as Peter of Montboissier, Abbot of the Benedictine Abbey of Cluny.

Ottoman power and its armies' significant incursions into the European continent.

What made the mission of defaming Islam and the Prophet easier, were precisely those valuable features recorded in the earliest of the Prophet's biographies, namely, the fact that they were open and honest, as well as the authors' simple and strong faith in Muḥammad. The situation was akin to a great man speaking about himself with simplicity and sincerity, only for the listener to ignore everything but the facts that malign him, then inflating these and publicising them while shouting: "Those were his precise words" or "as witnessed by one of their own".[25]

From that time until the present day, the principle embraced by the Orientalists writing the Prophet's biography – even the best among them – was that whatever they saw as insulting to the Prophet in the writings of the early Muslim historians must undoubtedly be true, while anything that would raise his stature must surely be doubtful, and should be subjected to the most rigid standards of research and criticism, on the premise that self-praise should not be taken seriously, while self-flagellation must inevitably be true.

Modern European Trends in Writing the Prophet's Biography

With the era of enlightenment in Europe and the attack on Christianity by many eighteenth-century philosophers and writers, some of these (such as Edward Gibbon[26] in *The History of the Decline and Fall of the Roman Empire*) expressed praise for Islam and Muḥammad in a crafty ploy to undermine the theological foundations of Christianity, which they resented, or to present a derogatory image of Christ. This new trend reached its peak by the mid-nineteenth century, when Thomas Carlyle[27] delivered a public lecture in

25 This is based on an Arabic authoritative expression to bestow legitimacy to a narrative, and which is taken from Q. 12:26: "*He said: 'She sought to make me yield (to her); and a witness of her own family bore witness: If his shirt is rent from front, she speaks the truth and he is one of the liars'.*"

26 Edward Gibbon (1737–1794), English historian, writer and Member of Parliament. In *The History of the Decline and Fall of the Roman Empire*, his most important work, published in six volumes between 1776 and 1788, and which is praised for its quality and use of primary sources, he uses irony to openly criticise organised religion.

27 Thomas Carlyle (1795–1881), Scottish philosopher, satirical writer, essayist, historian and teacher. He was considered one of the most important social commentators of his time.

Edinburgh, in May 1840, on Muḥammad and Islam,[28] which had a profound effect on the development of Islamic Studies in Europe. Carlyle defended Muḥammad in his lecture, which some gullible Muslims still cherish to this day (once again based on the concept of "as witnessed by one of their own"). Were they to know of Carlyle's thought and the rationale of his praise of Islam and its Prophet, they would have found no reason to feel proud. Islam was simply a vehicle through which the British philosopher chose to present his opinions about life, politics and religions.

Since then, the intellectual and religious climate in Europe, the spread of atheism, and the appreciation of the sciences and logic have encouraged a different view of Islam and the Prophet. If the declared principle was fairness and commitment to the scientific spirit, it is our opinion that, as in all other stages of Islamic Studies in Europe since its inception, this was often merely a reflection of passions, a subjective view that does not differ much in nature from the sudden interest of French painters in oriental arts, or the infatuation of an English band with Indian philosophies or the European and American fascination with black magic. However, it was the nineteenth-century scholars and orientalists, such as Weil,[29] de Perceval,[30] Wüstenfeld,[31] Sprenger[32] and Muir, who must be credited for using the early Muslim primary sources, unlike their predecessors, Sir Walter Raleigh,[33] Edward Gibbon and George Sale[34] and others, who relied on obscure secondary Arabic sources, such as *Tarīkh Abū-l-Fidā*" (d. 722 AH/1322 AD).

If we disregard the Western works from the mid-nineteenth century onward which offered nothing new about Muḥammad, such as the books

28 The lecture was titled: "Hero as Prophet; Mahomet: Islam" and was one of six lectures titled "On Heroes and Hero Worship, and the Heroic in History", and later published as a book in 1841 with the same title.

29 Gustav Weil (1808–1889), Jewish German orientalist.

30 Jean-Jacques-Antoine Caussin de Perceval (1759–1835), French orientalist and chair of Arabic at the Collège de France and later president of the Académie des Inscriptions.

31 Heinrich Ferdinand Wüstenfeld (1808–1899), German orientalist and later Arabist at Göttingen University.

32 Aloys Sprenger (1813–1893), Austrian orientalist and later secretary of the Asiatic Society of Calcutta and Professor of Oriental Languages at the University of Bern.

33 Sir Walter Raleigh (*c.* 1554–1618), Protestant English writer, poet, soldier, politician, courtier and explorer.

34 George Sale (1697–1736), British solicitor and orientalist, best known for his 1734 translation of the Qur'an into English.

by Émile Dermenghem,[35] Francesco Gabrielli,[36] and Maxime Rodinson,[37] we can discern three obvious and distinct trends that follow one another in an almost seamless succession. The first trend is represented by Sir William Muir, and reaches its peak in the writings of the Belgian Jesuit Henri Lammens.[38] It is a remnant of the hostile campaign of the Middle Ages, characterised by hatred of the Prophet (moderate in Muir's work and more pronounced in Lammens') and a genuine fear for Christianity from the spread of Islam to primitive societies. This trend differs from the former works in that it is more scientific and offers a more in-depth study of primary Islamic sources. However, the obvious desire to malign, which dictates the selection and presentation of the material, casts serious doubts on these books' objectivity and reduces their value.

The second trend (best represented by Goldziher,[39] Lane-Poole,[40] Frants Buhl,[41] Tor Andræ,[42] Margoliouth,[43] Richard Bell,[44] Nöldeke,[45] Wellhausen,[46]

---

35 Émile Dermenghem (1892–1971), French journalist, archivist and librarian.

36 Francesco Gabrielli (1904–1996), Italian Arabist and orientalist, later Professor of Arabic Language and |Literature at the University of Rome.

37 Maxime Rodinson (1915–2004), French historian, sociologist and orientalist, later librarian at the Bibliothèque Nationale in Paris, then Professor of Classical Ethiopian at the École Pratique des Hautes Études.

38 Henri Lammens (1862–1937), Belgian orientalist historian and Jesuit priest.

39 Ignác (Yitzhaq Yehud) Goldziher, also known as Ignaz Goldziher (1850–1921), Hungarian scholar of Islam and considered one of the founders of modern Islamic Studies in Europe.

40 Stanley Edward Lane-Poole (1854–1931) was a British orientalist and archaeologist and nephew of the famous British orientalist, translator and lexicographer, Edward William Lane (1801–1876).

41 Frants Peder William Meyer Buhl, also known as Frants Buhl (1850–1932), Danish orientalist and scholar of the Old Testament and later Professor of the Old Testament at the University of Copenhagen and Leipzig and member of the Royal Danish Academy of Sciences.

42 Tor Julius Efraim Andræ, known as Tor Andræ (1885–1947), Swedish scholar of comparative religion and bishop of Linköping, Professor of the History of Religions at University College of Stockholm and later in Uppsala and briefly Minister for Ecclesiastical Affairs (Minister of Education).

43 David Samuel Margoliouth (1858–1940), orientalist and briefly a priest in the Church of England, Laudian Professor of Arabic at the University of Oxford from 1889 to 1937, and member of the council of the Royal Asiatic Society and its director as of 1927.

44 Richard Bell (1876–1952) was a British Arabist at the University of Edinburgh.

45 Theodor Nöldeke (1836–1930), German orientalist, later chair of Oriental Languages at Strasbourg and considered one of the founders of modern Islamic Studies in Europe.

46 Julius Wellhausen (1844–1918) was a German biblical scholar and orientalist, later Professor Extraordinarius of Oriental Languages in the Faculty of Philology at Halle, and Professor Ordinarius at Marburg then Göttingen.

Demombynes[47] and Hamilton Gibb),[48] can be credited with explaining much that had remained a mystery in the history of Islam and the Prophet's biography, as well as facilitating the understanding of Arab history during *Jahiliyya* and after Islam. In writing the Prophet's biography, they were as objective as they could be, and considered the Prophet to be a strong, charismatic figure, who was able to provide a solution to the very difficult and complex challenge of building a state, and a great empire, out of the building blocks of scattered and warring Arab tribes, and to create an outlet for the Arab creative genius to contribute more positively to the world's history and civilisation. They acknowledged aspects of the Prophet's greatness, such as his equanimity, and they did not try – as did Muir – to compare Islam, Judaism and Christianity to prove the superiority of the latter two. However, their biggest failing was their inability to recognise the individuality of the figure of Muḥammad, and how his prophecy, ethics, personality and objectives differed from those of Christ and the prophets of the Old Testament. Furthermore, under the influence of Darwin's theories of evolution, the dominant belief in their studies was that the secret of every religion lies in its origins and its sources, and that the mere discovery of the sources from which Muḥammad drew the principles of Islam and the religious conditions prevailing prior to his appearance would be sufficient to shed light on his biography. The result was an exaggerated and disproportionate interest in these issues.

Montgomery Watt's Defence of Muḥammad

Such shortcomings were brilliantly side-stepped by the two leading scholars of the third and current trend in Western Islamic Studies, namely, Arthur Arberry[49] (author of the best English translation of the meanings of the

47 Maurice Gaudefroy-Demombynes (1862–1957), French Arabist and specialist in Islam and the history of religions and professor at the École nationale des langues orientales vivantes.

48 Hamilton Gibb (1895–1971), Scottish historian and orientalist, editor of the *Encyclopaedia of Islam*.

49 Arthur John Arberry (1905–1969), British orientalist and prolific scholar of Arabic, Persian and Islamic Studies. After heading the Department of Classics at Cairo University in Egypt, he became Chair of Persian at the School of Oriental and African Studies, University of London, 1944–1947, and subsequently the Sir Thomas Adams' Professor of Arabic at Cambridge University and a Fellow of Pembroke College, Cambridge.

Qur'an) and especially the Scottish orientalist Montgomery Watt,[50] who may be considered the most renowned Western biographer of the Prophet. Watt set out to defend Muḥammad and Islam, as enthusiastically as any Muslim defending his religion and his Prophet, yet adhering to a scientific research methodology to a large extent.

However, we feel an inexplicable, fundamental contradiction in his position which – in a way and in some cases – makes us prefer Muir's biography of the Prophet, with its clearly stated aims, to that of Watt.

Watt writes in the introductions to his books, *Muḥammad at Mecca*, *Muḥammad at Medina* and *What is Islam?* as well as in Richard Bell's *Introduction to the Qur'an* that he tried to take a neutral position between Christianity and Islam:

> For example, in order to avoid deciding whether the Qur'an is or is not the Word of God, I have refrained from using the expressions "God says" and "Muḥammad says" when referring to the Qur'an, and have simply said "the Qur'an says" . . . I have endeavoured, while remaining faithful to the standards of Western historical scholarship, to say nothing that would entail the rejection of any of the fundamental doctrines of Islam. There need be no unbridgeable gulf between Western scholarship and Islamic faith; if some of the conclusions of Western scholars have been unacceptable to Muslims, it may be that the scholars have not always been faithful to their own principles of scholarship and that, even from the purely historical point of view, their conclusion requires to be revised. On the other hand, it is probably also true that there is room, without any change in essentials, for some reformulation of Islamic doctrine.[51]

Watt does not see the adoption of a materialistic viewpoint as necessary for the historian's neutrality. He writes, as he says, from the point of view of a monotheistic believer: "I am not a Muslim in the usual sense, though I hope

50 William Montgomery Watt (1909–2006), Scottish historian, orientalist, Anglican priest and Professor of Arabic and Islamic Studies at the University of Edinburgh as well as visiting professor at the University of Toronto, the Collège de France and Georgetown University.

51 Watt, W. M., *Muhammad at Mecca*, Oxford: Clarendon Press, 1953, p. x.

I am a *muslim* as 'one surrendered to God'; but I believe that embedded in the Qur'an and other expressions of the Islamic vision are vast stores of divine truth from which I and other occidentals have still much to learn." Yet he also adds: "At the same time we cannot fully accept the standard Islamic view that the Qur'an is wholly true and the criterion of all other truth."[52]

He then writes: "With the greatly increased contacts between Muslims and Christians during the last quarter of a century, it has become imperative for a Christian scholar not to offend Muslim readers gratuitously, but as far as possible to present his arguments in a form acceptable to them. Courtesy and an eirenic outlook certainly now demand that we should not speak of the Qur'an as the product of Muḥammad's conscious mind; but I hold that the same demand is also made by sound scholarship."[53]

Hence, according to Watt, the need to write about the Prophet in such a courteous way which respects Muslim sensibilities stems from the need to forge closer ties between the modern Western world and the Muslim world: "In the modern world, where contacts between Christians and Muslims are closer than ever before, it is urgent that both should strive to reach an objective view of Muḥammad's character,"[54] and "Critics of my books on Muhammad have accused me of not stating my views clearly . . . but the matter is difficult when one is writing for a great variety of readers who will understand the key concepts in many different ways."[55] Despite our admiration for Montgomery Watt and his books, we can, frankly, neither understand nor condone such an attitude. How can the idea of forging ties between the West and the Muslim world today be the motivation for Westerners to vindicate Muḥammad and elevate his status? However, this position is in fact significant and should be studied. If at some point Europe's need for the region's oil led to growing European sympathy for the Arab cause, as manifested by the Islamic festivals and exhibitions held in Europe in the 1970s and the works of contemporary Arab writers translated on an unprecedented scale, it would not be surprising if in the near future we were to read research on the impact of the global energy crisis on *Sīra* writing in oil-consuming countries!

---

52 Watt, W. M., *What is Islam?* London/Beirut: Longmans/Librairie du Liban, 1968, p. 21.

53 Watt, W. M. and Bell, R., *Bell's Introduction to the Qur'an*, Edinburgh: Edinburgh University Press, 1970, p. vi.

54 Watt, W. M., *Muhammad: Prophet and Statesman*, Oxford: Oxford University Press, 1961, p. 229.

55 Watt, *What is Islam?* p. 21.

While this attitude is therefore not surprising, the astonishment and sadness lies in finding some Muslims cheering and swelling with confidence when orientalists or foreigners deign to praise or defend the Prophet (even if they were not scholars of Islamic Studies, such as Washington Irving,[56] Le Bon[57] and Thomas Carlyle), or in finding them to defame and malign those who did the same to him. Neither should their praise make us feel proud, nor ought we feel weakened or shaken by their disparagement. Why should we feel proud if praise often stems from an author's atheism, or from his eagerness to appear independent or objective, or from his desire not to shock his readers, or if it is motivated by national or materialistic interests, or prompted by an intellectual and political rapprochement with Islamic countries? Equally, why should we feel shaken if disparagement, in the best of cases, arises from a Western Christian's inability to understand the Prophet in the context of his Arab environment?

It is high time, in our opinion, for the Muslim world to produce a new biography of the Prophet. A biography that is neither defensive, nor apologetic nor ashamed. A biography that does not blur and invent facts to the point of becoming untruthful, or consists of a simple narration of facts to the point of becoming insipid. A biography that does not omit "some of the things which are reviled and which would upset people if mentioned". A biography that is not afraid to offend some people; one that does not impose any guardianship on anyone. A biography that revives an entire historical era and reconstructs its ethical standards and values, its environment, and its particular traditions and customs so that the Prophet's persona and his deeds become clear within their context. A biography that deals with history from a genuine religious perspective, written by a courageous Muslim proficient "in a clear Arabic tongue",[58] one who is not suffering from complexes and who takes great pride in his religion and has the utmost confidence in his Prophet. A biography that al-Waqidī or al-Ṭabarī may have written, were they alive today.

---

56 Washington Irving (1783–1859), American short story writer, essayist, biographer, historian and diplomat.

57 Charles-Marie Gustave le Bon (1841–1931), French polymath interested in anthropology, psychology, sociology, archaeology, medicine, invention and physics.

58 This is a reference to Q. 16:103: "*And certainly We know that they say: Only a mortal teaches him. The tongue of him whom they reproach is barbarous, and this is clear Arabic tongue.*"

3
Reflections on the Truth about Abū Lahab (the Judas of Banū Hāshim)

Q. 111:1: Perdition overtake both hands of Abū Lahab, and he will perish.
Q. 111:2 His wealth and what he earns did not avail him.
Q. 111:3: He shall soon burn in fire that flames,
Q. 111:4: And his wife, the bearer of fuel,
Q. 111:5: Upon her neck a halter of strongly twisted rope.

Chapter 111 of the Qur'an

Reading Qur'an Chapter 111 ("Al-Massad") raised a number of questions in my mind about the time and place the chapter was revealed, the use of certain tenses in the verses, the use of the *kunya* (epithet) instead of his given name, the meaning of certain phrases used in the verses, and, finally, why Abū Lahab in particular? This chapter attempts to answer these questions.

Meccan or Medinan? Past or Present Tense?

According to all, or most, of the Muslim exegetes and commentators, the *sūra* (Qur'anic chapter) was one of the first Meccan chapters revealed. It is claimed that when Q. 26.214[1] was revealed, the Prophet ascended

1 Q. 26.214: "*And warn your nearest relations.*"

al-Ṣafā[2] hill and shouted out until the people gathered around him, and then told them that he is a *nadhīr* (harbinger), foretelling them of severe suffering. Abū Lahab is said to have replied: "Damn you! Is this why you brought us together?," and left, calling upon the others not to gather around the Prophet. If it is true that Chapter 111 was revealed shortly after this episode, then what is the reason for using the past tense in this verse (Q. 111:1) and the one following it (Q. 111:2), when at that time Abū Lahab – as is evident – was still alive and enjoying his riches?

The answer is easy with respect to the first verse. It is common practice among the Arabs to use the past tense in cases where the verb refers to the present or the future. Examples of this can be found in Q. 16.1:[3] "*Allah's commandment has come*", meaning "it will come in the future", and in Q. 3.110:[4] "*You were the best of the nations*", meaning "you are in the present". Furthermore, in daily usage the Arabs say "*raḥimahu Allah*" ("God had mercy upon him"), "*ṣaḥibatka-l-salāma*" ("safety accompanied you") and "*bārak Allahu fikum*" ("God blessed you"), which denote the present or future tense. Hence, *tabbat* (lit. perished) here is a verb in the past tense, yet refers to the future.

However, the answer with regard to the second verse Q. 111:2 is more difficult.

The Qur'an does not use the words "*ma aghnā*" ("did not avail him") and similar phrases except to indicate an event that had already taken place in the past. For example, verses Q. 15.83[5] and Q. 15.84,[6] as well as verses Q. 26.206[7]

---

2 Al-Ṣafā is a small hill located in Mecca, together with another small hill named al-Marwah. Both hills are important for performing the Ḥajj, as Muslims travel back and forth between them seven times during the Ḥajj and Umrah (pilgrimages).

3 Q. 16.1: "*Allah's commandment has come, therefore do not desire to hasten it; glory be to Him, and highly exalted be He above what they associate (with Him).*"

4 Q. 3.110: "*You were the best of the nations raised up for (the benefit of) men; you enjoin what is right and forbid the wrong and believe in Allah; and if the followers of the Book had believed it would have been better for them; of them (some) are believers and most of them are transgressors.*"

5 Q. 15.83: "*So the rumbling overtook them in the morning*"; Q. 15.84: "*And what they earned did not avail them.*"

6 Q. 15.84: "*And what they earned did not avail them.*"

7 Q. 26.206: "*Then there comes to them that with which they are threatened,*"

and Q. 26.207.[8] See also other verses such as Q. 39.50,[9] Q. 40.82,[10] Q. 46.26[11] and Q. 9.25.[12]

If the intention of these verses was to refer to the future, then – and God knows best – the word "*yughnī*" ("shall avail") would have been used, as in verse Q. 3.10[13] or in verse Q. 45.10.[14] See also other verses such as Q. 3.116,[15] Q. 8.19[16] and Q. 58.17.[17]

We believe it is most likely that Chapter 111 was revealed after the news about Abū Lahab's death was received, shortly after the Battle of Badr in 2 AH/624 AD (Ibn Hishām reported that he died seven days after the battle). It is unsound to argue that the shortness of the verses in this chapter – which is what distinguishes the Meccan chapters from the Medinan chapters in general – is evidence that they were revealed in Mecca. There are Medinan chapters with very short verses as well, like, for example, Chapter 110. With regard to existing interpretations which say that the first verse Q. 111:1: "*Perdition overtake both hands of Abū Lahab, and he will perish*", came in response to Abū Lahab telling the Prophet "Damn you", we say that exegetes often fabricate stories in order to interpret the verses and explain the occasions of their revelation.

8 Q. 26.207: "*That which they were made to enjoy shall not avail them?*"

9 Q. 39.50: "*Those before them did say it indeed, but what they earned availed them not.*"

10 Q. 40.82: "*Have they not then journeyed in the land and seen how was the end of those before them? They were more (in numbers) than these and greater in strength and in fortifications in the land, but what they earned did not avail them.*"

11 Q. 46.26: "*And certainly We had established them in what We have not established you in, and We had given them ears and eyes and hearts, but neither their ears, nor their eyes, nor their hearts availed them aught, since they denied the communications of Allah, and that which they mocked encompassed them.*"

12 Q. 9.25: "*Certainly Allah helped you in many battlefields and on the day of Hunain, when your great numbers made you vain, but they availed you nothing and the earth became straight to you notwithstanding its spaciousness, then you turned back retreating.*"

13 Q. 3.10: " *(As for) those who disbelieve, surely neither their wealth nor their children shall avail them in the least against Allah, and these it is who are the fuel of the fire.*"

14 Q. 45.10: "*Before them is hell, and there shall not avail them aught of what they earned, nor those whom they took for guardians besides Allah, and they shall have a grievous punishment.*"

15 Q. 3.116: "*(As for) those who disbelieve, surely neither their wealth nor their children shall avail them in the least against Allah; and these are the inmates of the fire; therein they shall abide.*"

16 Q. 8.19: "*If you demanded a judgement, the judgement has then indeed come to you; and if you desist, it will be better for you; and if you turn back (to fight), We (too) shall turn back, and your forces shall avail you nothing, though they may be many, and (know) that Allah is with the believers.*"

17 Q. 58.17: "*Neither their wealth nor their children shall avail them aught against Allah; they are the inmates of the fire, therein they shall abide.*"

The strongest evidence of the validity of our thesis is the account reported in *al-Ṭabaqāt al-kubra* of Ibn Saᶜd, who is considered trustworthy. After Abū Ṭālib died and his brother Abū Lahab became his successor in the leadership of the Banū Hāshim clan, the Prophet rarely left his house. The Quraysh clan took advantage of the situation in a way they would not have imagined possible before. When Abū Lahab heard of that, he went to the Prophet and said: "O Muḥammad, do what you want, and what you would have done if Abū Ṭālib were alive. I swear by al-Lāt[18] that nobody will harm you for as long as I am alive!" According to another account, Abū Lahab punished Ibn al-Ghayṭala when the latter insulted the Prophet. Ibn al-Ghayṭala walked away yelling: "O tribe of Quraysh, Abū Lahab has become a Sabian!" The Qurayshi men gathered and stood before Abū Lahab. He told them, "I have not left the faith of ᶜAbd al-Muṭṭalib, but I will prevent any harm coming to my nephew until he has accomplished what he desires." They replied: "You have done the right thing, and upheld your family ties." The Prophet then spent a period of time coming and going without any interference from Quraysh who respected and feared Abū Lahab.

One cannot imagine that this incident, reported in *al-Ṭabaqāt al-kubra,* could have taken place after the revelation of Chapter 111 at the start of the call to Islam. It is unreasonable for Abū Lahab to insist on protecting the Prophet after Abū Ṭālib's death in 619 AD (only three years before migration to Medina), and for the Prophet to have accepted his protection after what the Qur'an revealed about him and his wife.

Be that as it may, it is our opinion that the *sūra* may be Medinan, and in that case the verb "*tabbat*" ("perished") would be a statement of fact or state. It would imply that all his money and wealth will not prevent his death or his torment in hellfire. However, if it was a Meccan *sūra*, as the exegetes and commentators insist, the purpose of the verb would be to invoke the descent of a curse upon him.

The Use of the Kunya *(Epithet)*

The Arabs used epithets as a means of glorification or recognition, as an honorific address or as a form of reverence to avoid disclosing the name.

18 Al-Lāt is the name of a goddess worshipped in pre-Islamic Arabia. Together with Manāt and al-ᶜUzzā, she was one of the three chief goddesses of Mecca.

Al-Suyūṭī (849–911 AH/1445–1505 AD)[19] wrote in his *al-Muzhir fī ᶜulūm al-lughah wa anwāᶜihā* (*The Luminous Work Concerning the Sciences of Language and its Subfields*): "only the most honourable of people are entitled to an epithet".

Why then would the Qur'an resort to using an epithet to honour this infidel? His name is in fact ᶜAbd al-ᶜUzzā b. ᶜAbd al-Muṭṭalib, but his father called him Abū Lahab ("He with a flame") because of the beauty and brightness of his face.

The answer again is easy. We find it in the *Tafsīr al-Kashshāf* by al-Zamakhsharī (457–538 AH/1075–1144 AD),[20] as well as in the *al-Jāmiᶜ li-aḥkām al-Qur'ān* by al-Qurṭubī (611–671 AH/1214–1273 AD)[21] and elsewhere. Abū Lahab is well known by his epithet and not by his name, hence, his epithet replaced his name. As he was doomed to hellfire and its flames, his epithet conformed to his future fate and therefore it was more suitable to call him by his epithet. Finally, his name ᶜAbd al-ᶜUzzā, means worshipper of, or slave to, al-ᶜUzzā,[22] one of the idols worshipped in *Jahiliyya*. God has not used the word *ᶜabd* (worshipper or slave) in conjunction with the name of any idol in the Qur'an.

Umm al-kitāb, *or* Urtext

Exegetes and Qur'an commentators interpret Q. 85:22[23] to mean the *Umm al-kitāb*, or *Urtext*,[24] from which the Qur'an and all other divine books were copied. They believed that this *urtext* included the explanations for all matters relating to all created beings, their life spans and death dates, their deeds, their fate and the consequences of their actions.

---

19 Abū-l-Faḍl ᶜAbd al-Raḥmān b. Abī Bakr b. Muḥammad Jalāl al-Dīn al-Khuḍayrī al-Suyūṭī (849–911 AH/1445–1505 AD), was a prolific Egyptian religious scholar, juristic exegetist and teacher.

20 Abū-l-Qāsim Maḥmūd b. ᶜUmar al-Zamakhsharī (457-538 AH/1075–1144 AD), known as al-Zamakhsharī, medieval Muᶜtazila scholar of Persian origin.

21 Abū ᶜAbd Allah Muḥammad b. Aḥmad b. Abū Bakr al-Anṣārī al-Qurṭubī (611–671 AH/1214–1273 AD), a famous exegete, traditionist and jurist from Cordoba.

22 Al-ᶜUzzā is the name of a goddess worshipped in pre-Islamic Arabia. Together with al-Lāt and Manāt, she was one of the three chief goddesses of Mecca.

23 Q. 85.22: "*In a guarded tablet.*"

24 An original, or the earliest version, of a text, to which later versions can be compared.

Was Chapter 111 therefore "*in a guarded tablet*" from the beginning of time, long before Abū Lahab's birth, such that there was no escape for him from hellfire and that it was impossible for him to convert to Islam? The attempt to answer this question would lead us into the long and painstaking debate about the eternal topic of whether human beings are *mukhayyar* (endowed with free will) or *musayyar* (pre-destined)? This debate filled hundreds and hundreds of pages in the books of Muslim scholars.

In any case, to say "*He shall soon burn in fire that flames*" offers more support to the thesis that the *sūra* is Medinan and not Meccan, and that it was revealed after Abū Lahab's death when his chance to embrace Islam and to repent and escape the fate of burning in hellfire had elapsed.

What is Meant by "the Bearer of Fuel"?

Some exegetes and Qur'an commentators opined that Umm Jamīl,[25] Abū Lahab's wife, used to carry firewood on her back so that she could dispense with servants, due to her being extremely parsimonious. They also said that she used to collect thistles and thorns at night and carry them to lay them on the path of the Prophet and his Companions.

We believe that in all likelihood the verse does not refer to what Umm Jamīl did during her lifetime, but instead to the fact that this woman will be collecting the firewood that will fuel the fire in hell. Perhaps what proves this point is that the word "*ḥammālata*" (bearer) is (according to *qirāʿatu ʿĀṣim*)[26] to be read with an accusative case ending, indicating that this verse is grammatically linked to the previous one, meaning that it depicts Umm Jamīl's state in Hell. If the word was simply a predicate or an adjective describing the wife's occupation during her lifetime, it would have had a nominative case ending. Others, meanwhile, believe that while the word may be in the accusative case, it is so due to an ellipsis implying censure, hence, the word "*ḥammālata*" is not used to simply describe Umm Jamīl, but to censure her.

It is also our opinion that the verse "*Upon her neck a halter of strongly twisted rope*" means that in hell she will have a rope, twisted from a stringy

25 Umm Jamīl bint Ḥarb, daughter of Ḥarb b. Umayya (a chief of Mecca), sister of Abū Sufyān and one of the leading women of the Quraysh tribe, she was also known as Arwā.

26 Qirāʿāt, literally the readings, is a term referring to the method of recitation of the Qur'an, here according to the recitation of ʿĀṣim b. Abū-l-Nujūd al-Kūfī (d. 127 or 128 AH/744 or 745 AD).

fibrous material, around her neck. We do not agree with what al-Ḍaḥḥāk[27] and others said, namely, that in her lifetime she would tie a rope around her neck and that God's punishment for her was such that she was strangled to death by that rope.

But Why Abū Lahab?

We believe that this question is the most important one: why did God single out Abū Lahab in particular, out of all the infidels, by naming him and allocating a *sūra* to him? Why not Abū Jahl,[28] or Umayya b. Khalaf,[29] or ᶜUqba b. Abū Muᶜayiṭ[30] or al-Naḍr b. al-Ḥārith,[31] who were all among the Prophet's worst enemies in Quraysh and the most cruel to him?

Of all the Prophet's contemporaries, the Qur'an only mentions two by name. One of them is a Muslim, Zayd b. al-Ḥāritha,[32] and the other an infidel, Abū Lahab. So what is the reason for the revelation of this particular chapter?

We know that the Companion ᶜAbd Allah b. Masᶜūd[33] – who considered himself one of the greatest trustworthy experts on the Qur'an – said that the Qur'an version approved by Caliph ᶜUthmān b. ᶜAffān was distorted and

---

27 al-Ḍaḥḥāk b. Muzāḥim (d. 105 AH/723 AD), traditionist and exegete.

28 ᶜAmr b. Hishām, known as Abū Jahl (Father of Ignorance) and not by his epithet Abū-l-Ḥakam (Father of Wisdom), from the powerful Banū Makhzūm clan and one of the leaders of Quraysh and known for his staunch opposition towards Muḥammad and the early Muslims in Mecca. He is credited with the plan to assassinate Muḥammad. He was fatally wounded in the Battle of Badr (2 AH/624 AD).

29 Umayyah b. Khalaf b. Safwān, head of the Banū Jumah clan and a leading member of Quraysh. He was fiercely opposed to the Prophet and the Muslims. He owned the slave called Bilāl b. Rabāḥ al-Ḥabashī, the first muezzin chosen by the Prophet, whom he brutally tortured for converting to Islam. He was killed in the Battle of Badr (2 AH/624 AD).

30 ᶜUqba b. Abū Muᶜayiṭ of the Banū ᶜAbd Shams clan of Quraysh and one of its leaders. He was one of the principal adversaries of Islam, assaulting Muḥammad verbally and physically. He was killed in the Battle of Badr (2 AH/624 AD).

31 al-Naḍr b. al-Ḥārith b. ᶜAbd Manāf, one of the leaders of Quraysh, a staunch enemy of the Prophet and one of the main strategists of the siege of Banū Hāshim. It is said that he was taken prisoner of war during the Battle of Badr and then beheaded (2 AH/624 AD).

32 Zayd b. al-Ḥāritha al-Kalbī (35 before *Hijra*–8 AH/581–629 AD) was once regarded as Muḥammad's adoptive son. He was married to Zaynab bint Jaḥsh, who married the Prophet after their divorce. He was killed during the Battle of Muᵓtah (8 AH/629 AD).

33 ᶜAbd Allah b. Masᶜūd, also known by his epithet Abū ᶜAbd al-Raḥmān (31 or 37 before *Hijra*–32 AH/594–653 AD), was an early convert to Islam and a Companion of the Prophet. He is a prominent transmitter of *ḥadīth*.

incomplete, and that he accused Zayd b. Thābit[34] and his companions, who collected the Qur'an, of excluding some verses that cursed the Umayyads. However, this accusation is unacceptable. ᶜAlī b. Abū Ṭālib and many other Companions were still alive at the time Zayd b. Thābit embarked on this mission, and we do not read that one of them supported Ibn Masᶜūd's allegation or protested against the exclusion of any verses.

Abū Lahab was the Prophet's uncle and was, at some point in time, on good terms with his nephew, as is evidenced by the story quoted from *al-Ṭabaqāt al-Kubra*. Another proof of the good relationship is that Abū Lahab's two sons, ᶜUtba and ᶜUtayba, were either engaged to or married to the Prophet's daughters: the first son to Ruqaya and the second to Umm Kulthūm. What happened after that to turn Abū Lahab into one of the leaders of the infidels and one of the Prophet's staunchest enemies?

Two words in the *sūra*, we believe, are key to the answer: his wealth and his wife. We will explain what we mean below.

The Merchants of Quraysh

We know that the pastoralist nomadic communities were always in great need of solidarity between their members in order to protect the tribes' existence. Therefore, it was the duty of every member of the tribe or clan to support "his brethren", be they right or wrong. It was also the duty of the leader to provide protection to those he led, as well as to help the needy and the vulnerable.

However, as Quraysh in Mecca gradually turned to trade, this led to a steady weakening of solidarity among the members of the tribe. The leaders and elders became more concerned with amassing wealth. This was facilitated by the fact that the merchants primarily dealt in luxury commodities that

34 Zayd b. Thābit (12 before *Hijra*–45 AH/611–665 AD), the personal scribe of the Prophet, who was assigned to collect and authenticate the Qur'anic verses by Abū Bakr after the death of many who had memorised the Qur'an in the Battle of Yamāmah. He completed the task and is said to have given the collection to Abū Bakr, who is said to have left it with ᶜUmar b. al-Khaṭṭāb before he died. ᶜUmar is said to have left it with his daughter, Ḥafṣa. ᶜUthmān revived the project and assigned Zayd and some other Companions to make copies of the manuscript in Ḥafṣa's possession to be sent to the Muslim provinces to become the standard copy of the Qur'an for all to use.

were small in size and easy to store, which enabled them to increase their wealth without limits. The definition of wealth in Bedouin societies, however, was different. It was defined as an abundance of camels in large herds, which made it very difficult to amass large amounts of wealth. These herds needed numerous men to care for them and protect them from enemy raids; men who had a strong feeling of loyalty to the flock's owner to motivate them to fulfil their tasks and risk their lives in the process.

The Qurayshi merchants then proceeded to exploit the vulnerable, especially widows and orphans. The leaders among them managed the tribe's entire capital by investing it in trade on their behalf and then keeping the profits exclusively for themselves. Nevertheless, only a small number of the Qurayshi merchants were able to amass a large amount of wealth. At the time when the Prophet started his mission (around 610 AD), the conflict was not so much between the rich and the poor, as between the moderately wealthy and the very rich. The moderately wealthy merchants were concerned about the steady weakening of the feelings of solidarity among the members of the tribe, the increasingly individualistic attitudes, and the collapse of traditional tribal values that had provided some kind of reassurance about the future for all members of the tribe.

The new commercial interests soon led to the establishment of new alliances between the big merchants of Quraysh. Two major groups with conflicting ambitions formed in Mecca. The Banū Hāshim, who were less affluent, led the *ḥilf al-fuḍūl* (League of the Virtuous), which was mainly composed of those who were unable to organise independent trade caravans to make the profit they were unjustly deprived of. They were in a feud with *al-aḥlāf* (The Alliance), which was set up by the wealthy merchants, who sought to impose a kind of trade monopoly. We believe that one of the motives that led the Prophet to direct more than half of the Muslims, at that time, to emigrate to Abyssinia (despite the commonly accepted account that the persecution they suffered was the only motive for this emigration), may have been a desire to break this monopoly, so that the Muslim emigrants could look for another trade route not dominated by the big merchants of Quraysh. This assumption is supported by two points: the first point is that the majority of emigrants to Abyssinia were members of *ḥilf al-fuḍūl*, and the second is that a number of them remained in Abyssinia until the seventh year of *Hijra*, that is, after the migration of the Prophet and the other Muslims to Medina and the end of their persecution.

Abū Lahab's Role

Around the year 616 AD (almost a year after the emigration to Abyssinia), the leaders of Quraysh agreed on a boycott of the Banū Hāshim and the Banū al-Muṭṭalib, who had close ties to the Banū Hāshim. They banned all commercial dealings with them and also banned marriage to anyone from these clans. The apparent reason for this was said to be Abū Ṭālib's refusal to cease his protection of his nephew, Muḥammad, and his inability to persuade him to abandon his call for a new religion. Despite the fact that the Arabs considered it most shameful for a clan to cease the protection of any of its members just because other clans threatened them with punishment, it would have been easy for Abū Ṭālib to find any excuse or other to give up on his nephew if he really wanted to avoid the Qurayshi boycott of the Banū Hāshim.

In fact, Banū Hāshim's continuing challenge of the boycott over three years is evidence that they had a genuine interest in the dispute, and that they were still able to engage in some trade, albeit on a much smaller scale than before. The boycott finally collapsed when some of the Qurayshi leaders withdrew from it after they realised that its success would lead to even greater power for the rich merchants behind it, to an extent not previously foreseen.

Around the year 619 AD (shortly after the end of the boycott), Abū Ṭālib died, and Abū Lahab succeeded him in the leadership of Banū Hāshim. We believe that about a year or so into Abū Lahab's leadership (a period in which Abū Lahab emulated his brother's approach to protecting the Prophet, as evidenced in the paragraph quoted from *al-Ṭabaqāt al-Kubra*), *al-aḥlāf* realised that they would not be able to exert pressure on the Prophet and the Banū Hāshim unless this pressure came from within the ranks of the Banū Hāshim themselves. They therefore sought to bribe Abū Lahab, and succeeded in persuading him to abandon his clan's traditions and betray their commercial and economic interests for purely personal benefits. It is likely that they seduced him by offering him a share of their profits, or inviting him to join their commercial operations and partake in the monopoly. Their success was due to three reasons:

First, his mean nature and his love of money, wealth and a life of luxury (Q. 111:2: "*His wealth and what he earns*"). Second, his marriage to Abū Sufyān's sister (Q. 111:4: ". . . *the bearer of fuel*"). Abū Sufyān was one of the leaders of the powerful Banū Umayya clan and one of the biggest two or three merchants of Quraysh. This woman must have exerted a great influence on her husband, otherwise why would she be paired with him the way we see in Chapter 111. Her influence could either be by virtue of belonging to the Banū Umayya clan, or due to personal characteristics such as her beauty or wealth. Third, the *al-aḥlāf* were able to find a convenient excuse for Abū Lahab to ease his guilt and to use with the Banū Hāshim should they blame him or humiliate him. The *al-aḥlāf* convinced him – or he chose to be convinced – that Muḥammad's cursing of the gods worshipped by ᶜAbd al-Muṭṭalib as well as his prediction that they were doomed to hell, were two perfect and sufficient reasons to abandon the protection of his nephew without any shame or loss of the people's respect.

Quraysh were not – as many believe – very strongly attached to their gods, nor were their pagan beliefs deeply rooted. They continued to worship the idols just like their forefathers and due to the lack – until the advent of Islam – of any organised opposition to these acts of worship. What strengthens this argument is that many of them belittled their gods and disregarded them, and that *al-Ḥunafā*[35] called to the worship of one God and disparaged the pagan beliefs of their people without any persecution or any harm coming to them. Furthermore, the ease of Quraysh's stunning and complete acceptance, after the conquest of Mecca, of the demolition of their idols without any regrets or indignation is another argument supporting this thesis. Quraysh's opposition to the Prophet stemmed essentially out of political and economic concerns. Despite the fact that the Prophet had no plans for complete control of Mecca, their recognition of him as a messenger of God would have ultimately led to his growing political influence. Since this recognition implied an acknowledgement that the provisions and orders he brought to them were from God, and that they had no option but to follow them, this would inevitably have caused a radical change in Mecca's

35 *Al-Ḥunafā* (also called *al-Ḥanīfiyya*) are, according to Islam, the followers of the religion of the Prophet Ibrāhīm. Before the advent of Islam, some followed what they believed to be Ibrāhīm's religion, the most famous amongst them being the prominent poet Ummayya b. Abū-l-Ṣalt and Zayd b. ᶜAmr b. Nufayl, the paternal uncle of ᶜUmar b. al-Khaṭṭāb. The Qur'an confirmed their ideas in several verses, such as Q. 4:125: "*And who has a better religion than he who submits himself entirely to Allah? And he is the doer of good (to others) and follows the faith of Ibrahim, the upright one, and Allah took Ibrahim as a friend.*" (See also Q. 2:135, 3:67, 3:95, 6:79, 6:105, 6:161, 16:120, 16:123, 22:31, 30:30 and 98:5.)

economic conditions, as well as in the balance of power within the clans of Quraysh.

Be that as it may, Abū Lahab terminated his protection of the Prophet and, hence, it became too dangerous for the Prophet to continue to advocate Islam in Mecca, or even to continue living there. If later on the Prophet accepted the asylum granted to him by al-Muṭᶜim b. ᶜAdiy,[36] leader of the Banū Nawfal clan, it is most likely that al-Muṭᶜim set some conditions to somewhat limit the scope of the Prophet's proselytising and imposed some restrictions on his freedom. Before that, the Prophet actively sought new grounds for his call to Islam beyond Mecca. His first thought was neighbouring al-Ta'if, especially since its people, the Banū Thaqīf, had in the past been the greatest rivals of the Qurayshi merchants, even though they had meanwhile come under their control. Despite the fact that their conversion to Islam could have led to their salvation from this financial dependency on Mecca, they refused to accept the Prophet's invitation to Islam (perhaps they too feared that this would grant the Prophet too much political influence), and the Prophet returned to Mecca unsuccessfully. We all know how successful the subsequent negotiations with the people of Yathrib (Medina) were, who were desperately seeking a strong political authority to put an end to the bloody feud between al-Aws and al-Khazraj.[37] We also know how in 622 AD he migrated to Medina with around seventy Muslims, and that one of the main factors in his victory over the Meccans was that the Muslims choked off Qurayshi trade until they were forced to yield and comply.

The bottom line is that this betrayal on Abū Lahab's part in order to make material gains at the expense of his clan, and under the strong influence of his wife, is the sole explanation for this extreme indignation against both of them in Chapter 111.

And Allah knows best what he intended.

---

36 al-Muṭᶜim b. ᶜAdiy, the chief of the Banū Nawfal clan. It is said that he, together with four other people, embarked on an initiative that resulted in the end of the Meccan boycott.

37 al-Aws (Banū Aws) and al-Khazraj (Banū Qayla) were the two main tribes in Medina, who later became al-Anṣār (the helpers) after Muḥammad's migration to Medina. The two tribes were sworn enemies and the historical books claim that they had been fighting for over 120 years. The Prophet was invited to resolve the feud between them and ultimately did so by absorbing both into the Muslim community and forbidding bloodshed among Muslims.

4
The Role of Aḥādīth *(Traditions) Ascribed to the Prophet in the History of Islamic Societies*

With the Prophet's death, divine communication ceased. The people – among them ᶜUmar b. al-Khaṭṭāb – imagined that he would remain in his *ummah*[1] to manage its affairs and be the last man standing, and then bear witness to this *ummah* on the Day of Resurrection. When, after Abu Bakr's sermon, they ascertained the news of his death, they became – in the words of ᶜAᵓisha – "like sheep on a rainy winter night at the loss of their Prophet".[2]

The Muslims were at once deprived of both heavenly guidance and the presence of the Prophet. However, they still had God's book, which His messenger was given. The Qur'an alone was enough to govern and regulate the conditions of the first Muslim community and its religious, social and political affairs. However, it was not long after the Prophet's death that the Arabs expanded from their desert like a giant genie released from its bottle. Within a century, they controlled territories from the Oxus River in Central Asia to the far north of Africa on the Atlantic Ocean, governing various nations with customs, morals and values, environments and civilisations very different from those of the people in the Arabian Peninsula. They founded new cities and inhabited existing cities already densely populated with their original indigenous inhabitants. All this resulted in a need for more complex and detailed laws than those that were sufficient for the simple desert

1 Nation/community.
2 As mentioned in the *Sīra* of Ibn Hishām.

community in Mecca and Medina. The rules governing the simple life of the first Muslims no longer met the needs of their grandsons, who were now living in new environments, mixing with followers of religions radically different from their own, and facing conditions that the Qur'an did not talk about, or addressed only in general terms, without elaborating on the details.

The Sunna as the Second Source of Law

Faced with this massive geographic expansion, the pressures of the new, historic and ever-changing conditions, as well as the changing times and places, the Muslims and their jurists sought guidance on how to deal with all these new circumstances. It was only natural for their piety to lead them to seek guidance at the same source that had received the revelation and proclaimed the divine message: Muḥammad, the decent human being, chosen by God and protected by Him from human afflictions, the Prophet, who did not speak out of whim or personal desire,[3] but was the one who best understood the will of God.

The next generation after the *Ṣaḥāba* (Companions), namely, the *tabiᶜūn* (followers), thus began to collect the accounts of the Prophet's words and deeds and all that which was common practice during his lifetime. They made this, the Sunna of the Prophet, the second source of law and a standard for moral judgements second only to the Qur'an. Despite the fact that the Prophet himself had never claimed to be infallible, except when dictating or reciting God's verses, and that the Qur'an even drew his attention to some minor misdeeds on his part,[4] the adherents of enforcing the Sunna believed that the divine providence would guide all the Prophet's actions and each word he uttered from the time of his call to prophethood until his death. They therefore believed that the rules and regulations of the Sunna are binding in all cases where there was no clear Qur'anic injunction.

This was followed by attempts to raise the status of the Sunna to the rank of Qur'anic rulings in legislative matters. It was said that the Prophet arrived at these rulings by God's orders and that they were also revealed to him, just

3 This is based on Q. 53.3: "*Nor does he speak out of desire*", and Q. 53.4: "*It is naught but revelation that is revealed*".

4 The verses are collectively called "*ayāt al-ᶜitāb*" (verses of reprimand). See, for example, Q. 4:105, 5:67 and 5:89, 8:67–69, 9:43, 18:23–24, 33:37–39, 39:36, 52:48, 66:1–2 and 80:1–16.

like the verses of the Qur'an. In the late second/eighth century, al-Shaybānī[5] opined that the Sunna may supersede Qur'anic injunctions. In his book *al-Sayr al-Kabīr* he writes: "the abrogation of the Qur'an through the *mashhūr* (known widely, famous) Sunna which scholars have accepted as probable is permissible". His pupil, al-Shāfiᶜī,[6] did not find anything objectionable about his teacher's opinion. We also find al-Qāḍī al-Khaṣṣāf[7] in the third/ninth century stating that the *mutawātir* (successive)[8] Sunna is equal to the Qur'an. Ibn Qutayba's contemporaries defended this opinion, claiming that the Sunna is divinely inspired.

Perhaps the most important reason prompting the jurists to collect the *aḥādīth* and establishing the Sunna as the second source of law was the great desire of the devout public, who did not live during the Prophet's time, to know everything he said or did so they could adapt their lives and behaviour to emulate him. Another factor was their fear of contradicting any religious provision or introducing any innovation that may not be consistent with the will of God.

A *ḥadīth* (cited by al-Nasāʾī)[9] became very popular among the people. It stated: "The most evil matters are those that are newly invented, for every newly invented matter is an innovation and every innovation is misguidance and every misguidance is in the Hellfire." Whenever a jurist articulated an opinion, they asked him: "Is it something you heard from the Prophet or is it your own opinion?" The jurists and scholars realised that there was no way that a legal opinion would be acceptable to the pious public unless it was based on a *mutawātir* Sunna or it was allegedly based on a *ḥadīth*.

Hence, the jurists and scholars resorted to supporting any view that they saw as viable and desirable by a *ḥadīth* that they ascribed to the Prophet, much

5 Muḥammad b. al-Ḥasan al-Shaybānī (131–189 AH/749/50–805 AD), was a prominent Muslim jurist, and a disciple of Abū Ḥanīfa, Mālik b. Anas and Abū Yūsuf, the leading jurists of their time. He is credited with being the father of Muslim international law.

6 Abū ᶜAbdullāh, Muhammad b. Idrīs al-Shāfiᶜī (150–204 AH/767–820 AD), also referred to as Imam al-Shāfiᶜī or "Shaykh al-Islām", was a theologian and jurist and credited with founding the Shāfiᶜī School of Jurisprudence.

7 Abū-Bakr Aḥmad b. ᶜUmar b. Muhayr al-Shaybānī al-Khaṣṣāf (d. 261 AH/874 AD), was a traditionist and Hanafi jurist.

8 This means that it was reported by a large number of narrators, such that it is inconceivable that they all agreed on a lie or fabrication, thus it is accepted as unquestionable in its veracity.

9 Abū ᶜAbd al-Raḥmān Aḥmad b. ᶜAlī b. Shuᶜayb b. Baḥr b. Sinān al-Nasāʾī (215–303 AH/830–915 AD), was a traditionist and author of one of the six canonical collections of traditions (*ḥadīth*).

like those who wrote the Book of Deuteronomy[10] then attributed it to Moses to give it an authoritative and trustworthy character. This practice became relatively easy after the death of the Companions' generation, who had alone been able to deny that the Prophet had uttered such and such *ḥadīth*. The jurists and scholars were reassured and their conscience rested easy, as they believed that putting words and sayings into the Prophet's mouth would serve the religion of Islam and stand against the worldly rule of the Umayyads.

The Impact of Sectarian Conflicts on the Fabrication of Ḥadīth

The majority of the pious who opposed the rule of the Umayyads were from *Shīᶜatu*[11] ᶜAlī b. Abū Ṭālib, and the *ahl al-bayt*,[12] who would have liked to see the descendants of the Prophet or those of his uncle al-ᶜAbbās exercise control over the state, to save the community of Islam from the evils of immersion in worldly affairs. They saw no shame or embarrassment in making up a number of *aḥādīth* attributed to the Prophet, some of which praised *ahl al-bayt* and raised the status of Banū Hāshim, while others vilified the Umayyads. This explains the emergence of *aḥādīth* making statements such as: "If I am someone's *mawla* (friend) then ᶜAlī is his *mawla* too and God will be the *mawla* of all who take ᶜAlī as their mawla and an enemy to those who are ᶜAlī's enemies", "Whoever harms my uncle, harms me", "If you see Muᶜāwiya preaching from my *minbar* (pulpit), kill him", "A woman consulted the Prophet about marrying Mu'awiya and he said to her: 'he is a wretch'", and on the authority of ᶜAbd al-Raḥmān b. Awf:[13] "Every new-born was brought to the Prophet." When Marwān b. al-Ḥakam[14] was brought to him as an infant, the Prophet said: "He is the weakling, son of the weakling, the cursed, son of the damned."

---

10 The fifth book of the Torah and the Christian Old Testament.

11 Lit. people of like persuasion, i.e., followers.

12 Lit. people of the house, i.e., the Prophet's family.

13 ᶜAbd al-Rahman ibn ᶜAwf (43 before Hijra–32 AH/580–656 AD) was one of the Companions of the Prophet and one of the first to convert to Islam.

14 Marwān b. al-Ḥakam, also known as Marwān I (2–65 AH/623–685 AD), one of the Prophet's *Ṣaḥāba* (Companions), cousin of ᶜUthmān b. ᶜAffān, the third of the Rightfully Guided Caliphs, and also the fourth Umayyad caliph. He succeeded Muᶜāwiya II, who abdicated in 64 AH/684 AD. His ascension to power marked the shift from the Sufyanids (descendants of Abū Sufyān) to the Marwanids (descendants of Ḥakam), both grandsons of Umayya (after whom the Umayyad dynasty is named).

Naturally, the Umayyad caliphs did not stand idly by as they watched these *aḥādīth* being disseminated – knowing they were forged by their enemies and accepted and welcomed by the gullible general public. However, it appears that they saw how futile it was to attempt to expose these as forgeries and fabrications, and that the easiest way to resist them would be to engage in the same practice as their opponents. The Umayyads and their supporters therefore resorted to fabricating *aḥādīth* that raised the status of the Banū Umayya, such as: "The days and nights will pass and then Muᶜāwiya will rule",[15] and "The Prophet made a supplication for Muᶜāwiya and said: 'O God, enable him to rule the land'." When they found it difficult to fabricate *aḥādīth* attributed to the Prophet defaming ᶜAlī or his descendants, they concocted some *aḥādīth* that defamed his father Abū Ṭālib and that said that his fate was hellfire on the Day of Resurrection (to which the Shi'ites responded by fabricating the story of Abū Ṭālib's conversion to Islam on his deathbed).

In addition, when the Umayyad caliphs failed to find an authentic *ḥadīth* in support of a particular view or a certain political decision that they wanted to impose, they had a *ḥadīth* fabricated for them. They always found among the pious jurists (who received their salaries from them) someone willing to advocate their rights of succession, help them to implement their policies or realise their aims by finding support for these rights or policies in the *ḥadīth* corpus. For example, when Caliph ᶜAbd al-Malak b. Marwān wanted to prevent people from going on Ḥajj (pilgrimage) out of fear that his rival ᶜAbd Allah b. al-Zubayr[16] would force them to pay allegiance to him as the Muslim caliph, he assigned the pious jurist al-Zuhrī[17] the task of finding (or fabricating) a *ḥadīth* equating the visit of ᶜBayt al-Maqdisᵓ[18] in Jerusalem with the pilgrimage to Mecca. Hence, when people complained about the

15 Meaning, it will not be long before Muᶜāwiya will rule.

16 ᶜAbd Allah b. al-Zubayr (1–73 AH/623–692 AD), was the son of al-Zubayr b. al-Awwām and Asmāᵓ bint Abū Bakr, nephew of ᶜAᵓisha, the Prophet's wife. He is regarded as the fifth Rightfully Guided Caliph as he revolted (unsuccessfully) against the ascension of Yazīd I and refused to swear allegiance to him or recognise him as caliph. He declared himself caliph in Mecca after the death of al-Ḥusayn, the Prophet's grandson, in Karbala. He was killed in battle and after his death the Umayyads re-established their control over the Islamic empire.

17 Muḥammad b. Muslim b. ᶜUbayd Allah b. Shihāb al-Zuhrī (d. 124 AH/741 or 742 AD), was one of the major collectors of *Sīra* (Prophet's biographies) and of the Prophet's *aḥādīth*.

18 Another name for the Masjid al-Aqsa (lit. "the farthest mosque"), which is the third most holy place in Islam, for being the place where the Prophet went on his night journey from Mecca.

ban on the pilgrimage to Mecca, ᶜAbd al-Malak answered them saying: "This is Ibn Shihāb al-Zuhrī narrating that the Prophet said: 'No journey is worthy except to three mosques: the Sacred Mosque (in Mecca) and my mosque (in Medina) and the Mosque of Bayt al-Maqdis (in Jerusalem)'." After this incident, when Makḥūl[19] spoke of al-Zuhrī he said: "he is the kind of a man who was spoiled [corrupted] by his own doing in the company of kings".

Thus, lies were spread in the Prophet's name. Every fabrication was fought by producing more fabrications, until every group, sect and follower of a doctrine was in possession of a huge array of *aḥādīth* that challenged other groups and doctrines. The standard became that the end justifies the means, and that any means, regardless of how much fabrication and slander it included, was acceptable as long as it served a noble purpose, such as strengthening the faith or remedying wrongs, and preventing heretics from managing Muslims' affairs, or rooting out sedition. The opponents of the Umayyads from among the Shi'ites, the Kharijites and others, believed that in order to achieve their goals they needed to tint their opposition to the rule with religious overtones. The Umayyads' response to this was to use political *aḥādīth* – authentic as well as forged – urging Muslims to obey their rulers ("He who obeyed a prince, has obeyed me, and he who disobeyed him, has disobeyed me"). Other *aḥādīth* reminded people that obedience is a religious duty which only infidels would shirk from performing, and that, even if the government was corrupt and unjust, the governed were obliged to leave the matter to God, as its continuity may be due to a certain wisdom that only the Almighty can see.

Hence, *aḥādīth* were spread that urged the governed to be patient even if they were dissatisfied with the actions of their rulers, such as "Be patient until you meet me". Other *aḥādīth* urged compliance with the will of the prince, whether he is righteous or an evildoer, and said that an unjust sultan is better than lasting strife. The opponents of the Umayyads responded by spreading contradictory *aḥādīth* saying: "Do not dislike discord, as it will root out the hypocrites!" Yet other *aḥādīth* advocated silence to overcome the authorities, or that opposition in one's heart alone is sufficient: "Whoever witnessed it and hated it, is like someone who missed it". They also responded to those

19 Makḥūl al-Hadhlī (d. *c.* 112 AH/731 AD), scholar, traditionist and jurist in the Levant, and contemporary of al-Zuhrī.

calling for leadership to be restricted to the Prophet's descendants by spreading a *ḥadīth* saying that only a ruler who has the allegiance of the Muslims has the right to rule, and another saying: "If there were to be a prophet after me then it would be ᶜUmar b. al-Khaṭṭāb."

The Umayyads did not stop at fabricating *aḥādīth*, they also severely punished those who promoted *aḥādīth* defaming their ancestors or praising their opponents. The ᶜAbbāsids resorted to the same tactics when they assumed the succession, punishing everyone who narrated *aḥādīth* that referred favourably to Muᶜāwiya or Banū Umayya. When the ᶜAbbāsids fell out with the Shi'ites, they also punished people who claimed that ᶜAlī b. Abū Ṭālib's descendants should have been the rightful heirs of the Prophet and his successors, or who bestowed sanctity on them. It also became punishable to narrate the *ḥadīth* attributed to the Prophet where, shortly before his death, he allegedly recommended that ᶜAlī should be his successor. Sunnis at that time promoted the *ḥadīth*: "What we have left is charity which cannot be inherited" in order to prove that nobody had the right to inherit from the Prophet, neither money nor office. When the ᶜAlīds took umbrage at that, they distorted the text of the *ḥadīth* by changing one word to make it: "Whatever charity we have left cannot be inherited" (meaning that only that which is left in charity cannot be inherited). The Sunnis therefore added a word to ensure the matter is unambiguous and could not be distorted by the ᶜAlīds: "*We do not leave an inheritance, whatever we leave is charity.*"

The Roots of the Tragedy

It seems to us that the trend to forge and fabricate *aḥādīth* to defame some or bolster a doctrine started at the time of Caliph ᶜUthmān b. ᶜAffān, when people were dissatisfied with his rule. We read that ᶜUthmān forbade people from narrating *aḥādīth* that were unheard of in the days of Abū Bakr and ᶜUmar. This may have been prompted by the *aḥādīth* circulated by his enemies, which defamed his Umayyad relatives while extoling the Banū Hāshim, in order to destabilise his rule and force him to either improve his performance or abdicate. His opponents accused him of having had 500 words deleted from his *muṣḥaf* (codex), which were found in other copies of the Qur'an belonging to revered Companions, such as the one belonging to ᶜAbd Allah b. Masᶜūd. Among the allegedly deleted passages is one that supposedly says: "*Yes, ᶜAlī is the guidance.*" They also claimed that he deleted ᶜUmar's name and replaced it by *fulān* (so and so, such a one) in Q. 25:28,[20] and accused him of concealing a short *sūra*, akin to Chapter 111, that cursed his relative Abū Sufyān.

However, there is evidence to suggest that, even before the time of ᶜUthmān, some had started to ascribe sayings to the Prophet that he did not say, even though the amount of fabrication at that time was less dangerous. It is both remarkable and laudable that some of the Prophet's senior Companions – like Abū Bakr, ᶜUmar and ᶜUthmān – narrated only a limited number of *aḥādīth* in spite of their proximity to the Prophet, which should have qualified them to narrate more of his sayings. The reason for this reluctance was their piety and their fear that their memory would fail them, and that they would inadvertently add or omit something (as Ḥudhayfa b. al-Yamān[21] said: "We are Arabs, we exaggerate and we hold back, we add and we omit, but we do not intend to lie").

ᶜAbd Allah b. Masᶜūd is said to have been so fearful of changing the words of the Prophet that he followed every *ḥadīth* he narrated with the words: "The *ḥadīth* is either more than this, or similar to this, or less than this." ᶜAmr b. Maymūn[22] says, "I frequently visited ᶜAbd Allah b. Masᶜūd over a one-year period, during which I never heard him narrate from the Prophet or say 'The Prophet said'. Only once did he narrate a *ḥadīth*, saying 'the Prophet said', and I saw how distressed he became, the sweat running down his forehead." There were some of the Companions who, when asked about the traditions narrated by the Prophet, refused to narrate any, saying: "I'm afraid that if I narrate one *ḥadīth*, you would narrate one hundred from me."[23] Furthermore, when ᶜAbd Allah b. al-Zubayr, whose narrations do not exceed thirty-three *aḥādīth* in the different collections, was told: "We do not see you narrating from the Prophet like *fulān* and *fulān*," he replied: "I followed the Prophet since I was a boy, and I was close to him after I accepted Islam, and I memorised many of his sayings, yet I heard him say: 'Whoever (intentionally) ascribes to me what I have not said then (surely) let him occupy his seat in hell-fire.'"

20 Q. 25:28: "*O woe is me! Would that I had not taken such a one for a friend!*"

21 Ḥudhayfa b. al-Yamān (d. 36 AH/656 AD), revered Companion, known for his intelligence, quick wittedness and his ability to keep a secret.

22 ᶜAmr b. Maymūn al-ᶜAwdī (d. 74 or 75 AH/693 or 694 AD), was one of the Anṣār and a Companion of the Prophet.

23 This means that he was afraid that they would forge traditions and name him as their narrator.

However, other Companions were not like this minority. Abū Hurayra,[24] for example, who only accompanied the Prophet during the last three years of his life, narrated about 3,500 *aḥādīth* in the different collections (according to Ibn al-Jawzī,[25] they are 5,374), which occupy approximately 300 pages of *Musnad Ibn Ḥanbal*. His numerous *aḥādīth* raised the doubts of listeners, especially since he was known to be "a joker" (see *Ṣaḥīḥ al-Bukhārī*: "*Faḍāʾil al-aṣḥāb*" (*Virtues of the Companions*)). He used to say to them: "You say that Abū Hurayra overdoes it with his narrations from the Prophet, and that the *Muhājirūn* (immigrants) and the *Anṣār* (helpers) do not narrate from the Prophet like he does. My brothers from the *Muhājirūn* were occupied with their deals in the markets, while my brothers from the *Anṣār* were occupied by tending their own lands. I, on the other hand, was dedicated to the Prophet's company, being there when they were absent, and memorising when they forgot." Abū Hurayra explained the power of his memory and his ability to absorb the exact words of the Prophet's *aḥādīth* by saying: "The Prophet told me one day: 'Whoever extends his robe until I finish my talk, and then holds it close to him, will never forget anything I said.' So I extended my robe and he spoke to us and when he finished I gathered my robe tightly around me. By God, since that day I have never forgotten anything I heard from him." Nevertheless, there were some Companions – like ᶜAbd Allah b. ᶜUmar b. al-Khaṭṭāb – who did not trust him. Some people called him "the pious liar". Al-Bukhari narrated a *ḥadīth* where the Prophet allegedly ordered the killing of all dogs except hunting hounds. When ᶜAbd Allah b. ᶜUmar was told that Abū Hurayra added "or the plantation dogs" he responded sarcastically that Abū Hurayra added this phrase after he became the owner of a farm!

Leniency in the Isnād *(Chain of Narration) of the* Aḥādīth *about Virtuous Deeds*

The pious did not see any harm in approving *aḥādīth* ascribed to the Prophet, as long as they urged virtuous deeds and forbade evildoings. The examples include: "The Muslim is the one from whose tongue and hands the Muslims

24 Abū Hurayra al-Dawsī al-Yamānī (19–57 AH/599–676 AD) was the most prolific narrator of traditions ascribed to the Prophet. He converted to Islam about three years before the Prophet's death.

25 Abuᶜl-Faraj Ibn al-Jawzī (510–597 AH/1116–1201 AD) was a Muslim scholar, theologian, exegist and traditionist.

are safe," "You will not impress people with your wealth, impress them with your manners," "Blessed is he who focuses on his own defects rather than the defects of people," "The ignorant person should not hide his ignorance and the scholar should not hide his knowledge," and "The Prophet said: Beware of Khaḍrāᵓ al-Dammin. They asked: O Messenger of God, what is Khaḍrāᵓ al-Dammin? He said: The beautiful woman in an improper environment."

The standard here was not whether or not people believed that the Prophet really said something, but instead whether or not these sayings concurred with the norms of the religious teachings. The common attitude was characterised by leniency with regard to fabricated *aḥādīth* that were thought would serve Islam and promote virtues and strengthen the faith. Hence, they fabricated *aḥādīth* such as: "Whatever good was said, I have said it" (*Sunan Ibn Māja*),[26] and a *ḥadīth* where the Prophet advised comparing what has been attributed to him with the Qur'an and if it agrees with the book of Allah, then "it is to be attributed to me whether I said it or not". This is akin to what the Talmud says: "Everything that the faithful students of the sages will ask in the future, God has already revealed to Moses on Mount Sinai."[27] As we have said, for them, the end justified the means and there was nothing wrong in lying if it resulted in something good. Abū ᶜAṣim al-Nabīl[28] referred to them when he said: "We have not seen the righteous lie as much as when they lied about the *ḥadīth*." Wakīᶜ narrated from Ziyād b. ᶜAbd Allah saying: "Despite him being honourable, he lied when narrating *aḥādīth*."

If this was the attitude of the pious Muslims and the jurists, then it is no wonder that the general public neglected to thoroughly investigate and examine the *aḥādīth* and believed all or at least most of the sayings attributed to the Prophet. In fact, the general populace hardly took the authenticity of the *isnād* into account, if at all, as long as the *matn* (textual body of the narrative)

---

26 Abū 'Abd Allāh Muḥammad b. Yazīd b. Māja al-Rab'ī al-Qazwīnī (209–273 AH/824–886 AD), is known as Ibn Māja. He was a theologian and traditionist, and his book *Sunan Ibn Māja* is one of the six canonical collections of Sunni Islam.

27 One Midrash recounts that on Sinai, God told Moses everything that was to be said about the written Torah, "even what a faithful student was someday to ask his teacher". This quote is found in Exodus Rabbah 47:1 as translated in Hayim Nahman Bialik and Yehoshua Hana Ravnitzky (eds), *The Book of Legends: Sefer Ha-Aggadah* (New York: Schocken, 1992).

28 Abū ᶜĀṣim al-Nabīl (122–212 AH/740–827 AD) was a trustworthy traditionist, who collected a large quantity of *aḥādīth* from several *tābiᶜīn* (Successors). His biographers assert that he never fabricated a single one.

was good, or morally sound, or was serving a doctrine in which they believed. Abū Ḥayyān al-Tawḥīdī[29] recorded an amusing anecdote which illustrates this perfectly. He narrates that he went to visit a friend who was sitting in front of an open book. The book included the wise sayings by Bozorgmehr, the famous Persian philosopher.[30] Next to every wise saying, his friend was writing the name of one of the four Rightfully Guided Caliphs and some of the Prophet's Companions and Arab sages. When Abū Ḥayyān asked him what he was doing, he replied calmly: "I am attributing the wisdom to the *ahl al-ḥikma* (lit. people of wisdom)."

Thus, some people did not hesitate to attribute a wise or witty saying from the time of *Jahiliyya* to the Prophet, as they did with sayings by the prophets of the Old and New Testaments. The phrase "support your brother whether he is right or wrong", for example, is an old Arab proverb. The saying "Goodness is knotted to a horse's forehead" is part of a verse from the poetry of Imraʾul-Qays.[31] Any saying that impressed the jurists or found resonance in their preferred creed was transformed into a *ḥadīth*, which in turn helped to shape Islamic thought. ʿAbd Allah b. Lahīʿa[32] narrated that one of the eminent *ḥadīth* scholars advised him, after he had repented, to stop believing the *aḥādīth*: "because when we liked something, we turned it into a *ḥadīth*".

The *isnād*, which was supposed to confirm the authenticity of a narration and bestow credibility upon it, was easily fabricated and merely a formality. Any forger or fabricator could forge a *ḥadīth* and introduce it with a "golden chain"[33] in which he would make sure that the narrators all met one another, or even without making sure of that. There are those who neglected the *isnād*

29 ʿAlī b. Muḥammad b. ʿAbbās, known as Abū Ḥayyān al-Tawḥīdī (310–414 AH/922–1023 AD), was a man of letters and a philosopher and one of the influential thinkers and writers of his time. He was described as "the philosopher of litterateurs and the litterateur of philosophers".

30 Wuzurgmihr ī Bōxtagān (Bozorgmehr-e Bokhtagan) or in Arabic Abūzarjmehr, Bozorjmehr or Būzorjmehr, was the Grand Vizier of Khosrow I. Persian and Arabic sources call him a man of "exceptional wisdom and sage counsels". His name appears in the *Shāh-nāma*. He is credited with the authorship of *Ẓafar-nāma*. Some writers attributed the preface to the famous book *Kalīla wa Dimna* and even the translation of the whole work to him, but there is no evidence for this claim.

31 Imraʾul-Qays b. Ḥujr al-Kindī (520–565 AD), was an Arabic poet in the sixth century AD, and the son of one of the last kings of Kinda. His poems are said to be the best examples of pre-Islamic Arabian verse.

32 ʿAbd Allah b. Lahīʿa al-Ḥaḍramī (97–174 AH/715–790 AD), was an Egyptian scholar of *ḥadīth*.

33 This is considered the soundest of all chains of transmission.

completely: Ḥafṣ b. Ghayyāth[34] once asked al-Aᶜmash[35] about the *isnād* of a *ḥadīth*. He took his earring and placed it next to wall and said, "This is its *isnād*."[36] Ibn al-Sammāk[37] narrated a *ḥadīth* and a man asked him about its *isnād*. He replied: "It is from the known *mursalat*" (sing. *mursal*).[38] These forgers and fabricators were not subjected to any harm, on the contrary, the pious honourable people who raised doubts about the veracity of a *ḥadīth* or its chain of narration, often faced grave danger from the populace, sometimes even being called heretics. An old proverb says: "The most deserving of mercy is a scholar who is judged by an ignorant."

Undoubtedly, all those should be assumed to have acted in good faith. When people narrated "Whoever (intentionally) ascribes to me what I have not said, then (surely) let him occupy his seat in hell-fire" (which is also potentially a fabricated narration to combat the barrage of fabrications and forgeries ascribed to the Prophet!), they added after the word "intentionally" the phrase "to deceive the people". This was done to allow for fabrication of that which is not intended to deceive the people. In addition, the words "to me" was interpreted as "against me", as opposed to "for me", in the sense that there is nothing wrong in lying for the benefit of religion!

When confronted with evidence exposing their lies, the forgers were not embarrassed; instead they openly admitted their lies and fabrication. For example, there are *aḥādīth* about certain Qur'anic verses such as: "Chapter 112 is one third of the Qur'an," or others that narrate that God will write down the amount of 1 *qinṭār*[39] of good deeds for whoever reads a thousand verses of the

34 Ḥafṣ b. Ghayyāth (d. 95 AH/713 AD), a Qāḍī and *ḥadīth* scholar from Kufa.

35 Sulaymān b. Mahrān al-Aᶜmash (61–147 or 148 AH/ 680–764 or 765 AD), was well-known traditionist from Kufa.

36 This is a pun on the word *isnād*, as *isnād*, other than chain of narration, can also mean "leaning", so that leaning the earring against the wall can also be called *isnād*.

37 Abū-l-ᶜAbbās Muḥammad b. Ṣabīḥ, also known as Ibn al-Sammāk (d. 183 AH/799–800 AD), was a pious ascetic, preacher and professional storyteller known for his witticism and courage, who frequently advised Hārūn al-Rashīd, the ᶜAbbāsid caliph. Not to be mistaken for Abū ᶜAmr ᶜUthmān b. ᶜAbd Allah b. Yazīd al-Baghdādī al-Daqāq, also known as Ibn al-Sammāk (d. 344 AH/955 AD), a *ḥadīth* scholar from Iraq.

38 *Mursal* (lit. hurried): if the narrator between the Successor and the Prophet is omitted from a given *isnād*, the hadith is considered *mursal*, based on the belief in the uprightness of all Companions, hence, it was not considered problematic when a Successor did not mention which Companion narrated the *ḥadīth* to him.

39 Unit of weight equivalent to 143.8 kg.

Qur'an in one night (and in another account, 2 *qinṭār*!). When one of the ascetics who frequently narrated similar *aḥādīth* was asked about its source, he replied: "When I saw that people have ceased reading the Qur'an and have concerned themselves with the jurisprudence of Abū Ḥanīfa[40] and the *ᶜMaghāzī'* by Ibn Isḥāq, I fabricated this *ḥadīth out of ḥisba to God*" (meaning to draw closer to Him by getting people to start reading the Qur'an again).

The jurists were lax about the *isnād* of narrations that dealt with morality and behaviour. This is referred to in the phrase "a weak *ḥadīth*, but one feels content with it". However, strict scrutiny was applied to the narrations concerning *ḥalāl* (permissible) and *ḥarām* (prohibited). Or in the words of Aḥmad b. Ḥanbal: "If we narrated from the Messenger of Allah about *ḥalāl* and *ḥarām*, the Sunan and regulations, we applied strict scrutiny to the *isnād*."

Aḥādīth *about Prophecies*

However, the traditionists (*ḥadīth* scholars) went beyond the *aḥādīth* about morals and virtues. They attributed narrations to the Prophet that contain prophecies about the course of events in the Islamic state, and what will happen in its different parts, such as revolts, revolutions and strife. They attributed a *ḥadīth* prophesying the establishment of the ᶜAbbāsid state to the Prophet in a narration that talks about black flags moving from Khorasan without any resistance until they reach Iliyāᵓ (Jerusalem).[41] It was also claimed that the Prophet disclosed the secrets of the unseen to Ḥudhayfa b. al-Yamān, and so his name was cited in the chains of narrations in most of the traditions that predict future events. ᶜAlī b. Sulaymān said that the strangest thing that happened to him was when he narrated a *ḥadīth* prohibiting scholars from fraternising with the sultan. One of the listeners attacked him saying: "How could the Prophet have said that when there were no sultans at his time?!" ᶜAlī b. Sulaymān commented about the questioning by this "unbeliever", saying: "As if this wretch is not aware that the Prophet was able to predict everything

40 Nuᶜmān b. Thābit al-Kufī, also known as Abū Ḥanīfa (80–150 AH/699–767 AD), an important Muslim scholar, jurist and theologian. He is considered the founder of the Ḥanafī School of Jurisprudence. He is called "The greatest Imam".

41 Aelia Capitolina, a Roman colony built under Emperor Hadrian on the site of Jerusalem. It remained the official name of Jerusalem until 17 AH/ 638 AD, when the Arabs conquered the city and kept the first part of it as Iliyāᵓ.

that will happen until the Day of Judgment!" It is clear to us that ᶜAlī b. Sulaymān has forgotten Q. 6:50: "*Say: I do not say to you, I have with me the treasures of Allah, nor do I know the unseen . . .*"[42]

The followers of the four schools of Islamic jurisprudence also circulated *aḥādīth* that were supportive of this or that school and commended its founder. For example, the followers of the doctrine of Abū Ḥanīfa circulated a *ḥadīth* saying: "there will be a man known by his epithet Abū Ḥanīfa who will be the *sirāj* (lamp) of my nation" and they attributed it to the Prophet by way of Abū Hurayra. The followers of the Mālikī School also circulated a *ḥadīth* saying: "the most knowledgeable of the jurists are the jurists of Medina". Mālik was a Medinan, while Abū Ḥanīfa was from Iraq.

In addition to all of this, the people of the various geographical regions, nations and cities also fabricated *aḥādīth* to commend this or that region, or its population or making it one of God's preferred spots on Earth from among all the regions: "You will conquer Egypt. Treat its people kindly since they have a right of kinship upon you," "When you conquer Egypt after I am gone, take many soldiers from there, for their soldiers are the best soldiers on earth" and "Allah Allah, behold the Copts of Egypt, you shall take them over and they shall be your instrument and help in the way of Allah." Other *aḥādīth* attributed to the Prophet predicted that the Muslims would conquer Basra and that the best Qur'an reciters would be there, as well as God-fearing people, the world's most knowledgeable scholars and most charitable populace. Further predictions foretold that a city would be built in Morocco and named Fez, whose righteous inhabitants are the best at performing their prayers and that God will protect them from all harm. Even a negligibly small, insignificant town in Algeria by the name of Cherchell is subject of numerous *aḥādīth* listing its virtues and those of its people!

Pigeon Racing

In fact, there was no big difference between the ᶜAbbāsid and the Umayyad caliphs in terms of lifestyle. Perhaps the only difference was that the ᶜAbbāsids saw it as their responsibility to revive interest in the Sunna, to keep the jurists

42 The full verse reads as follows: Q. 6:50: "*Say: I do not say to you, I have with me the treasures of Allah, nor do I know the unseen, nor do I say to you that I am an angel; I do not follow aught save that which is revealed to me. Say: Are the blind and the seeing one alike? Do you not then reflect?*"

in their close proximity, as well as to colour their dynasty with a religious character to guarantee the devotion and loyalty of the populace. The ᶜAbbāsid jurists, meanwhile, fabricated a seemingly endless amount *aḥādīth* ascribed to the Prophet, to please the princes and to satisfy their whims and desires. Caliph al-Mahdī, for example, loved pigeon racing, which the Sunnis prohibited. He managed to convince a traditionist named Ghayyath b. Ibrahim[43] to fabricate a *ḥadīth* which said: "Do not race except in sandals, hoofs and wings." Al-Mahdī rewarded him generously and continued racing pigeons.

The jurists and scholars attended gatherings in the caliphs' courts where wine and song flowed in abundance. During such events they would discuss the legal rulings and punishments for drinking and getting drunk. The jurists' efforts to reconcile what the rule of law stated and the lifestyle of the ᶜAbbāsid caliphs by fabricating numerous *aḥādīth*, and their proximity to those caliphs, was undoubtedly more harmful to the faith and to religion than the distance that they had kept from the Umayyad caliphs.

The Storytellers' Aḥādīth

Piety, political and ideological factors, regional pride and the desire to please the caliphs, were not the only reasons to fabricate *aḥādīth*. In addition, traditions were fabricated purely for fun and financial gain, which made matters worse, leading to complete chaos. The professional storytellers found their way to the mosques and the streets, telling stories about the Prophet and putting words into his mouth. These storytellers were attuned to the level of public understanding and they fed their listeners stories according to their tastes and whims. They also narrated *aḥādīth* that the general public relished for its content, such as: "The Prophet said: 'Whoever fasts the months of Rajab, Shaᶜbān and Ramaḍān, God will build him a palace in heaven, its courtyard will be a thousand *farsakh*[44] long'." The poet Bashār b. Burd[45]

43 Ghayyāth b. Ibrāhīm al-Tamīmī al-Baṣrī, also known as Abū ᶜAbd al-Raḥmān (d. before 183 AH/799 AD), was Kufan, traditionist, cousin of Ḥafṣ b. Ghayyāth and well known for fabricating *aḥādīth*.

44 Farsakh is an ancient measurement unit, probably originating in Iran as *parasang*, and is equivalent to the European "league" covering a distance of between 4 and 6 km.

45 Bashār b. Burd (96–168 AH/714–783 AD), was a very famous blind poet during the late Umayyad and early ᶜAbbāsid periods. He was called the "Imam of Poets". His poetry was deemed to be licentious, and he was condemned as a heretic and executed by Caliph al-Mahdī. He claimed to have written more than 12,000 poems, yet what survives is a fraction of this amount and therefore was possibly an exaggeration on his part.

commented on that, saying: "By God, cursed is such a house in winter!" An anecdote tells of a poet named Kulthūm b. ᶜAmr al- ᶜAttābī,[46] who became famous during the rules of Harūn al-Rashīd, al-Amīn and al-Maᵓmūn, and who narrated the following *ḥadīth* in a Baghdad mosque: "Whoever can reach the tip of his nose with his tongue will not enter Hell." Thereupon the entire audience present in the mosque stuck out their tongues, trying to touch the tips of their noses!

These storytellers were particularly fond of fabricating stories about the prophets of the Old Testament. They never left a question about them unanswered, and replied with great confidence, even if they had to make up the answer then and there. They were anxious that replying "we do not know" would damage their reputation with the general populace. When asked about the donkey's name, whose jawbones Samson used to fight his enemy, they supplied a name.[47] It was reported that when Abū Kaᶜb al-Qaṣṣāṣ (the storyteller) was telling stories in a mosque, he said: "the wolf that ate Yūsuf was named such and such". When a man from the audience reprimanded him saying: "but Yūsuf was not eaten by a wolf", he quickly retorted: "You are right! This, then, was the name of the wolf that did not eat Yūsuf"!

The *isnād* did not stand in their way either: they initiated their *aḥādīth* with good solid chains of narration. It was reported that Aḥmad b. Ḥanbal[48] and his companion Yaḥya b. Maᶜīn[49] went to a particular mosque to pray. There they heard a preacher talking to the people saying: "I heard from Aḥmad b. Ḥanbal and Yaḥya b. Maᶜīn, who narrated from ᶜAbd al-Rāziq, who said that he heard from Muᶜammar, who heard this tradition from Qatāda, who narrated it from Anas b. Mālik that the Prophet said: 'Whoever says "There is no god but Allah", God will reward him on the Day of Resurrection by creating a special bird for every word he uttered. The bird's beak is made of gold, and

46 Kulthūm b. ᶜAmr al-Aṭābī (d. 220 AH/835 AD), was a famous poet during the ᶜAbbāsid rule and a protégé of the Barmakids.

47 Judges 15:16: "He found a fresh jawbone of a donkey, so he reached out and took it and killed a thousand men with it. Then Samson said, 'With the jawbone of a donkey, Heaps upon heaps, With the jawbone of a donkey I have killed a thousand men.'"

48 Aḥmad b. Muḥammad b. Ḥanbal, also known by his epithet, Abū ᶜAbd Allāh al-Shaybānī (164–241 AH/780–855 AD), was an important Muslim scholar and theologian. He is considered the founder of the Ḥanbalī School of Jurisprudence. He is called "Shaykh al-Islam".

49 Yahya b. Maᶜin (158–233 AH/774–847 AD), a famous traditionist and an expert of *Ilm al-rijal* (lit. "Knowledge of Men", but more commonly understood as the Science of Narrators, or biographical evaluation of narrators) and a close friend of Ahmad b. Ḥanbal.

its wings of sapphire.'" Aḥmad b. Ḥanbal turned to his companion in utter shock and asked him to go and ask the preacher from whom he heard this tradition. The preacher replied: "from Aḥmad b. Ḥanbal and Yaḥya b. Maᶜīn". Yaḥya replied: "I am Yaḥya b. Maᶜīn and this man there is Aḥmad b. Ḥanbal, and we never narrated this tradition to you." The preacher replied: "Do you think that you are the only ones called as Yaḥya b. Maᶜīn and Aḥmad b. Ḥanbal? I for one have met seventeen people other than you two who were are called Yaḥya b. Maᶜīn and Aḥmad b. Ḥanbal in my lifetime!"

The classes of these storytellers in the mosques – if indeed they can even be called classes – were far more popular than the gatherings or classes of the jurists. In fact, the people's respect for the storytellers exceeded that for the senior scholars. It has been reported that Abū Ḥanīfa's mother consulted her son about a religious issue, and when she did not like his opinion she went to one of the storytellers called Zarᶜa to tell him her son's opinion and ask for his. When the storyteller supported Abū Ḥanīfa's opinion she was convinced and reassured of its veracity.

The general public found the storytellers' tales easy to understand, as well as entertaining, something they did not find in the jurists' complex phrases and difficult words. While the scholars and jurists tolerated the storytellers and condoned their activities, as they saw that their stories and tales could strengthen the public's faith, the majority of the storytellers did not respect the jurists and scholars. They even mocked them in the mosque to elicit laughs from the general public. The sources report that the great jurist and traditionist al-Shaᶜbī[50] saw a number of people gathered around a shaykh with a long beard, writing down the *aḥādīth* he dictated to them. Among them was one with a long *isnād*, its summary was that the Prophet said that on the Day of Resurrection there will be two horns that will be blown. With the first horn, everybody will be rendered a corpse and with the second one they will all be resurrected again. When al-Shaᶜbī reprimanded the shaykh about his narration, the shaykh shouted: "How dare you deny a properly attested *ḥadīth* with a correct *isnād*, which had been heard from the Messenger of Allah?" Then, he took off his shoe and motioned to the people to follow suit. They all beat al-Shaᶜbī until he swore that God allocated thirty horns for Doomsday.

50 ᶜAmir b. Sharāḥīl al-Shaᶜbī, also known as al-Imam al-Shaᶜbi (16 or 21–100 AH/642–723 AD), jurist and traditionist.

The famous exegete and historian, al-Ṭabarī, was subjected to a similar situation when he contradicted a storyteller who said that God would make room for the Prophet on His throne on the Day of Resurrection. Al-Ṭabarī shouted out loudly and exasperatedly: "Glory to Him Who has no comrade nor companion sitting with Him on His Throne!"[51] The public fumed with anger and marched on his house pelting it with stones until all doors and windows were blocked.

In general, these storytellers had no political, sectarian or doctrinal tendencies. They simply wanted to entertain their listeners and teach them manners and morals. Above all else, their interest was purely financial. They habitually collected money from the "audience" after they finished their stories. The sources report that in the fifth/eleventh century the storytellers distributed *Ṣuqūq al-Ghufrān* (lit. forgiveness bonds, akin to the Christian Indulgentia).[52]

It was often observable that a storyteller would hold his session at one end of a road, and would praise ᶜAlī b. Abū Ṭālib, recounting all his merits, while at the other end of the road his partner would be praising Abū Bakr and recounting his merits. At the end of such a session, they would collect money from the Sunnis and Shi'ites and divide it between them after the people left.

Al-Muᶜammirūn: *The Centenarians*

Another type of fraud was practised by those elders who appeared in the third/ninth and fourth/tenth centuries, claiming to be centenarians blessed with longevity[53] and that they were Companions of the Prophet. They claimed to have heard his *aḥādīth* directly from him and hence did not require an *isnād*. In the late third/ninth century a man named ᶜUthmān b. al-Khaṭṭāb appeared, claiming to be ᶜAlī b. Abū Ṭālib's friend and narrated numerous *aḥādīth* on his authority. Around the year 350 AH/961 AD another

51 This is found quoted in the biography of al-Ṭabarī in *Muᶜjam al-Udabāʾ – Irshād al-Arīb ila maᶜrifat al-adīb* by Yāqūt al-Ḥamawī (574–626 AH/1179–1229 AD).

52 In the Catholic Church the Indulgentia (Penitential Redemptions, Certificate of Absolution or Certificate of Indulgence) was "a way to reduce the amount of punishment one has to undergo for one's sins".

53 See, for example, *Kitāb al-Muᶜammirīn min al-ᶜArab wa ṭaraf min akhbārihim wa mā qālūhu fī muntahā aᶜmārihim* by Abū-l Ḥātim Sahl b. ᶜUthmān al-Sijistānī al-Baṣrī (d. 235 AH), or *al-Muᶜammirūn* by Muhammad Abū-l-Yusr Abdīn (1307–1401 AH/1889–1981 AD).

man appeared, named Jaᶜfar al-Rūmī, who claimed to have accompanied the Prophet during the Battle of Tabūk and that the Prophet's whip fell out of his hands, so Jaᶜfar dismounted and picked it up, handing it back to him. The Prophet prayed for his longevity and this prayer was the reason of his long life, which exceeded had three centuries!

The phenomenon of these "centenarian" imposters spread, particularly in India and Central Asia. One of these was an Indian named Sarbatak,[54] who, at the alleged age of 725 years, pretended to have been the Indian prince to whom the Prophet had sent his missionaries. He claimed to have then travelled to Hijaz where he saw the Prophet twice, in Mecca and in Medina. He is said to have died in the year 333 AH/944 AD when he was 894 years old.

Another Indian, named Ratan b. ᶜAbd Allah (d. 632 AH/1234 AD), said he was six years old when he received an inspiration telling him of the birth of the Prophet of Islam in Mecca. He then rushed to Mecca (note the parallels to the biblical Magi or the wise men from the East at the birth of Christ). He said that he carried Muḥammad in his arms when he was a little boy on the road between Mecca and Jeddah. He said that God rewarded him for this deed by extending his life. This Ratan narrated almost three hundred *aḥādīth* (all of a Shi'ite character) that he claimed he had heard from the Prophet. Many scholars travelled to India from different parts of the Islamic world to hear him.

Al-Majinūn *(the Bawdy and the Frivolous)*

It was not surprising in all of this chaos to see some of the frivolous and bawdy Arabian poets (the likes of Abū Nuwās,[55] Isḥāq al-Mawṣilī[56] and Muḥammed b. Munadhir[57]) use the *ḥadīth* and its *isnād* as a source for anecdotes, humour

54 Harsavardhana is an old king of Qinnawj in India and a contemporary of the beginning of Islam. The Prophet had sent some of his Companions to him, at whose hands he accepted Islam. Sarbatak seems to be a truncation of his name combined with the Persian suffix -ak.

55 Abū Nuwās al-Ḥasan b. Hānī al-Ḥakamī (*c.* 129 to 145–198 AH/*c.* 747 to 762–814 AD) was known as Abū Nuwās. He was one of the greatest classical Arabic poets, renowned for his witty and humorous poetry, as well as his poems about the joys of wine and drinking (*khamriyyāt*), and ribald humour (*mujuniyyāt*). He was infamous for his mockery and satire.

56 Isḥāq al Mawṣilī (150–235 AH/767–850 AD) was a musician and famous singer at the court of ᶜAbbāsid Caliph Hārūn al-Rashīd. He was also the teacher of the famous Ziryāb.

57 Muḥammed b. Munadhir, known as Ibn Munadhir (d. 199 AH/814 AD), was professional panegyrist and famous poet, particularly known for his satire and malicious wit.

and irony. They authored obscene anecdotes in verse and stories in prose, introducing them with an *isnād*-like beginning, such as, for example:

> Abū Bilāl has once narrated to us . . . that his teachers heard Sharīk narrating thus[58]

(this is the verse directly preceding a lewd joke in the poem about the story of Aladdin). Or one of the verses of Abū Nuwās about a lover who broke his promise:

> Al-Azraq narrated to me from ᶜAmr . . . Ibn Shammar, who narrated from Ibn Masᶜūd
> Whoever breaks a promise is ungrateful . . . an infidel chained in Hell for good[59]

Another story is about the famous Ashᶜab,[60] the "King of the *ṭufayliyyūn*" (party gatecrashers or social parasites), which goes as follows: people told him that if he narrated prophetic traditions instead of jokes and anecdotes, it would be much better for him. He replied: "By God, I have heard many *aḥādīth* and narrated them." They said: "Narrate some for us." He said: "I heard from Nāfiᶜ, who narrated from Ibn ᶜUmar that the Prophet said: 'two attributes, if found in anyone, are purely from God'." They asked him: "This is a good *ḥadīth*, what are they?" He said: "Nāfiᶜ forgot one and I forgot the other!"

This *mujūn*[61] (lit. shamelessness) and ridicule came about as a reaction to the behaviour of the traditionists, to mock the great myths which permeated

58 This is quoted from *al-Luṭf wa-l Laṭāʾif* by al-Thaᶜālibī (350–429 AH/961–1038 AD).

59 This is quoted as part of a poem by Abū Nuwas in *al-Bidāya wa-l-nihāya* by Ibn Kathir (701–774 AH/1301–1373 AD) and *Tarikh Madinat Dimashq* by Ibn Asakir (499–571 AH/1106–1175 AD).

60 Ashᶜab b. Jubayr, also named al-Tammaᶜ (the Greedy) (d. 154 AH/771 AD) was a singer, poet, comedian and professional entertainer, who lived in Medina in the second/eighth century and was the subject of many jokes and anecdotes. See, for example, Franz Rosenthal, *Humour in Early Islam*. Leiden: Brill, 1956, who devotes this book to translating the jokes and anecdotes about him.

61 *Mujūn*, according to the *Encyclopaedia of Arabic Literature*, is throwing off of societal restraints and refers to open and unabashed indulgence in prohibited pleasures, particularly drinking wine, homoeroticism and, above all, sexual profligacy. It literally described and celebrates this hedonistic way of life, frequently using explicit sexual vocabulary, graphic descriptions and humorous intent, an exotic blend of the *raffiné* and *recherché* along with coarseness and vulgarity, mixed with scatological humour.

their fabricated narrations. It was also to poke fun at the very specific details concerning the most trivial issues of daily life that were found in their narrations, such as what to say to anyone who sneezes, or God's hatred for yawning or which foot to start with when putting on one's sandals. Their derision was also directed at the general public's appetite for hearing such things, and their willingness to believe that such narrations were actually said by the Prophet, as well as their willingness to believe that a society's acceptance of a *ḥadīth* is the standard of its veracity.

Ḥadīth *Compilations*

Thus, the field of *ḥadīth* became a murky sea, where the truthful was mixed with the forged and fact was mixed with superstition. Some dealt with it as a merchandise to extract money from the people or to seek privilege from the governors, and hence all limits were exceeded. This mighty chaos resulted in a massive turmoil among the pious and revered religious scholars, who were alarmed by all these fabrications and their adverse effect on the evolution of Islam. They feared that the religion would be exposed to the same dangers that had affected other religions before it, when their followers abandoned the holy books in favour of books penned by rabbis and priests. In fighting this wave of fabrication, some fabricated *aḥādīth* that prohibited the fabrication of *aḥādīth*! But others – such as al-Bukhārī[62] and Muslim[63] – refused to stoop to this level, and instead endeavoured to set the foundations of the science of *ḥadīth*, by formulating rigorous standards for the selection of the authentic traditions. Al-Bukhārī narrated that he started the task of collecting the authentic traditions when he saw himself in a dream expelling flies from the Prophet, and someone interpreted this dream to him saying that these flies are the lies and fabrications that had infiltrated the Prophet's sayings.

The standard by which they checked the narrators, their identity, piety, probity and integrity was the *isnād.* If they were proven to be pious and trustworthy, not known to have engaged in deliberate lies about the Prophet

62 Abū 'Abd Allāh, Muḥammad b. Ismā'īl al-Bukhārī, commonly referred to as Imam Bukhārī (194–256 AH/810–870 AD), was a renowned traditionist who authored the collection titled *Sahih al-Bukhari*, which is regarded as the most authentic collection.

63 Muslim b. al-Hajjāj, commonly referred to as Imam Muslim (206–261 AH/822–875 AD), was a renowned traditionist and considered al-Bukhārī's student. His collection *Ṣaḥīḥ Muslim* is considered second only to that of al-Bukhārī.

caused by lack of faith, a whim or adhering to a certain doctrine or creed, they were considered trustworthy. If it was proven that these narrators were contemporaries and the *aḥādīth* collectors, narrators and writers could have met, then the narration was regarded as authentic. Al-Bukhārī is said to have collected 600,000 *aḥādīth* when he embarked on writing his *Ṣaḥīḥ*, of which he only regarded 7,397 as authentic enough to be written into his collection. Leaving aside the repeated *aḥādīth* found in various sections of his book, what remains is 2,762 *aḥādīth* (this means only one out of more than 200 *aḥādīth* circulated by the general public).

Al-Bukhārī's selection of authentic *aḥādīth* – as mentioned – was on the basis of the correct *isnād*, not the *matn* (body of text or the actual wording of the *ḥadīth*). For him, and for others, the *isnād* was the pillar of *ḥadīth*. If the *isnād* falls, the whole *ḥadīth* is disregarded, but if the *isnād* is found to be correct, the *ḥadīth* is accepted whatever its content. By focusing on the *isnād* at the expense of scrutinising the *matn*, the *ḥadīth* compilers thus neglected to study the motives that may have led the forgers and fabricators to put such narrations into the Prophet's mouth or to circulate them among the public. They did not allow historical facts to guide them, and denounced anyone questioning the veracity of a *ḥadīth* with a solid *isnād*, even when the *matn* contained obvious superstitions and myths or defied logic or contradicted documented history. For example, they did not discuss the issue of how the Prophet could have predicted the emergence of Abū Ḥanīfa. Although Ibn Khaldūn called for the criteria of "what is possible and impossible" to be the basis of distinction between the fabricated and authentic traditions, and Ibn ᶜAbd al-Barr[64] and al-Nawawī[65] disregarded the traditions that defied logic, these were mere formalities, as most compilers used the *isnād* to judge the veracity of the traditions. When they were confronted with contradictory traditions that both appeared to have an equally solid *isnād*, they tried to reconcile between them, and if they could not, they applied the theory of *al-nāsikh wa-l-mansūkh* (abrogation).[66]

64 Yūsuf b. ᶜAbd Allah b. Muḥammed b. ᶜAbd al-Barr al-Andalusī al-Qurtubī al-Mālikī, commonly known as Ibn ᶜAbd-al-Barr (368–463 AH/978–1071 AD), was a prolific jurist and theologian in al-Andalus.

65 Abū Zakaria Yaḥya Ibn Sharaf al-Nawawī, popularly known as al-Nawawī or Imam Nawawī (631–676 AH/1234–1277 AD), was a theologian, jurist and traditionist.

66 This is a term used in Islamic legal exegesis for seemingly contradictory material within or between the two primary sources of Islamic law: the Qur'an and the Sunna.

Despite our criticism of that position, due to the ease of fabricating a golden chain of *isnād*, we have to recognise that their position stemmed out of pure piety and had a logic of its own, as they believed that the general public might not have the intellectual capability to grasp everything the Prophet meant. They also believed that it would be arrogant and pompous to reject everything that was not understood.

Conclusion: "A Book Other than the Book of God?"

It is undeniable that the *aḥādīth* and the provisions of the Sunna have played a most serious role in shaping the lives of Muslims to this day. Because of the sheer amount of *aḥādīth*, they compete with the Qur'anic provisions in the depth of their impact. Indeed, many of the sectarian conflicts, the behaviour of our nations' religious youth, and the discontent of those clinging to religion with some aspects of our modern life, is based on the *ḥadīth*, whether authentic or fabricated. Therefore, the most sacred duty of any religious reformer seeking to lay the foundations of proper Islam and to go back to the pure origin of the religion, is to address and eradicate all the falsehoods and concealed motives that have tainted the *ḥadīth*.

However, it is not beneficial to dismiss what has been proven to be forged or fabricated from within the *ḥadīth* corpus. These forged and fabricated traditions emerged as a result of religious, social and historical developments in the Islamic state. Studying these forgeries will serve our understanding of these developments, especially as they often mirrored the ambitions of the followers of different sects and political groups. However, at the same time, these fabrications should never be relied upon to study the Prophet's thought, nor the religion of Islam. They should not be allowed to play any role in shaping our beliefs and our way of life.

But how can we identify the authentic traditions? It is easy for us to identify the *aḥādīth* that were fabricated by followers of different political groups like the Shi'ites, the Khawarij, the Umayyads or the ᶜAbbāsids (such as those that claim that the right of succession was rightfully ᶜAlī's, or those that curse Muᶜāwiya, or glorify ᶜAbbās, or those that predict the ascent of Banū Umayya to the rule). It is also easy to detect the forgeries from among the predictions of events that actually happened in the Islamic state, or those that contain ludicrous descriptions of the Day of Resurrection, or those that list the virtues of certain regions or cities, and those forged by the storytellers, as well as all those that defy logic and reason (for example, Yazīd b. Hārūn said that Hishām b. ᶜAbd Allah narrated from Haffān, who narrated from Anas b. Mālik, who said: "The Messenger of Allah said: 'If any of you eat, let them eat with their right hand, for the devil eats with his left hand and drinks with his left hand!'").

However, two types of *aḥādīth* are particularly difficult to judge in terms of their correct or false attribution to the Prophet. The first type of *aḥādīth* are those that Ibn Ḥanbal termed "virtues and virtuous deeds", which urge the adherence to morals, good behaviour and restrains bad deeds. We believe – like Ibn Ḥanbal – that there is no harm in accepting those or in being lenient about accepting them. The second type of *aḥādīth* are those that relate to what is *ḥalāl* (permissible) or *ḥarām* (prohibited) and those relating to the provisions of the law. There is a real danger in being lenient about accepting those.

The fundamental disagreement between jurists was about whether the nation of Islam can articulate laws to fit the needs of every generation, or whether it is imperative to adhere to the Sunna of the first generation of Muslims. The jurists realised in the second/seventh century and third/eighth century, as they embarked on laying the foundations of Islamic law, how little the previous generations had preserved from the Prophet's *aḥādīth* that could lend themselves to establishing these foundations. Abū Ḥanīfa and jurisprudents known as "*aṣḥāb al raᶜy*"[67] had a more honest, courageous and independent opinion. They believed that the only way to avoid the fabrication of traditions in order to fill gaps in the law was to fill these gaps with juristic rulings formulated by scholars and jurists through *qiyās* (deductive analogy), *ijtihād* (independent reasoning) and the diligent adherence to the guidance of the general spirit of Islam.

We believe this position has pointed the *umma* (community) towards the one true path. The major disaster was not the fabrications by the Shi'ites, the Umayyads or the storytellers, but the reaction to Abū Ḥanīfa's position by those known as "*aṣḥāb al-ḥadīth*", as well as the dissent of Abū Ḥanīfa's followers, even those closest to him like Abū Yūsuf and al-Shaybānī,

67 This term literally translates as advocates of common sense or rational discretion, and who are sometimes called rationalistic jurisprudents. They were prominent during the Umayyad period in Kufa, in Iraq. For a more detailed explanation about the struggle between them and the *aṣḥāb al-ḥadīth* (traditionalists) see, for example, Christopher Melchert, *The Formation of the Sunni Schools of Law: 9th-10th Centuries C.E.*, New York: Brill, 1997.

who turned their backs on this rational trend. The opposition, which had become the majority and therefore more powerful in the state, prevailed and managed to dictate that all laws should have textual support from either the Qur'an or Sunna and refused any law based on rational discretion, *qiyās* and *ijtihād*.

> If an opponent jurist engages in *qiyās* . . . resulting in an inappropriate innovation
> We present him with the words of God . . . or a clear Prophetic tradition[68]

The available *aḥādīth* at the time of laying the foundations of Islamic law were insufficient, as mentioned, hence, people resorted to fabrications. These fabrications increased exponentially with the jurists' insistence, as well as that of the general public, to use the *aḥādīth* as a basis for the formulation of laws and provisions (i.e., the supply increased with the growing demand). They also increased with the jurists' persistence that a tradition with a weak *isnād* is better than sound independent reasoning, and that only trustworthy narrators should be allowed to say "*fulān* narrated to us from *fulān*", and nobody else should have a say.

Subsequently, doctrines emerged that believed innovation to be not only everything that contradicts the Sunna, but also everything that could not be proven to be Sunna. Such doctrines prohibited things like drinking coffee, using spoons and knives, as well as printing. All we can say is that such doctrines, if they were destined to be applied, would have prohibited any different living conditions from those that prevailed during the Prophet's time and the time of the Rightfully Guided Caliphs!

Is it acceptable to allow the fabricated *aḥādīth* to form a barrier between us and the social and political progress of the Muslims?

Ijtihād, common sense or rational discretion did not stop with the death of Abū Ḥanīfa and the abuse of his memory after his demise. Although the *aḥādīth* had the same elevated and authoritative position in all schools of jurisprudence or creeds (including the doctrine of Abū Ḥanīfa himself, after

68 Part of a poem against Abū Ḥanifa cited in *Tārīkh Baghdād* by Abū Bakr Aḥmad b. ʿAli b. Thābit b. Aḥmad b. Mahdī, commonly referred to as al-Khaṭīb al-Baghdādī (392–463 AH/1002–1071 AD)

Abū Yūsuf engaged in the *aḥādīth* and al-Shaybānī embarked on finding *aḥādīth* which support the *fiqh* of his teacher), jurists continued to apply their rational thinking and arrive at their judicial opinions through *ijtihād*. However, when they wanted to publicise their opinions or teach them, they resorted to fabricating *aḥādīth* or to interpreting existing *aḥādīth* in a way that supported their opinions, so that the rulers and the general public would accept their opinions and their opponents would be silenced.

In our opinion, this attitude is an affront to rational opinion and to the freedom of thought. It amounts to shackles placed on the hands of scholars and thinkers who follow their conscience and refuse to fabricate traditions. We also see it as a corruption of their opponents, who, upon seeing the followers of all other creeds and doctrines and the "*ashab al-ra*ᶜ*y*" resort to fabrications to ensure their own victory, would follow suit and emulate them.

5
Is Sufism Islamic?

Some of the *Ṣaḥāba* (Companions) – even during the lifetime of the Prophet – were not content to simply observe the religious rituals, obey the provisions of the Qur'an and emulate the Prophet in his actions and his conduct, but wanted to enter into a spiritual relationship with God, which they claimed was closer and allowed them to free their soul from the yoke of the flesh. Hence, they overdid their acts of worship, their seclusion and contemplation. They chose asceticism, refrained from the worldly pleasures, and imposed restrictions on themselves and on their desires, which were never imposed by the religion.

The Prophet resisted and denounced this trend to his Companions. He used to say to those who were preoccupied by prayer and worship during the night, neglected the care for their families and ignored their rights that sexual intercourse with one's wife was a form of charity. To those who saw in marriage a worldly pillar, he said: "*If you're one of the Christian monks, then follow them, but if you are one of us, then marriage is of our Sunna.*" And to those who emulated the monks' way of life, he said: "*There is no monasticism in Islam.*" There are verses in the Qu'an that confirm this, for example, Q. 7.32: "*Say: Who has prohibited the embellishment of Allah which He has brought forth for His servants and the good provisions? . . .*", Q. 2:172: "*Oh, you who believe! eat of the good things that We have provided you with, and give thanks to Allah . . .*", Q. 2:185: "*. . . Allah desires ease for you, and He does not desire for you difficulty . . .*", Q. 20:2: "*We have not revealed the Qur'an to you that you may be distressed*", and, finally, Q. 22:78: "*. . . He has chosen you and has not laid upon you a hardship in religion.*"

The Prophet, knowing the extent to which some people were affected by the Christians and the lifestyle of the monks during *Jahiliyya*, was anxious that they would introduce innovations and force them onto the religion. The *Sīra* books mention four of them: Waraqa b. Nawfal, ᶜUbayd Allah b. Jaḥsh, ᶜUthmān b. al-Ḥuwayrith and Zayd b. ᶜAmr b. Nufayl. They did not believe in idol worship, and sought another form of faith or religion in which to believe. Waraqa b. Nawfal had become a Christian and was well versed in its teachings, while ᶜUbayd Allah b. Jaḥsh remained undecided, until he converted to Islam. He then migrated with the Muslims to Abyssinia, where he left Islam, converted to Christianity and died a Christian. ᶜUthmān b. al-Ḥuwayrith went to the Roman emperor and converted to Christianity and was well regarded there. Zayd b. ᶜAmr b. Nufayl did not adopt Judaism or Christianity, but he detached himself from the religion of his people and society, abstained from idol worship, and eating carrion and blood, condemned the practice of burying girls alive and said that he would worship the Lord of Ibrāhīm (Abraham).

Perhaps ᶜUthmān b. Maẓᶜūn was one of those known as *al-Ḥunafāʾ*.[1] The *Sīra* books mention that he was "one of those who prohibited the consumption of alcohol in *Jahiliyya*." The books allude to him practising a form of asceticism and austerity so extreme, that the Prophet reprimanded him. Some orientalists believe that ᶜUthmān, ᶜUbayd Allah and others who migrated to Abyssinia were men with strong religious beliefs, some of whom had adopted these beliefs even before the advent of Islam. They also believe that their doctrine, which set them apart from the rest of the Muslims, was the reason why the Prophet selected them to migrate to Abyssinia, and may also be the reason why many of them stayed in Abyssinia and did not return with the other Muslims to Medina until the seventh year after *Hijra*.

While the other famous ascetics from among the Companions – such as Abū-l-Dardāʾ and Abū-l-Dhar al-Ghaffārī – based their asceticism on several Qur'anic verses urging asceticism and abstinence from pleasures and vanity, it is certain – in the light of the biography of the Prophet and the above-mentioned verses – that these verses did not mean an asceticism that rejects the pleasures of this world. The verses meant that one should not indulge in them in such a way that they take over one's life and distract the believer

---

1 *Al-Ḥunafāʾ* (also *Ḥanīf*) is used in the Qur'an as a designation for true monotheists who were neither Jews nor Christians, nor worshipers of idols.

from thinking about God. As for the life of destitution and hardship, which the ascetics saw as a requirement for spiritual perfection, there is not a single verse in the Qur'an that speaks of "the virtue of poverty". It was narrated that al-Ḥasan b. ᶜAlī, upon hearing that Abū-l-Dhar al-Ghaffārī said "poverty is preferable to me over riches", replied: "God have mercy on Abū-l-Dhar. And I say that whosoever trusts in God's choice, should not like other than what He has chosen."

The Impact of the Expansion of the Islamic State on the Growth and Trends of the Movement

The influence of Christianity and the monastic way of life in the Arabian Peninsula and around its edges was the main source for the trend towards asceticism in the lifetime of the Prophet and the Rightfully Guided Caliphs. However, with the expansion of the Islamic empire and the intellectual contact with the Aramaic Christians and Jews and followers of Indian and Persian religions in Central Asia, the movement expanded and became stronger and more complex. Non-Arab peoples of the conquered countries who converted to Islam retained some of the tenets of their old religions which leaned towards asceticism and the suppression of the desires of the flesh. They introduced innovations to their conquerors' religion to which they converted, based on elements of Eastern and Western religions and philosophies: Greek, Christian, Platonic, Zoroastrian, Indian Vedanta and Buddhism. It was only natural that the Sufi movement first intensified in the civilisations outside the Arabian Peninsula: in Iraq, Syria, Palestine and Egypt. However, with the end of the second/seventh century, it had spread to Mecca and Medina, and afterwards beyond that to Yemen.

The leaders of this phase of the movement – the most important of them being al-Ḥasan al-Baṣrī (d. 110 AH/728 AD) – sought to highlight the Qur'anic basis for their movement as well as hide its foreign influences. At the beginning, they chose not to abandon their community, but to remain part of it, in the role of mentors, counsellors or simply as role models. However, very quickly, their worship of God drove them to avoid the world and withdraw from their community. They sought refuge in the caves and deserts, where they lived a life of hardship and self-denial. They believed that poverty was a key to piety. They donned robes of white wool, which several centuries earlier, were the sign of repentance and atonement for the

Christian monks. When others stated that this outfit was nothing but a reprehensible foreign fad, they responded that it was the Prophet of Islam who chose the wool garments for the ascetics. This was denied by their opponents, who claimed that Muḥammad hated woollen robes!

Reasons for the Spread of the Sufi Movement

Throughout the first generations of Islam, the Sufis remained a marginal phenomenon in the Islamic community. Hence, it is rare to find any mention of them in the non-Sufi literature. However, the movement gradually started to occupy the minds of the people, rulers as well as the general public, until it took its place along with the Sunni doctrines.

A large number of devout Muslims were encouraged to pursue this route, due to the overly worldly indulgence of the Umayyads, which they found repulsive, and the life of luxury resulting from the influx of wealth from the conquered Byzantine and Persian regions, which threatened to sweep away the feelings of piety and distract from thinking about the afterlife. Furthermore, these people witnessed long hollow arguments about the tiniest details of *Sharīᶜa*, rituals and worship from the schools of jurisprudence in the ᶜAbbāsid era. In addition, they saw the wholly unreasonable, extravagant celebration of matters as completely unrelated to the pure spiritual relationship between man and his God. They also witnessed the disgraceful worldliness of the jurists and their reprehensible submission to the will of the caliphs and emirs. There is no better example of this than the *Miḥna*, initiated by Caliph al-Maᵓmūn.[2] Contributing to the spread of the movement was the deterioration in the quality of political life in Iraq due to the arrival of Turkish soldiers. People turned to nurturing their spiritual life and their concern about the afterlife when it became difficult, or almost impossible, to effectively contribute to any political activity. Moreover, the extraordinary activity within the Muslim community during the first/sixth century of its history, the constant struggle for status, wealth or glory, which were facilitated by the conquests,

2 *Miḥna* is the Arabic word for trial, ordeal or test and refers to the events that took place between 218 and 233 AH/833 and 847 AD, initiated by the seventh ᶜAbbāsid Caliph al-Maᵓmūn to enforce the officially sponsored doctrine that the Qur'an was the created (rather than the uncreated or eternal) word of God. In this context, it is usually translated as "inquisition", though it only vaguely resembles the Spanish Inquisition.

inevitably resulted in the emergence of a minority who were unable to keep up with these developments or those whose nature rejected such competition. They chose to step away from the thicket and to instead assume a position of superiority and transcendence. This reminds us of an old saying: "If you hear a man say: 'what is from God is better and more lasting', know that there was a banquet in the vicinity to which he was not invited!"

As in other religions, mysticism in Islam focused on the relationship between the servant (believer) and his God, purification of the self and the soul, with an increasing neglect of rituals and the legislative side of the Qur'an and Sunna, which was the aspect of most interest to the jurists. Sufism is, in part, a strong reaction on the part of gentle, sensitive and transparent souls to the excessive concern of the schools of jurisprudence with the superficial behaviour of the individual. It is also an affirmation of the fact that the apparent manifestations of the law are not what Islam is all about, and that the jurists' logic is not a sincere expression of this religion. This was the only positive contribution of Sufism to the framework of Islam. It reinstated the personal religious experience and raised the status of the essence at a time when the superficial and the conventional had overshadowed it, to the point of almost destroying religion.

The Sufis thus preferred the narrow gate,[3] especially those who had converted to Islam from other religions, as they were not convinced by the simple rites and rituals of the new religion and its teachings. They adhered to their memory of a different role model, and of different modes of applying self-restraint and pursuing spiritual perfection. They saw in the image of religion projected by the Sunni jurists and the theologians an image lacking the lustre of salvation, an image that was so simple that it did not convince anyone but shepherds and fighters, a society such as that of the *Jahiliyya* Arabs. They contemplated the verses of the Qur'an and the prophetic traditions that said that deeds are judged by their intentions, and concluded that they mean that emphasis should be placed on the individual's conscience, which should be held accountable in the strictest way possible. In their view, the *Sharīca* of the scholars does not care about the details of the individual's spiritual life or conscience, as it judges only the visible actions and condemns

3 This is a reference to Mathew 7:13: "Enter in by the narrow gate; for wide is the gate and broad is the way that leads to destruction, and many are those who enter in by it."

only sins against society, without providing any weapons against hypocrisy. There is more to religion than a simple adherence to a literal form of *Sharīᶜa*. How can – in the words of al-Ghazālī[4] – the debate about divorce, buying and selling and the like help the pious and prepare them for Judgement Day? Or how can we accept the idea of the vast distance between a person and his God, which is perpetuated by the Sunni jurists when the Qur'an itself has stated in verse 50:16[5] that God is closer to a human than his jugular vein?

The Religion of the Seen and of the Unseen

The Sufi shaykhs, especially in the third/ninth century (the time in which Sufism turned from a simple form of asceticism to a complex theory), tended to exaggerate the irreverence for the rites and rituals and for the *Sharīᶜa*, just as the Sunni scholars exaggerated their reverence for these. This situation is perfectly encapsulated by the words of Abū Ḥāmid al-Marwazī:[6] "If it were not for the Khawarij saying that ᶜAlī was an unbeliever, the *ghulāt*[7] would not have said that ᶜAlī is a god!" These Sufi shaykhs regarded the literal and apparent meanings of the *Sharīᶜa* and the rites as a mere first stage, or a ladder leading from one stage to the next. They opined that whoever reached the ultimate goal could dispense with the means and the intermediaries, and was therefore free from the obligation of performing the rituals, which to them were mere symbols. They even went so far as to opine that performing these rituals could – in some instances – lead to the creation of obstacles to the salvation of the soul.

They then even went beyond that, claiming that their *awliyā*ᵓ[8] ranked higher than the Prophet's, as the link between these *awliyā*ᵓ and their God

4 Abū Ḥāmid Muḥammad b. Muḥammad al-Ghazālī, called al-Ghazālī for short and known to the Western medieval world as Algazel (450–505 AH/1058–1111 AD), was a Muslim theologian, jurist, philosopher and Sufi of Persian origins. He is considered to be a *mujaddid* (renewer of the faith), and therefore received the honorific title *Ḥujjat al-Islam* (Proof of Islam).

5 Q. 50.16: "*And certainly We created man, and We know what his mind suggests to him, and We are nearer to him than his life-vein.*"

6 Abū Ḥāmid al-Marwazī (d. 362 AH/972 AD), was an Iraqi jurist, judge, theologian and scholar.

7 Arabic term that literally means "exaggerators". It is used in theology to denote a minority group of Shi'a Muslims who ascribe divine characteristics to some members of *ahl al-bayt* (the Prophet's household), such as Ali or al-Husayn.

8 Arabic word with several meanings, including custodian, supporter, guardian, ally, protector, helper or friend. In Sufism, it denotes someone who is a friend of Allah and later developed towards the English meaning of "saint".

was a direct one. Sometimes they unite with Him or become dissolved into Him, while prophets only connect with Him through an intermediary. See, for example, "I traversed the tossing ocean, on whose shore the prophets stood!"[9] They regarded themselves as closer to God and more knowledgeable of religion than the most devout Sunni jurist, whose religion, they claimed, was the religion of the seen, while theirs was the religion of the unseen (insights or vision). They declared the superiority of "knowledge", divine wisdom and contemplation over the "science" of the scholars. Furthermore, they claimed that when a man anchored in scholarship lost his vision: "you have received your dead knowledge from the dead, and we take the best of our knowledge from the 'Ever Living'[10] who does not die". People like us say: "my heart has told me of God", while you say: "So and so narrated from such and such." But where are they? They reply: "They are dead!"[11]

It was therefore not surprising, in view of this growing boldness and the increased popularity of these teachings among the public, as well as the focus on the individual at the expense of the overall needs of the nation, that the religious scholars and jurists sounded a wake-up call and issued a denunciation that reverberated across the Muslim world. They saw Sufism – like Christianity – as seeking to achieve spiritual ecstasy through strange and dubious practices, such as listening to music, and even dancing to it, and the use of poetry, even raunchy love poems (such as the *ghazal* poems by ᶜUmar b. Abū Rabīᶜa[12] and Abū Nuwās addressing both women and men), interpreted and explained in a Sufi fashion and sung by handsome *ghilmān* (beardless youths), which for them were a symbol of God's perfect creation! These religious scholars and jurists had also heard the extraordinary sayings attributed to Dhūl Nūn al-Miṣrī,[13] Abū Yazīd al-Bistāmī and

---

9 This is a saying attributed to Abū Yazīd Ṭayfūr b. ᶜĪsā b. Surūshān al-Bisṭāmī, a Persian Sufi commonly known in Iran as Bāyazīd Bisṭāmī (188–261 AH/804–874 AD). He was called *Sultān-ul-Ārifīn* (King of the Gnostics), and was famous for the boldness of expressing the mystic's complete absorption into God.

10 One of the ninety-nine names of God, which according to Islamic tradition were revealed by God in the Qur'an.

11 Another saying attributed to Abū Yazīd Ṭayfūr b. ᶜĪsā b. Surūshān al-Bisṭāmī.

12 ᶜUmar b. Abū Rabīᶜa (23–93 AH/644–711 AD) was a famous Arab poet from Quraysh in Mecca. He was most famous for his love poetry and is attributed as being the originator of the genre of *ghazal*. He is also known for *mujūn* poetry.

13 Dhūl Nūn al-Miṣrī (179–245 AH/796-859 AD) was an Egyptian Sufi saint. He is credited with having formulated the concept of Gnosis in Islam.

al-Ḥallāj[14] and the likes of them, which they misunderstood and equated to polytheism. They did not appreciate that such sayings were uttered by the mystics when they felt complete unity with God and total immersion in Him. Furthermore, they misunderstood the fact that it is God who is speaking in some of these utterances, such as "I am God and God is I",[15] "Glory to Him, how great am I",[16] "our banner is greater than that of Muḥammad",[17] "Beware of monotheism!",[18] "Satan and Pharaoh are both my friends and guides", "he who differentiates between disbelief and belief, has disbelieved",[19] "May God hide from you the apparent of *Sharīᶜa* and reveal to you the truth of disbelief, for the apparent of *Sharīᶜa* is a hidden disbelief and the truth of disbelief is an evident knowledge"[20] and, finally, upon hearing the muezzin's call for prayer, chanting "Allahu Akbar" (God is great), answering "I am greater!"

The Ghulāt *(Extremists) and the Moderates*

Sufi teachings thus began to flagrantly depart from those of mainstream Islam. Sufism's real face started to show, and it opened its doors to foreign influences to such an extent that these almost erased the original features of the religion. The sincerity of the Islamic belief of some Sufis came under suspicion. For example, the Persian al-Ḥallāj, whose grandfather was a Zoroastrian, and who advocated dropping intermediaries between the believer and his God and replacing obligatory rituals with other deeds, was believed to be a Christian hiding his real belief from the people, an assertion made by the orientalists Müller[21] and d'Herbelot.[22] What allowed these people to unleash themselves in word and deed, and to deal with the religion in such an irreverent manner,

14 al-Ḥusayn b. Manṣūr al-Ḥallāj, known as al-Ḥallāj (244–309 AH/858–922 AD), was a Persian mystic, writer and teacher of Sufism. "I am the Truth", is the most famous saying attributed to him.

15 This saying is attributed to al-Ḥallāj.

16 A saying attributed to Abū Yazīd Ṭayfūr b. ᶜĪsā b. Surūshān al-Bisṭāmī.

17 A saying attributed to Abū Yazīd Ṭayfūr b. ᶜĪsā b. Surūshān al-Bisṭāmī.

18 A saying attributed to al-Ḥallāj.

19 A saying attributed to al-Ḥallāj.

20 A saying attributed to al-Ḥallāj.

21 Friedrich Max Müller (1823–1900), was a German philologist and orientalist, who lived and studied in Britain for most of his life.

22 Bartélemy d'Herbelot de Molainville (1625–1695), was a French orientalist.

was the fact that Islam has no supreme religious authority, such as the Catholic Church, whose function would be to restrict and channel its course, to prevent the misguided and the "misguiders" from tarnishing it, and to adopt and adapt newly emerging intellectual trends.

However, some Sufi shaykhs at the time recognised the consequences of their brothers' persistence in such eccentric behaviour. They sensed a danger of disastrous proportions that would eventually engulf them all once this sort of behaviour led to a clash with the authorities and the established Sunni scholars. They tried to remedy the situation before it was beyond redemption, and to assure the Muslims that Sufism was neither a threat to religion nor an independent Islamic doctrine, such as those that had previously shaken Muslim unity. They argued that the Sufis believed that Islamic thought was in need of reform, renewal and revival, and they chose to reform it from within rather than through dissent and the provocation of more disunity. They resorted to the Qur'an and Sunna – like the most pious of jurists – in order to prove that the teachings of Sufism emanated from these sources.

In his book *al-Riᶜāya li-ḥuqūq Allah*, al-Muḥāsibī[23] wrote that the Sufis are the purest and most genuine of Sunnis. To prove this statement, he interpreted Qur'anic verses in ways which only the Sufis could think of, and which agreed with the Sufi doctrine. For example, Q. 8:17: ". . . *you did not smite when you smote, but it was Allah Who smote* . . ."; Q. 2:115: "*And Allah is the East and the West, therefore, whither you turn, thither is Allah* . . ."; Q. 5:119: ". . . *Allah is well pleased with them and they are well pleased with Allah* . . ."; Q. 34:46: "*Say: I exhort you only to one thing, to rise up for Allah* . . ."; Q. 51:50: "*Therefore flee to Allah* . . ."; Q. 50:16: "*And certainly We created man, and We know what his mind suggests to him, and We are nearer to him than his life-vein*"; Q. 6:52: "*And do not drive away those who call upon their Lord in the morning and the evening, they desire only His favour* . . ."; Q. 5:83: "*And when they hear what has been revealed to the apostle you will see their eyes overflowing with tears on account of the truth that they recognise* . . ."; and, finally, Q. 23:60: "*And those who give what they give (in alms) while their hearts are full of fear* . . ."

23 al-Ḥārith al-Muḥāsibī (170–243 AH/781–857 AD) was a Sufi and the founder of the Baghdad School of Islamic Philosophy. He authored many books about theology and *tasawwuf* (Sufism).

Those Sufis attempted to prove their concept of unification and *ḥulūl* (fusion or incarnation) by referring to Q. 8:17: "*So you slew them not but Allah slew them.*" They undertook a slight distortion to Q. 54:49: "*Surely We have created everything according to a measure*" by reading the word *kull* ("all") with a nominative ending (*kullu*) rather than an accusative ending (*kulla*), thus changing the meaning to "*Surely We are everything . . .*" in order to refute the duality. They further resorted to a symbolic interpretation of the Qur'an, stating, for example, that Surah Yūsuf (Chapter 12) symbolises the forces of the spirit, with Yaᶜqūb (Jacob) representing the mind and Yūsuf the heart. The heart, in their interpretation, had become the victim of the ten siblings' envy, five of whom represent the internal senses while the other five represent the external senses, and so on. In addition, the Sufis – as many others before and after them – also resorted to fabricating *aḥādīth* and attributing them falsely to the Prophet. An example of that would be: "the greater *jihad* is against the lust of the flesh, and that is more valuable than the lesser *jihad*, which is fighting those who reject religion". They also translated many of Christ's sayings from the New Testament and attributed them to Muḥammad. Furthermore, they made a great effort to disseminate stories about the Prophet – which the public believes and narrates to this day – talking about the poverty and hunger he endured even in Medina. These include stories on how he sometimes tied stones to his stomach, or how he once met Abū Bakr and ᶜUmar [b. al-Khaṭṭāb], when they were all driven out to the streets by hunger. Such stories angered Aḥmad Ibn Ḥanbal, who leapt to attack al-Muḥāsibī and others, refuting their claims.

The Jurists and the Authorities and their War on Sufism

While the Sufis accused the Sunni jurists and scholars of hypocrisy, because they were preoccupied with the apparent meaning of the truth without its core, the Sunni jurists and scholars accused the Sufis of heresy, as they neglected all what is apparent and is enjoined by the Qur'an, the Book of God. The jurists were not alone in their opposition to the Sufis: they were joined by the Khawārij and some of the Shiʿite sects, followed by the Muᶜtazila and the Ẓāhirīs and finally by the Wahhabis. These sects or doctrines often fought among themselves, but they all agreed on the hatred of Sufism, which some considered as the best evidence that Sufism was alien to Islam.

Their Responses to the Sufis can be Summarised as Follows

Obedience to *Sharīʿa* alone is enough to please the Creator and it is the way to spiritual perfection. The Qur'an and the Prophet never asked Muslims to follow anything else and whatever goes beyond that is misguidance and heresy. As for the "divine love" which the Sufis describe as being devoid of desire and dread, how can that be reconciled with Q. 32:16, which speaks of the believers' choice saying: "*Their sides draw away from (their) beds, calling upon their Lord in fear and in hope . . .*"? We do not recognise anything but obedience, patience and the servant's sense of weakness with regard to the Creator's ability. The Sufis' focus on meditation at the expense of prayer, and their pursuit of "divine love" is only to permit themselves freedom from performing the rituals. Their talk about *ḥulūl*, union with God, ecstasy and total annihilation into God is merely the devil's deception!

Islam censures the words of the Christian prayer: "Our Father who art in heaven", for being an attempt to narrow the wide gap between God and His servants, and considers it a form of heresy. The Prophet of Islam himself – the most perfect of all human beings – was only the carrier of a message to the people. He did not receive this message from God directly, but through an angel, Jibrīl (Gabriel). Is it then conceivable that God could have singled out the Sufi shaykhs to receive something he denied the Prophet? As for the Sufi's call to choose a life of poverty, this is wrong, astray and reprehensible, and is only an emulation of the Christian monks, just as they emulate them in wearing woollen robes. "They show humility in their clothes and but hide their arrogance in their hearts. They are prouder of their woollen garments, than the wearer of fur with his precious fur." As for the self-imposed asceticism and hardship, this is evil, for these people think that God does not have mercy on them unless they torture themselves. How true are ʿUmar b. al-Khaṭṭāb's words, when he saw an ascetic feigning expiration, he told him: "Do not kill our religion for us, may God kill you!"

What, furthermore, are we to make of these strange teachings, rituals and expressions, which Islam is completely innocent of, and with which they want to swamp it, for a certain motive in their hearts? Many of their expressions are translated from Syriac books of Greek philosophy, while many of their teachings are taken from the Upanishads and the Indian Yoga Sutras and many of their rituals – like the movements during *dhikr* – are derived from either those of the Indian mystics or the Christians. Furthermore, the system of the *murshid* (spiritual guide) whom the *murīd* (student or committed one) must follow blindly, like a corpse in the hands of the undertaker to turn as he pleases, is not from within Islam at all, but is of purely Christian origin. They say that the *murīd* 's obedience to his shaykh is the first religious obligation. They also say that the shaykh could order his aspiring student to abandon the rituals if he deems that this is in his spiritual interest. Is it possible that the abandonment of an obligatory ritual can be in someone's spiritual interest? From which verse of the Qur'an or which text in the Sunna do these shaykhs draw their power, which is akin to the authority of priests and rabbis? Did not Q. 9:31[24] condemn the Jews and Christians for taking "*their rabbis and their monks as lords besides God*"?

In response to the uproar caused by the Sunni jurists, scholars and theologians, the authorities carried out a relentless campaign against the Sufi *ghulāt*. It has been claimed that the ᶜAbbāsid persecution of the ᶜAlīds, who were conducting clandestine operations against them, drew their attention to the Sufi groups that had begun to increase. As a result, Dhul-Nūn was summoned from Egypt to the court of Caliph al-Mutawakkil[25] (in 240 AH/853 AD) to respond to accusations of heresy, while Nūrī[26] and Abū Ḥamza[27] were tried between 262 and 269 AH/875 and 882 AD. The persecution of the Sufi shaykhs continued until it culminated in the crucifixion of al-Ḥallāj (in 309 AH/922 AD).

Al-Ḥallāj's crucifixion marked the end of the first stage in the evolution of Sufism, which covered the first three centuries after *Hijra*. It had undergone a gradual evolution, from asceticism, austerity, fear of God and self-restraint (as exemplified by al-Ḥasan al-Baṣrī),[28] to divine love and complete obedience

---

24 Q. 9:31: "*They have taken as lords beside Allah their rabbis and their monks and the Messiah son of Mary, when they were bidden to worship only One Allah. There is no Allah save Him. Be He Glorified from all that they ascribe as partner (unto Him)!*"

25 Jaᶜfar b. Muḥammad al-Muᶜtaṣṣim biᶜllah, known by his regnal name al-Mutawakkil ᶜala Allah (He who relies on God) (205–247 AH/822–861 AD), was an ᶜAbbāsid caliph, who reigned 232–247 AH/847–861 AD.

26 Abū-l-Ḥusayn Aḥmad b. Muḥammad al-Nūrī (d. 295 AH/902 AD) was a famous early Sufi of Persian origins. He was popularly known as "Nūrī" because he was said to radiate light when talking.

27 Abū Ḥamza al-Bazzāz al-Baghdādī (d. 269 AH/882 AD) was a leading Sufi shaykh in Baghdad in the third/ninth century.

28 al-Ḥasan al-Baṣrī (21–110 AH /642–728 AD) was a well-known Muslim preacher, theologian, scholar and Sufi. He was famous for his piety and condemnation of worldliness. His mother was said to have been a servant in the Prophet's household.

devoid of desire and dread (as exemplified by Rābiᶜa),[29] and, finally, to the complex theory of adoration, *fanāʾ* (annihilation within God) and *ḥulūl* (as exemplified by al-Junayd[30] and al- Ḥallāj).

The Second Phase

The second phase was during the fourth/tenth and fifth/eleventh centuries. It began with the panic that hit most of the Sufi shaykhs, due to the impact of the trials, crucifixions, the revolt of the Sunni jurists and scholars, and the wrath of the authorities. It was characterised by the endeavour of the Sufis to restrain their movement, and to exercise extreme caution in their teachings and rituals, showing reverence for the "apparent" *Sharīᶜa*. It was also characterised by a return to an acceptable pattern of behaviour and pretending disapproval of what the jurists had accused their *ghulāt* of engaging in, such as statements that were interpreted as disbelief. They attempted reconciliation with these jurists and scholars and a balanced middle way that was easily acceptable to everyone.

This phase was also marked by the efforts of a large number of Sufi scholars to organise their movement and set rules and boundaries. They formulated theories, explaining them in books with selective texts and sayings of moderate Sufi shaykhs. Some of these books became essential for the Sufis and were viewed as second only to the Qur'an and *ḥadīth*. Among them are *al-Lumaᶜ* (*The Luminous*) by Abū Naṣr al-Sarrāj al-Ṭūsī,[31] *Qūt al-qulūb* (*Nourishment of the Hearts*) by Abū Ṭālib al-Makkī,[32] *Kitāb al-taᶜrīf li-madhhab ahl al-taṣawwuf* (*The Doctrine of the Sufis*) by Abū Bakr al-Kalābādhī,[33] *Ṭabaqāt al-ṣufiyya*

29 Rābiᶜa al-ᶜAdawiyya al-Qaysiyya (d. 717 AH/801 AD) is regarded as the most famous and influential Sufi woman of Islamic history. She was renowned for her virtue, piety and extreme asceticism. She wrote poetry about divine love.

30 Abū-l-Qāsim al-Junayd b. Muḥammad al-Khazzāz al-Baghdādī (221–297 AH/830–910 AD) was one of the most famous of the early Sufis. He was of Persian origins.

31 Abū Naṣr al-Sarrāj al-Ṭūsī (d. 378 AH/988 AD), was a Sufi shaykh and ascetic. He was called "*ṭāwūs al-fuqarāʾ*" (the peacock of the poor).

32 Muḥammad b. ᶜAlī Abū Ṭālib al-Makkī (d. 386 AH/996 AD) was a traditionist, Shafiᶜi jurist and a Sufi mystic. He is credited with setting the foundation of Sufi practices in his book *Qūt al-qulūb fī muᶜāmalat al-maḥbūb wa wasf ṭarīq al-murīd ilā maqām al-tawḥīd* (*The Nourishment of Hearts in Dealing with the Beloved and the Description of the Seeker's Way to the Station of Declaring Oneness*).

33 Abū Bakr Muḥammad b. Isḥāq al-Kalābādhī (d 380 AH/990 AD) was a jurist, traditionist and a famous Persian Sufi.

(*Biographical Dictionary of the Sufis*) by Abū ᶜAbd al-Raḥmān al-Sulamī,[34] *Kashf al-maḥjūb* (*The Revelation of the Veiled*) by al-Hujwirī[35] and *al-Risāla* (*The Epistle*) by al-Qushayrī.[36] The majority of them adhered to the moderate principles formulated by al-Junayd's teacher. All of them almost completely ignored al-Ḥallāj, neither quoting any of his sayings nor including his biography in order to calm tempers and divert suspicion.

These books succeeded in creating a large measure of agreement on the meaning of Sufism, its objectives and its theoretical and practical concepts. The greatest credit for the removal of other obstacles that stood in the way of reconciliation with the Sunnis is undoubtedly attributable to Imam al-Ghazālī's efforts. Some may even go as far as saying that it gave new life to the Sunni doctrines by infusing them with a spiritual dimension. Others may argue that it benefitted Sufism by reigning in its *ghulāt* and reducing their excesses. Yet a third group might argue that it benefitted neither.

By the late fifth/eleventh century, al-Ghazālī sought to codify a complete methodology of the Sufi doctrines as formulated by the previous moderate Sufi shaykhs. He added them to the teachings of the early Muslim scholars in his wonderful book *Iḥyāʾ ᶜulūm al-dīn* (*Revival of Religious Learning*). Al-Ghazālī – thanks to his reputation, piety, unified thought and respect for the "apparent" of the *Sharīᶜa*, as well as his distinguished moderation – contributed significantly to the consensus on accepting the principles from which Sufism arose. He also succeeded in the desired reconciliation between Sufism and *Sharīᶜa*, or mysticism and law. While he managed to elevate the status of the Sufi theory of divine knowledge and wisdom, he also rejected the possibility of *fanāʾ* and the theory of *ḥulūl*, which the majority of Sufis believed in. Although he warned the jurists and theologians not to heave

34 Abū ᶜAbd-al-Raḥmān al-Sulamī (325–412 AH/937–1021 AD) was a traditionist, Sufi and hagiographer of Persian origins. He was said to have been a prolific writer. According to his biographers, he authored about 100 works, most of which are no longer extant.

35 Abū-l-Ḥasan ᶜAlī b. ᶜUthmān al-Jullābī al-Hujwirī al-Ghaznawī, also known as ᶜAlī al-Hujwirī (d. 465 AH/1072 AD), was a Persian Sufi and scholar who was credited with significantly spreading Islam in South Asia.

36 ᶜAbd al-Karīm b. Hūzān Abū-l-Qāsim al-Qushayrī al-Naysābūrī (376–465 AH/986–1073 AD), was a jurist, exegete, traditionist, poet and a famous Sufi. Despite his other works, he was mostly known for his *al-Risāla*, also known as *al-Risāla al-Qushayriyya* (*Epistle on Sufism*), a defence of Sufism against the doubters. He was called *Zayn al-Islam* (adornment of Islam).

charges of heresy and unorthodoxy haphazardly whenever they disagreed with people having slightly different views, he also warned the Sufis of neglecting Islamic rites and performing the rituals, which, he argued, could offer the mystics valuable assistance in achieving their goals.

Nevertheless, the Christian influence is evident in the thoughts presented by *Ḥujjat al-Islam*,[37] which aroused the hatred of Ibn Taymiyyah,[38] the Ḥanbalīs and Wahhabis for al-Ghazālī, to the extent that the Wahhabis banned the reading of his books when they rose to power in the Arabian Peninsula in the late eighteenth century. In addition to the frequent references to Christ and biblical quotes, he wrote that if it were not for the doctrine of the Trinity and the denial of Muḥammad's message, Christianity would have been the pure expression of the "Truth". We see him include many of Christianity's commandments and practices into his works, as when he recommends that the *murīdūn*[39] confess all that weighs on their consciences to their shaykhs and mentors, and to accept whatever punishment they propose to them as penance and for curing whatever defect. However, he omitted from this Christian practice of confession its authority to forgive sins.

One of the most prominent of al-Ghazālī's views is twofold: the first is that there are some supreme, divine truths that should not be shared with the general public for fear of the dire consequences that may result. The "Truth" should be presented to the individual only to the extent that he could tolerate. The second is that, nonetheless, the essence of the Sufi teachings must not remain the reserve of the scholarly elite and the shaykhs, but it is in the general interest that everyone should be privy to it, so that they can adapt to it and so that their daily lives may be filled with a sense of God's existence and a desire to accomplish His will.

The impact of al-Ghazālī's dualistic view produced two distinct trends in Sufism. The first was purely intellectual and metaphysical, represented by *al-khāssa* (the elite), which was led by Shaykh Muḥyī al-Dīn Ibn al-ᶜArabī

37 Honorific title given to al-Ghazālī, meaning "Proof of Islam".

38 Taqī al-Dīn Abū-l-ᶜAbbās Aḥmad b. ᶜAbd al-Salām b. ᶜAbd Allāh b. Muḥammad b. Taymiyyah, known as Ibn Taymiyyah (661–728 AH/1263–1328 AD), was an Islamic Ḥanbalī scholar, theologian and logician. He was a prolific writer and his works are extant, which is why he is thought by many to be the main influence behind the emergence of Salafism.

39 Plural of *murīd*, student or committed one.

al-Andalusī,[40] who was of the opinion that Sufism is a scholarly discipline and that only the elite of the devotees should be privy to its secrets. He advised caution in the disclosure of such secrets. The second trend included popular features, and called for leniency in the conditions imposed on the devotees so that its pure teachings can reach the masses, even if most of them were from the lowest of people. Naturally, it was the second trend that prevailed and proliferated. This resulted in the spread of strange and eccentric phenomenon throughout the Islamic world, known as the Sufi *ṭuruq* (orders).[41]

The Third Phase: the Sufi Orders

Throughout the first centuries of the movement, Sufism remained a personal affair of the individual, a movement that did not unite its followers in any type of organisation. Eventually, these individuals began to connect with others to review their spiritual experiences, and to benefit from these experiences. In addition, many youths gathered around the senior Sufi shaykhs seeking guidance and knowledge. These congregations of youths became known as following the teachings of this shaykh or the other. Initially, the Sufis met to hold their meetings in the homes of the shaykhs or in the mosques. There they listened to the lessons and practised their spiritual exercises. But in the fourth/tenth century the group members moved to private buildings which they inhabited, and which provided shelter for members from different neighbourhoods and food and drink to the poor and wayfarers. They became known as *tekije*, *zāwiya*, *ribāṭ* or *khanqah*.[42] Usually such a building

---

40 Muḥyī al-Dīn Abū ᶜAbd Allāh Muḥammad ibn ᶜAlī ibn Muḥammad ibn al-ᶜArabī al-Ḥātimī al-Ṭāᵓī Ibn al-ᶜArabī (560–638 AH/1165–1240 AD) was a celebrated Sufi mystic, Sunni scholar, poet and philosopher. He is said to have given the esoteric, mystical dimension of Islamic thought its first philosophic expression. He was a prolific writer and his major works are the monumental *al-Futūḥāt al-Makkiyyah* (*The Meccan Revelations*) and *Fuṣūṣ al-ḥikam* (*The Bezels of Wisdom*), which is the first work that discusses the concept of *al-Insān al-Kāmil* or the perfect being. He was given the honorific title *al-Shaykh al-Akbar* (Greatest Master).

41 Plural of *ṭarīqah* (lit. road, path, way, and in Sufism it denoted the Muslim spiritual path towards *maᶜrifah* (direct knowledge) of God or the *ḥaqq* (reality, truth). Eventually, *tarīqa* came to mean the Sufi order itself.

42 All these words denote a building designed specifically for gatherings of a Sufi order, brotherhood or *ṭarīqah*, and the building is a place for spiritual retreat and character reformation; *tekije* is Turkish, *zāwiya* is Arabic, while *ribāṭ* and *khanqah* are Persian.

was either owned by the shaykh and his family, or was a *waqf* (endowment)[43] set up by a prince or a wealthy individual, which used the proceeds from the lands, estates or villages attached to it to cover its expenses.

Thus, groups emerged which were governed by some regulation and whose members engaged in certain forms of collective worship, such as the *dhikr*.[44] *Dhikr* was originally a meeting of a group of people who would read verses of the Holy Qur'an together and then sit in silence to ponder them. However, *dhikr* later evolved to become an uninterrupted, repetitive chanting of the name of God: "Allah . . . Allah . . . Allah . . .", accompanied by rhythmic movements or circular dances (like the dance of the Dervishes), in order to reach a state of mystical ecstasy: they would focus all their thoughts on the word, until their tongues and lips could no longer move and the word became imprinted on their hearts.

As a result of these collective rituals, this form of communal experience and organisation and – above all – the desire to ensure the continuation of traditions, the individual groups crystallised into a permanent form, leading to the emergence of the Sufi orders in the late sixth/twelfth century. Since then, and to this day, the *ṭuruq* have dominated the Sufi movement, exercising an almost complete dominance over it. They attracted the broad masses, especially in the cities, more than any other Islamic movement or doctrine before them, even though some Sufis preferred to keep a distance and remain outside these orders. Power and submission characterised the relationship between shaykh and *murīd* within these orders. Each *ṭarīqah* (order) had its own initiation rituals to receive devotees, as well as its own distinct rituals of worship and organisation. Each had large estates and much money at their disposal, which came from endowments and donations. Each order fabricated long *isnāds* to attribute its spiritual lineage all the way back to one of the Prophet's Companions known for his asceticism.

---

43 *Waqf* literally means confinement and prohibition, but the practice meant an endowment made by a Muslim to a religious, educational or charitable cause. Typically, it meant donating a building, plot of land or several and even cash for Muslim religious or charitable purposes with no intention of reclaiming the assets.

44 *Dhikr*, also spelled *zikr* (lit. reminding oneself, or to mention), it was a form or ritual prayer or litany practised by the Sufi Muslim mystics to glorify God and achieve spiritual perfection. It was said to be based on the Qur'anic injunctions in Q. 18:24: "*Remind thyself* (udhkur) *of thy Lord when thou forgettest*" and Q. 33:41: "*O ye who believe! Remember (udhkurū) Allāh with much remembrance.*" It essentially is a form of remembering God by the frequent mention and repetition of his names.

It is not easy to make a general statement on whether the stand taken by the authorities since that time has been for or against the Sufi orders. It is also difficult to determine whether the Sufi orders have resisted or assisted the authorities in the Muslim world. There have been authorities and rulers who persecuted the Sufis to protect the creed or the state, such as, for example, the Shi'ite *mujtahidūn*[45] in Iran, the Wahhabis in the Arabian Peninsula and the government of Kemal Atatürk in Turkey. Likewise, there were rulers and authorities who believed that they needed the *baraka* (blessings)[46] from one of the Sufi shaykhs to continue to rule or to remain in power. Though we read about the involvement of Sufi orders in some insurgencies against some governments, we also know of other Sufi orders that supported other authorities effectively against their enemies. The best evidence of this is the position of al-Ṭarīqah al-Tijānīyah[47] during the French occupation of North Africa. While the Algerian Tijānīyah supported that occupation, the Tunisian and Moroccan Tijānīyah waged a desperate *jihad* against it. Be that as it may, some governments, in order to tighten control over the Sufi orders and to ensure their good behaviour, resorted to establishing the system of "*Shaykh al-Shuyūkh*", a kind of supreme Sufi shaykh for all orders, whom the government appointed, either openly or secretly. This "Supreme Shaykh" had power over the Sufi orders throughout the country. The "*Shaykh al-Shuyūkh*" in Egypt has always been a descendant of Abū Bakr, and for this reason was known as al-Shaykh al-Bakrī.

The oldest of all the Sufi orders is al-Ṭarīqah al-Qādirīyah,[48] founded by ᶜAbd al-Qādir al-Jīlānī in Iraq in the sixth/twelfth century. It is one of the

---

45 *Mujtahid* is a term for a qualified jurist who had the right to exercise original thinking, mainly *ra'y* (personal judgement) and *qiyās* (analogical reasoning) to interpret legal issues not explicitly addressed in the Qur'an.

46 *Baraka* (pl. *barakāt*, lit. blessings, God's grace) is a prominent concept in Sufism, and symbolises the spiritual connection between the divine and the worldly through God's direct and intentional blessing in the form of a flow of blessings and grace.

47 Al-Ṭarīqah al-Tijānīyah is a Sufi order found especially in North and West Africa. It was founded by Aḥmad al-Tijānī (1737–1815), who was previously a member of the Khalwatī order, around 1781 in Fez, Morocco. This order places great emphasis on good intentions and actions rather than on elaborate or extreme rituals.

48 Al-Ṭarīqah al-Qādirīyah is probably the oldest Sufi order. It was founded by the Ḥanbalī theologian ᶜAbd al-Qādir al-Jīlānī (470–561 AH/1078–1166 AD) in Baghdad. The order emphasises philanthropy, humility, piety and moderation. It is loosely organised, meaning that it allows each regional community to develop its own ritual prayers (*zikrs or dhikrs*). It has many offshoots, and is widespread, particularly in the Arabic-speaking world. However, it is also found in Turkey, Indonesia, Afghanistan, India, Bangladesh, Pakistan, the Balkans, Russia, Palestine, Israel, China and East and West Africa.

most tolerant and philanthropic orders, as well as being closest to the Sunni doctrine. Its followers are known for their piety, their propensity for charitable work, their humility and their distaste for religious and political fanaticism. One of its offshoots is al-Ṭarīqah al-Rifāᶜīyah,[49] which is rather fanatical and has the greatest tendency to self-torture (or *jihad* against the self). Their followers are known to eat glass, swallow fire, play with snakes and walk barefoot on fire or hot burning coals. Its founder, Aḥmad al-Rifāᶜī named himself "*khātam al-awliyāʾ*" (the Seal of the *Awliyāʾ*), in the same manner as the Prophet was called "*khātam al-anbiyāʾ*" (the Seal of the Prophets), which is to say, the last Prophet sent by God to mankind. His followers and admirers claimed that all the Prophet's merits were found in him. In order not to be misled, his followers prohibited any links with any other Sufi orders. Another famous order is al-Ṭarīqah al-Mawlaw'īyya,[50] which was named in honour of the great Persian poet Mawlānā Jalāl al-Dīn al-Rūmī.[51] It is famous for its circular dance of the dervishes, which symbolises the unending search for the divine beloved, and is its fundamental religious rite. There are numerous other orders, of which Massignon[52] counted 175 major ones, not to mention the innumerable offshoots of these orders.

Sufi women were not organised in any orders exclusively for women, although they sometimes owned a number of *zāwāya* (sing. *zāwiya*). The usual route for Sufi women mystics was either to engage in an already existing order or to lead a private spiritual life away from the orders. If women

49 Al-Ṭarīqah al-Rifāᶜīyah is an offshoot of the Qādirīyah, which was founded by Ahmed al-Rifāᶜī (512–578 AH/1118–1181 AD) in Iraq. It is found primarily in Egypt and Syria and in Turkey until it was outlawed in 1925. The order stresses poverty, abstinence, and self-mortification. Their *zikr* or *dhikr* is very distinctive: its members link arms in a circle and move their upper parts back and forth until they achieve ecstasy, then they fall on a dangerous object, such as swords or snakes. They are known to engage in magical practices, which is why they have been rejected by orthodox Islam.

50 Al-Ṭarīqah al-Mawlaw'īyya is a Sufi order in Konya, Turkey, which spread during the Ottoman Empire into the Balkans, Syria, Lebanon, Egypt and Palestine, especially in Jerusalem. It was founded by the followers of Jalal al-Din al-Rumi. They are also known as the Whirling Dervishes due to their famous practice of whirling as a form of *zikr* or *dhikr*.

51 Jalāl al-Dīn al-Rūmī, also known by his honorific title as *Mawlānā* (Our Master) (604–672 AH/1207–1273 AD), was a Persian Sunni poet, jurist, scholar, theologian and Sufi. His most famous work, *Mas̆navī-yi Maᶜnavī* or *Mathnawī* (*Spiritual Couplets*), is considered one of the greatest poems of the Persian language. After his death, his disciples were organised as the Mawlawīyah order.

52 Louis Massignon (1883–1962) was a French scholar of Islam and a pioneer of Catholic–Muslim mutual understanding.

attended lessons or *dhikr* -circles, they sat at a distance from the men, separated from them by a curtain. History tells us that Awḥad al-Dīn al-Kirmānī's daughter, in the third/ninth century, was a shaykha in seventeen separate *zāwāya* in Damascus.

It was inevitable that the teachings of the various Sufi orders would differ, and for conflict and differences to arise between them. Whereas some of the orders favoured celibacy, such as al-Ṭarīqah al-Bektāshiyya,[53] others followed Islam's approach of extolling the virtue of marriage. Muḥyī al-Dīn Ibn al-ᶜArabī was over sixty years of age when he added an eighteen-year-old girl to his wives in Damascus. While Aḥmad al-Rifāᶜī – as already mentioned – claimed to be "*khātam al-awliyā*ᵓ", Shaykh Aḥmad al-Tijānī claimed that Prophet Muḥammad handpicked him to be the seal of the *awliyā*ᵓ . Some of the orders mixed their teachings with Shi'ite teachings, such as Shaykh Rajab al-Bursī,[54] who (much like Christianity) held the view that the love of *ahl al-bayt* (the Prophet's family) atoned for all sins. Some of them claimed to be *al-Mahdī al-muntazar* (awaited ultimate saviour of humankind), such as Muḥammad Nūrbakhsh[55] in Afghanistan and Iran, and Muḥammad Aḥmad[56] in Sudan in the nineteenth century. Over time, Sufi orders became very similar to the political parties of today, each with their own beliefs and preferences, rituals, dress codes and colours, with each a shaykh boasting about the number of followers he has in his order.

The Decline of Sufism

By the end of the seventh/thirteenth century, the creative phase of Sufism was gone forever. The movement began – especially since the tenth/sixteenth century – to deteriorate rapidly, to take on features of frivolity and charlatanry, and to become materialistic, exceeding even the levels reached against the Sunni jurists during its early years.

---

53 al-Ṭarīqah al-Bektāshiyya is a Sufi order named after Haji Bektash Vali (1209–1271 AD) and is found mainly in Anatolia and the Balkans.

54 Rajab b. Muḥammad b. Rajab al-Bursī al-Ḥillī, also known as al-Ḥāfiz al-Bursī (d. 813 AH/1411 AD), was an Iraqi theologian, jurist, traditionist, poet and Sufi.

55 Muḥammad b. Muḥammad b. ᶜAbd Allah Nūrbakhsh al-Qahistānī (795–869 AH/1392–1464 AD) was a Persian theologian, jurist and Sufi.

56 Muḥammad Aḥmad b. ᶜAbd Allah (1843–1885), a Sudanese religious leader who proclaimed himself the Mahdi, the messianic redeemer of the Islamic faith, and led a successful military campaign, culminating in the liberation of Khartoum from General Charles Gordon.

With the early Sufi mystics continually promoting the virtues of poverty and of an austere ascetic life, people came to assume that Sufism is about abandoning worldly baggage and focusing on the salvation of the soul. Hence, it was highly peculiar to find the Sufi shaykhs courting the sultans, and seeking favour with the princes and the elite. They became interested in marrying the daughters of wealthy prestigious families, possessing elegant houses and vast estates, and having poets sing their praises and commend their virtues. When the naive and gullible questioned them about whether ownership, possession and riches burdened the soul and deterred it from attaining spiritual perfection – a matter which was subject to much debate in the first centuries – they responded that this was a question that could be asked or contemplated only by ignorant people, obsessed with appearances, who missed the fact that the essential core was the spiritual path, patience during poverty and destitution, and gratitude for God's grace and his blessings, while ownership and wealth as such did not mean a thing.

It was also strange to find some Sufis involved in warfare and joining battles, whether these were *jihad* against non-Muslims or revolts against Muslim rulers. History tells how the famous Sufi Shaykh al-Fāsī,[57] with an army of his followers, led an attack on Portugal and conquered parts of it by force of arms.

As for the hollow debates and sophistry, which the earlier mystics deprecated and held against the jurists, theologians and philosophers, these soon leaked into the Sufi movement itself. We saw a bitter conflict arise between the Khorasani and the Iraqi School about Q. 9:100:[58] ". . . *Allah is well pleased with them and they are well pleased with Him* . . ." The Iraqi School regarded "*riḍā*" (pleasure or satisfaction)[59] as a *maqām* (stage), since God's "*riḍā*" precedes that of his worshipers. The Khorasani School regarded it is a *ḥāl* (state), which is the fruit resulting from the worshiper reaching the *maqām* of *tawakkul* (trust in God).[60] Others tried to reconcile

57 Yūsuf b. Muḥammad b. Yūsuf al-Fāsī, also known as Abū-l-Maḥāsin al-Fāsī (937–1013 AH/1530/31–1604 AD), was a Moroccan scholar, theologian and Sufi.

58 Q. 9:100: "*And (as for) the foremost, the first of the Muhajirs and the Ansars, and those who followed them in goodness, Allah is well pleased with them and they are well pleased with Him, and He has prepared for them gardens beneath which rivers flow, to abide in them for ever; that is the mighty achievement.*"

59 The term "*riḍā*" literally means "the fact of being pleased, contentment or approval". It is one of the Islamic virtues discussed in Sufism. In this context, it is interpreted as satisfaction or "perfect contentment with God's will or decree".

60 *Tawakkul* in Arabic is the word for the Islamic concept of reliance on God or "trusting in God's plan".

between both opinions by stating that "*riḍā*" starts out as a *maqām* and ends up as a *ḥāl*![61]

If Sufism – thanks to al-Ghazālī's efforts – is now looked upon favourably and finds acceptance with most of the rulers and the masses of the people, the irreverence of al-Ḥallāj and al-Basṭāmī has now made a comeback and afflicted some of its shaykhs. Some of them have reaffirmed their contempt for the "apparent" *Sharīᶜa*, and then extended their disregard even further to include the established ethics, traditions and moral judgements that the Qur'an stipulated. Some preceded Rasputin[62] by hundreds of years in the call to refrain from fighting worldly desires, even advising their devotees to indulge in them, and arguing that such indulgence and depravity are the best way to recognise that desire is an illusion and to then uproot it. Al-Ṭarīqah al-Malāmatiyya in Khorasan[63] went as far as to say that committing the most heinous sins and the most depraved vices is in some instances the duty of devotees, as it would humiliate and crush their self-pride, and demonstrate the ability of the devotee to disregard public opinion and human rules.

Over the ages, some beliefs, rituals and patterns of behaviour, which were in clear violation of the provisions of Islam as taught by the Prophet, grew in the Sufi movement. It is true that some of its rational leaders made the distinction between the acceptable innovations and the corrupt ones; however, the efforts of these few were lost in the midst of the superstitions, which became one of the main features of the movement: the Egyptian *zār*[64]

61 In Sufi literature, a *maqām* is one of the many stages marking the path leading the mystics to God, and it is earned by the worshiper through his own effort, while the *ḥāl* (state) is a spiritual gift, a gratuitous favour of God, which is usually transitory.

62 Grigori Yefimovich Rasputin (1869–1916) was a Russian, who is best known for his role as a mystical adviser in the court of the Russian Tsar Nicholas II and whose name became synonymous with debauchery, lust and power.

63 Al-Ṭarīqah al-Malāmatiyya was a Sufi order founded in the third/ninth century in Nishapur, Khorasan. Their name derives from the Arabic word *malāmah* (blame), because the order believed in the value of self-blame.

64 The *zār* is a ritual that aims at exorcising spirits from an individual believed to be possessed or to cure mental illness, because it is believed to have powerful therapeutic effects. The *zār* became popular in the urban culture, especially of Cairo, as a form of women-only entertainment, providing a unique form of relief to women in strict patriarchal societies. The *zār* gatherings involved food and musical performances, and culminated in ecstatic dancing. In rare instances it involves sacrificing animals.

and the Tunisian *būrī*,[65] which aim at inducing a trance-like state in the afflicted patient to create an outlet in his or her soul in order to evict the spirits that torture him or her; the *majādhīb*,[66] who behave abnormally and engage in deviant practices and outrageous acts, all of which are excused and forgiven by the people, who claim that they are loved by God; the West African Haddāwa – the followers of Ibn Mashīsh[67] – who revere cats (*mashīsh* in the Berber language means kitten), who move from place to place, in their rags, begging and using drugs, and who venerate a huge pipe, which they claimed belonged to the founder of their order; and the followers of the Qalandariyya order,[68] who shave their heads and eyebrows and smoke hashish and openly disregard Islamic rites. The influence of Kurdish beliefs on the Sufi orders in the East has resulted in the establishment of two contrasting groups: the first, formed in the west of Iran, called themselves *ahl al-ḥaqq* (People of Truth) and worshipped ᶜAlī [b. Abū Ṭālib]; the second, formed in northern Iraq, were the Yazidis, who considered Yazīd b. Mu'awiya, the Umayyad caliph, an angel! It is worth mentioning that the Yazidis do not consider themselves to be Muslims, and they formerly revered the devil, whom they saw as a symbol of unification, as he refused to bow down to Adam, preferring the wrath of God over having someone share respect with Him.[69]

Since the seventh/thirteenth century in particular, the Sufis ascribed to Muḥammad the same position enjoyed by Jesus in Christianity (which sparked Ibn Taymiyyah's wrath on them). The union with Muḥammad became the goal of every religious activity. They introduced the custom of annually celebrating

65 The *būrī* ritual, also called *ḥadra*, is similar to the *zār* in that it is a sort of exorcism. Unlike the *zār*, it is more extravagant. It is divided into two parts, one collective, which is loud, and fast, where all dance vigorously together to loud music to enter into an ecstatic trance. The second part is an individual dance by the willing participants. Like the *zār*, this aims at allowing the trance to mollify the spirits that are said to possess the patient. Unlike the *zār*, the *būrī* involves self-mutilation and animal sacrifice.

66 *Majādhīb* (sing. *majdhūb*) are depicted in popular culture as being *makshūf ᶜanhu al-ḥijāb*, meaning that the veil that covers the unseen world has dropped and the unseen has become known to them.

67 ᶜAbd al-Salām Ibn Mashīsh al-ᶜAlamī (559–626 AH/1163–1228 AD) was a Moroccan Sufi.

68 Al-Ṭarīqah al-Qalandariyya includes a variety of different orders that are not centrally organised and its members are wandering ascetic Sufi dervishes. It was founded by Qalandar Yūsuf al-Andalusī of Andalusia, Spain.

69 This is a common misconception in the Muslim world due to the parallels between the story of the angel known as "Tawuse Melek" (the Peacock Angel), who is worshipped by the Yazidis, and the Qur'anic story of Iblis or Satan, as they both refuse to bow to Adam.

the *Mawlid* (the Prophet's birthday), which began in northern Iraq around 1200 AD and then spread to all Islamic countries over the following century. In addition, Sufis also tended to sanctify their mentors and shaykhs to a degree almost amounting to worship. When the claims of their divine wisdom found public acceptance, the public increasingly expected *karāmāt* (extraordinary abilities) from the *awliyā*ʾ, who responded to this desire and rushed to meet it. Although the Sufi theories exhort the *awliyā*ʾ to hide their "*karāmāt*", and to downplay their value as much as possible, many of them did not abide by this principle. Some orders went as far as to call for these "*karāmāt*" to be displayed and publicised, due to the positive effects they have on the general public. Hence, the biographies of the early Sufis are replete with anecdotes about such "*karāmāt*" : some Sufis drank poison, or stabbed themselves with daggers, or entered into hot burning furnaces or jumped down from steep mountains, so the people could plainly see God's ability manifest itself in these "*karāmāt*".

Conclusion

Sufism has come a long way from the era of al-Ḥasan al-Baṣrī to the time of the Haddāwa and *majādhīb*. For fourteen centuries it swayed between piety and charlatanry, inspiration and degradation, bravado and submissiveness; adoration of God and drugs; *fanā*ʾ and playing with snakes. However, in the interest of fairness, and much like the critique of a poet or artist is based on the assessment of their best work, we will – in responding to our two questions below – only consider Sufism in its golden age, disregarding the levels it has degenerated to.

The questions are: what has Sufism added to Islam?; and is it Islamic?

Indeed, Sufism performed a great service to Islam by exposing the hollow religion of the scholars and jurists, their controversies, their insubstantial empty debates on the tiniest minutiae without any spiritual dimension, and their polite behaviour in the streets and markets without any conscientiousness. Their efforts uncovered a shortcoming that had occurred in Islam, but that was not inherent to it. But they did not try – as Ibn Taymiyyah and Ibn Qayyim al-Jawziyyah[70] – to return Islam to its foundations and to remove the

70 Shams al-Dīn Abū ʿAbd Allah Muhammad b. Abū Bakr, also known as Ibn al-Qayyim or Ibn Qayyim al-Jawziyyah (691–751 AH/1292–1349 AD) was a famous Ḥanbalī scholar, jurist, theologian and exegete. He was Ibn Taymiyyah's student.

accumulated, superfluous innovations that crept into it after the first three generations. Their idea of reform was to add new building blocks to Islam, which were different from its original building blocks, and did not resemble Islam. Hence, the resulting edifice was neither purely Islamic, nor purely Christian, Indian, Persian or Greek, but rather a bit of all of these combined. If its founder returned to this world of ours, he would have denied that this was Islam, and if he met one of their shaykhs, he would be unable to understand him.

Sufis benefitted Islam by making it clear that the apparent truth without an inner core is nothing but hypocrisy. However, they also harmed Islam by not realising that the inner core without that which is apparent is disbelief. In this respect they resemble the Lutherans, who benefitted Christianity by attacking the corruption of the Church, and then distorting the religion in a way that was even more serious than what they had been fighting. There was another way to reform the religion than the one they embarked on, and that is, in our opinion, Ibn Taymiyyah's way and not that of al-Ghazālī.

Having said that, we would not want to be misunderstood as not believing in the development of the *Da^cwah*.[71] In fact, any *Da^cwah* has to develop in line with the changing needs of the times. However, there is a vast difference between development and dressing up the *Da^cwah* in garments that are not indigenous to it and hiding alien ideologies behind it. Sufism was not alone in resorting to this sort of cover-up. The history of Islam is replete with dozens or even hundreds of doctrines or sects that did exactly that, either out of fear of persecution and of being branded as heretics, or the desire for an easier access to the masses and general public, since the appearance of the Khawārij, all the way to the socialists in this day and age. If all these were courageous and honest enough to establish and found new philosophical schools or even new religious doctrines without attributing them to Islam, or calling them Islamic, they would not have garnered all that contempt and censure. But resorting to forcing meanings upon the Qur'an which were never intended, attributing traditions and sayings to the Prophet which he never said, as well as injecting Buddhist, Zoroastrian and Christian elements into Islam which were not inherent to it is, in our opinion, cowardly and dishonourable. The result can only be a contrived, phony "concoction" of disparate, incongruous elements.

71 The word *Da^cwah* in Arabic has a variety of meanings, invitation, proselytising, preaching, call or movement.

Schopenhauer[72] saw Sufism as the height of Islamic thought, a view shared by Massignon. The former thought so because it confirmed his view that what is perceived is pure evil, while the latter thought so because Sufi doctrines are the closest "Islamic" schools to Christianity. However, our question is: is Sufism Islamic at all?

Only one issue remains, namely, that of the relationship between Sufis and the weak and corrupt rulers. It has been mentioned that among the factors that helped it spread was the arrival of the Turks to the ᶜAbbāsid state, which caused the deterioration of the quality of political life. We also know that the Tatar hordes sweeping the eastern regions of the Islamic state gave Sufism an enormous new impetus, akin to the one given to it after the Arab defeat in June 1967. It is apparent that the ethics of every religion and *Daᶜwah* are aimed, among other things, at facilitating the nation's acceptance of new conditions and compliance with them. The Christian moral and ethical codes, for example, were the best way to ensure a peaceful co-existence between the people of Palestine and their Roman rulers, while the ethics of the Pharisee Jews impeded this harmony. If we applied this to Sufism, it becomes clear that their ethical and moral codes aimed at facilitating reconciliation with and acceptance of any conditions. If the Tatar armies were defeated and repelled this was thanks to the Mamluk army and not because of Sufi ethics – one might even say despite the Sufi ethics. Should the Arab world rise again after the setback of June 1967 to return to the right path, it would be despite the popular Sufi trends that have permeated the Arab world.

72 Arthur Schopenhauer (1788–1860), German philosopher.

6
Reflections on the Status of the Awliyāʾ

And they serve beside Allah what can neither harm them nor profit them, and they say: These are our intercessors with Allah. Say: Do you (presume to) inform Allah of what He knows not in the heavens and the earth? Glory be to Him, and supremely exalted is He above what they set up (with Him).

Verse 18, Chapter 10 (Yūnus)

Religion is a combination of a sacred text and the text's interpretation. The former is from God and is therefore constant and unchanging, while the latter is man-made and variable, depending on individuals, societies and eras. Since the sacred text is irreplaceable, humans often find ways of circumventing it by interpreting it to their liking, to fit their whims and inclinations.

Some ancient Greek and Roman thinkers, such as Pythagoras[1] and Numa Pompilius,[2] refused to leave behind any texts so as not to shackle the minds of their successors. They burnt their works before they died or recommended that their writings be buried with them. They wanted to enable every generation in the country to produce the thought that befits their time and environment. It may be argued that the Prophet of Islam did not order the collection of the Qur'an either, as evidenced by the fact that Caliph Abū Bakr hesitated when ʿUmar b. al-Khaṭṭāb suggested the idea to him, saying: "I cannot attempt to do what the Prophet did not do. He did not recommend the collection of the Qur'an before his death." Yet the main assumption of religion – any religion – is

1 Pythagoras (570–*c.* 495 BC) was a famous Greek philosopher and mathematician.
2 Numa Pompilius (753–673 BC) was the second king of Rome and reigned 715–673 BC.

that the teachings contained in the sacred text are valid for all, for every time and every place.

However, humans were often too weak to commit themselves to the provisions of the sacred text, too cowardly to revolt against them, and too devious to admit their inability or unwillingness. While they always needed religion for the unwavering certainty it provides and for protection from the humiliation of doubt, they saw nothing wrong, in view of their weakness, with providing interpretations that pleased them, and that deluded them that they are the loyal guardians of religion.

The Psychological Need for a Mediator or Intercessor

The most challenging concept imposed by religions was the abstract concept of the God. In the ancient world, worship was unimaginable without an idol or an image. The gods of the ancients were always embodied and tangible, whether they were an idol, a planet, a king or a natural phenomenon. It thus took several centuries for this new, abstract concept of a god to take root in the peoples' minds. However, the awareness of this enormous gap that now separated them from their god persisted. They therefore pictured God as a father to them, or closer to them than their jugular vein.[3] This pressing, "pagan" wish to close the gap by any means possibly reflected a psychological need that some clerics thought was wise to respond to, albeit to a limited extent. This may have been for fear that the common people may forgo the religion in its entirety or in an attempt to preserve their own power. Thus, religious statues and icons quickly replaced the idols and the sanctification of the *awliyā'*[4] replaced the worship of gods, kings and ancestors. In his book *Taḥqīq mā lil-hind min maqūlah maqbūlah fī al-'aql aw mardhūlah* (*Critical Study of What India Says, Whether Accepted by Reason Or Refused*),[5] al-Bīrūnī[6] wrote:

> It is well known that the popular mind leans towards the sensible world, and has an aversion to the world of abstract thought which is only understood by highly educated people, of whom in every

3 As found in Q. 50:16.

4 Lit. companions, friends, but also pious people and saints.

5 Translated as *Alberuni's India* by C. Edward Sachau, 2 vols (London: Truber, 1887–88; reprinted 1910).

6 Abū Rayḥān Muḥammad b. Aḥmad al-Bīrūnī (362–440 AH/973–1048 AD) was a Persian polymath and Muslim scholar excelling in mathematics, astronomy, natural sciences, physics and geography, as well as a historian and chronologer of the history of religions.

> time and every place there are only few. And as common people will only acquiesce in pictorial representations, many of the leaders of religious communities have so far deviated from the right path as to give such imagery in their books and houses of worship, like the Jews and Christians, and, more than all, the Manichaeans. These words of mine would at once receive a sufficient illustration if, for example, a picture of the Prophet were made, or of Mekka and the Kaʿba, and were shown to an uneducated man or woman. Their joy in looking at the thing would bring them to kiss the picture, to rub their cheeks against it, and to roll themselves in the dust before it, as if they were seeing not the picture, but the original, and were in this way, as if they were present in the holy places, performing the rites of pilgrimage, the great and the small ones. This is the cause which leads to the manufacture of idols, monuments in honour of certain much venerated persons, prophets, sages, angels, destined to keep alive their memory when they are absent or dead, to create for them a lasting place of grateful veneration in the hearts of men when they die. But when much time passes by after the setting up of the monument, generations and centuries, its origin is forgotten, it becomes a matter of custom, and its veneration a rule for general practice.[7]

Even under a regime such as the communist one, which has no place for religion in its "scientific" thought, faith in dialectical materialism carried clear overtones of religious fervour. Assemblies and parades took on features of religious ceremonies and processions. Their ideologues and founding fathers were bestowed an aura akin to that of the *awliyāʾ* and prophets. They were described as immortal or compared with the sun that never sets. Their larger-than-life pictures and sculptures, which replaced the religious icons and statues, looked over the people in the squares and public buildings, and even over individuals in their own homes. Their graves were turned into holy pilgrimage shrines, visited by millions of people who lined up in long queues for hours just for a glance. Their books are as good as sacred, and attributing an error to their ideas was considered as blasphemy. Some (like the Red Guards in China) even keep these books beside them or under their pillows at night to ward off any evil.

---

7 al-Bīrūnī, Muḥammad b. Aḥmad. *Alberuni's India: An Account of the Religion, Philosophy, Literature, Geography, Chronology, Astronomy, Customs, Laws and Astrology of India about A.D.1030*, trans. Edward Sachau, 2 vols, London: Kegan Paul, Trench, Trübner, 1910, vol. 1, pp. 111–12.

This psychological need among the common people for the tangible or concrete was accompanied by another psychological need for an intercessor or mediator. However much rulers insist that their doors are open to their subjects, and however much religions confirm that there is no intermediary between a person and his God, people will remain obsessed with the idea of a royal audience or a divine *ḥaḍra* (presence), and they will always prefer to have a mediator whom they deem closer to them and whom they see as one of them. Therefore, instead of turning to God with their *duʿāʾ* (prayer or supplication), they direct it to the Prophet, his grandson or any of his descendants from *ahl al-bayt* or to the local *walīy* (singular of *awliyāʾ*) in town or in the village, asking his help and intercession and resorting to him in times of tribulation or distress.

There is no doubt that religions had a profound impact on the beliefs, behaviour, habits and patterns of living of the people who embraced them. However, there is also no doubt that the ancient ideas and beliefs, which religions were revealed to uproot and replace, managed to creep into these religions and to adapt them to the psychological and social needs of the people. Often the basic teachings and tenets of a particular religion were mixed with local beliefs, resulting in a new concoction, where the original teachings became unrecognisable. Being resourceful and cunning (or perhaps, misguided), people were always able to provide a "religious" basis for their continued adherence to ancient beliefs, colouring these beliefs, rites and rituals, which they had no intention of giving up, with the new religion and placing them within its framework. An example for this would be the continued aversion towards marrying widows in India, even after the introduction of Islam and the attempts to find an "Islamic" interpretation for it, even though it is contrary to the spirit of Islam (especially given that the Prophet of Islam himself married many widows). Another example is that of some African tribes whose pagan religion forbade the slaughter and eating of roosters. After their conversion to Islam, they continued to forbid the same, but argued "Islamically" that the roosters' crowing awakened people from their sleep to perform the dawn prayer, and that they are, therefore, sacred birds!

Overcoming the Obstacles to the Sanctification of the Awliyāʾ

The prime opportunity for people to retain some aspects of their ancient religions came in the form of the veneration of *awliyāʾ*. Those who had converted to Christianity had found a replacement for their pagan idols in the statues of

Mary and Christ and in the religious icons. For those who converted to Islam, the sanctification of the *awliyāʾ* was the main way to replace their paganism and idol worship, due to the categorical prohibition of idols and images in Islam ("Angels do not enter a house, where there is a dog or a picture", *Sunan Ibn Majah*). This practice of sanctification was something they had in common with followers of other religions, including Judaism.

Muslims faced two major obstacles in their attempt to find a place for the sanctification of the *awliyāʾ* within the framework of their new religion, and to ascribe miracles (or *karāmāt*, as they call them) to those *awliyāʾ* to justify this sanctification.

The first obstacle was that Islam does not recognise mediators between God and the people. As such, there is no a place in Islam for such sanctification of individuals. The Qur'an has explicitly denounced the sanctification of rabbis by the Jews and that of the monks by the Christians:

Q. 9:31: "*They have taken their rabbis and their monks for lords besides Allah, and (also) the Messiah son of Maryam and they were enjoined that they should serve one God only, there is no god but He; far from His glory be what they set up (with Him).*"

Q. 25:16–17: Q. 25:16: "*They shall have therein what they desire abiding (in it); it is a promise which it is proper to be prayed for from your Lord*; Q. 25:17: "*And on the day when He shall gather them, and whatever they served besides Allah, He shall say: Was it you who led astray these My servants, or did they themselves go astray from the path?*"

Q. 2:48: "*And be on your guard against a day when one soul shall not avail another in the least, neither shall intercession on its behalf be accepted, nor shall any compensation be taken from it, nor shall they be helped.*"

Q. 10:18: "*And they serve beside Allah what can neither harm them nor profit them, and they say: These are our intercessors with Allah. Say: Do you (presume to) inform Allah of what He knows not in the heavens and the earth? Glory be to Him, and supremely exalted is He above what they set up (with Him).*"

The second obstacle was that the Prophet of Islam did not ascribe to himself the ability to manipulate the laws of nature, nor did he claim prescience. The early Muslims, likewise, did not ascribe any miracles to him, other than those mentioned in the Qur'an. They were satisfied with God's favours bestowed upon him and only saw him as a righteous human being who received divine revelations. How then can the common people attribute to the *awliyāʾ* miracles or extraordinary deeds and abilities, the likes of which the Prophet never possessed or performed?

Q. 6:50: "*Say: I do not say to you, I have with me the treasures of Allah, nor do I know the unseen . . .*"
Q. 7:188: "*Say: I do not control any benefit or harm for my own soul except as Allah please; and had I known the unseen I would have had much of good and no evil would have touched me . . .*"
Q. 6:109: "*And they swear by Allah with the strongest of their oaths, that if a sign came to them they would most certainly believe in it. Say: Signs are only with Allah . . .*"
Q. 13:7: "*And those who disbelieve say: Why has not a sign been sent down upon him from his Lord? You are only a warner and (there is) a guide for every people.*"
Q. 17:90–93: Q. 17:90: "*And they say: We will by no means believe in you until you cause a fountain to gush forth from the earth for us*"; Q. 17:91: "*Or you should have a garden of palms and grapes in the midst of which you should cause rivers to flow forth, gushing out*"; Q. 17:92: "*Or you should cause the heaven to come down upon us in pieces as you think, or bring Allah and the angels face to face (with us)*"; Q. 17:93: "*Or you should have a house of gold, or you should ascend into heaven, and we will not believe in your ascending until you bring down to us a book which we may read. Say: Glory be to my Lord; am I aught but a mortal apostle?*"

The first obstacle – the sanctification of the *awliyāʾ* being a violation of the spirit of Islam – has been completely ignored by the public. They simply circumvented this obstacle without removing it. Similarly, most jurists turned a blind eye to this violation, as long as the sanctification did not blatantly contradict the principle of *tawḥīd* (the oneness of God). The sanctification was even supported by some of the greatest thinkers of Islam, such as Ibn Sīnā[8] (in his *al-Ishārāt wa-l-tanbīhāt*), al-Ghazālī (in his *Iḥyāʾ ʿulūm al-dīn*) and Ibn

8 Abū ʿAlī al-Ḥusayn b. ʿAbd Allāh b. al-Ḥasan b. ʿAlī b. Sīnā, also known as Ibn Sīnā and Avicenna (370–427 AH/980–1037 AD), was a Persian polymath and one of the most significant thinkers and writers of Islam's Golden Age.

Khaldūn (in his *al-Muqaddima*). Others, such as the Mu˓tazila, their enemies the Ḥanbalīs and after them the Wahhabis, have fought this innovation and other traces of paganism. They based their reasoning on ˓Umar b. al-Khaṭṭāb's words to the Black Stone[9] in the Ka˓ba: "By God, I know you are just a stone, unable to do any harm or benefit, and if it weren't for me seeing the Messenger of God kissing you, I would not have kissed you." However, ˓Umar quickly regretted his words and even cried when ˓Alī b. Abū Ṭālib explained his mistake to him and clarified the Black Stone's importance and sanctity!

The second obstacle was swiftly and successfully surmounted by the general public. They saw that it was not possible to ascribe "*karāmāt*" to the *awliyā˒* without changing the purely Islamic concept of prophecy, nor would it have been appropriate to talk about *awliyā˒*'s *karāmāt* that were more spectacular than those of the Prophet, whose stature and abilities should always rise above them. The easiest way to overcome this obstacle was to attribute to the Prophet hundreds of miracles. Some of them described how he fed an entire army from one basket of dates, or how he caused water to spring up in a well in the desert by sticking his lance into the sand, or how he cured one of his Companions of conjunctivitis by spitting into his eye. Whenever the Sunni jurists objected to attributing some *karāmāt* to one of the *awliyā˒* that the Prophet had not performed, some more spectacular and superior miracles were quickly ascribed by the public to the Prophet.

Some examples from *Tārīkh al-khamīs fī aḥwāl anfas nafīs* by al-Diyārbakrī[10] are:

> "Asmā˒ bint ˓Umays[11] narrated, with two different chains of narration, that the Prophet received revelation (in Khaybar) while his head was in ˓Alī's lap. For that reason, ˓Alī did not perform his *˓asr* (afternoon)

---

9 The Black Stone is built into the eastern wall of the Ka˓ba. According to popular Islamic legend, the stone was given to Adam on his fall from Paradise and was originally white, but has become black by absorbing the sins of the thousands of pilgrims who have kissed and touched it.

10 Ḥusayn b. Muḥammad b. al-Ḥasan al-Diyārbakrī (d. 966 AH/1559 AD) was a jurist, scholar, historian and Qāḍī in Mecca.

11 Asmā˒ bint ˓Umays b. Ma˓ād (d. 38 AH/ 658 AD or 60 AH/679 AD) was one of the early believers. Her first husband was Ja˒far b. Abū Ṭālib, who immigrated with her to Abyssinya. She returned to Medina in 7 AH/628 AD. After his death in 8 AH/629 AD, she married Abū Bakr after the death of his wife, Umm Rūmān. After his death in 13 AH/634 AD, she married ˓Alī b. Abū Ṭālib. She narrated many prophetic traditions and is considered a trustworthy narrator.

prayers until the sun had set. The Prophet asked him: '[c]Alī, Did you pray?' He replied: 'No.' The Prophet said: 'Oh God, he was obedient to You and to Your messenger, backtrack the sun for us.' Asmā[ʾ] said: 'I saw the sun backtrack and rise after it had set.' This is an authentic *ḥadīth*, narrated by trustworthy narrators."

Afterwards, it became necessary to also ascribe such extraordinary powers to some of the Prophet's senior Companions, to pave the way to the sanctification of the *awliyā*[ʾ] :

"[c]Alī b. Abū Ṭālib pulled down the door of the Khyber fort which was made of cast iron. After pulling it down, he used it as a shield, carrying it while fighting. Afterwards, he carried it on his back and used it as a bridge for the Muslims to enter the fort. Then, when the war ended, he threw that iron door over his shoulder around eighty spans.[12] Abū Rāfi[c] narrated: 'seven people, me being the eighth, struggled to turn over that door and we failed'."

In *al-Mawāhib al-laduniyya bi-l-minaḥ al-Muḥammadiyya* by al-Qastallānī another version is reported as: "[c]Alī pulled down Khaybar's door. Seventy men could only move it after great effort." Ibn Isḥāq's version reports seven men. In *Sharḥ al-mawāqif* by al-Sharīf al-Jirjānī, the same narrative is reported as: "[c]Alī pulled down the door of Khyber with his bare hand, and said: 'I did not pull down the door using physical strength, but it was by divine force!'"

Attempts to Give a Religious Foundation to the Krāmāt *of the* Awliyā[ʾ]

Once these miracles had established themselves on the pages of books, in the sermons of preachers and in the minds of the people, the gap separating the divine and the human was bridged. The way to ascribing divine miracles to humans – the *awliyā*[ʾ] – was paved. The word *awliyā*[ʾ] is used in the Qur'an to denote pious individuals who are close to God, yet it does

12 A span is the distance measured by a human hand, from the tip of the thumb to the tip of the little finger. In ancient times, a span was considered to be half a cubit, which is taken to be equal to 18 inches (457 mm). Hence, a span is taken to be 9 inches (228.6 mm).

not ascribe any extraordinary abilities or miracles to them. See, for example, Q. 10:62–63:

> Q. 10.62: "*Now surely the friends of Allah (awliyāʾ) – they shall have no fear nor shall they grieve.*"
> Q. 10.63: "*Those who believe and guarded (against evil).*"

Nevertheless, the scholars sought to find support for the *awliyāʾ*'s *karāmāt* in the Qur'an. Qur'an 3:37 tells of the sustenance that God sent to Maryam (Mary) in her sanctuary:

> Q. 3:37: "*. . . whenever Zakariya entered the sanctuary to (see) her, he found with her food. He said: 'O Maryam! whence comes this to you?' She said: 'It is from Allah. Surely Allah gives to whom He pleases without measure'.*"

Qur'an 27:40[13] describes an unknown person or entity that brings the throne of the Queen of Sheba from her country to Sulaymān (Solomon) within the blink of an eye. As neither Maryam nor Sulaymān's companion were prophets, it follows that it is possible for God to bestow *karāmāt* or miracles on "non-prophets".

However, these scholars were careful, out of respect for the prophets, not to refer to the *karāmāt* as miracles or *ayāt* (signs from God). Instead, they called them *karāmāt* or *barakāt* (blessings), which, they argued, were extraordinary paranormal feats, different from miracles. While miracles are God's way to demonstrate the truth of the prophets' messages, the *karāmāt* are not coupled with any particular divine message, nor do they aim to challenge the unbelievers. They also differ from both the *maʿūna* (divine aid) received by a Muslim, which is not conditional on a particular religious experience, and the *irhāṣ* (wondrous event), which is a miracle that God sends as a sign to the prophet before his call to prophethood to let him know that he will be chosen. They also said that the *walīy* may be ignorant of his ability to perform any *karāmāt*, while a prophet cannot help but feel his ability. In addition,

---

13 Q. 27:40: "*One who had the knowledge of the Book said: 'I will bring it to you in the twinkling of an eye'. Then when he saw it settled beside him, he said: 'This is of the grace of my Lord that He may try me whether I am grateful or ungrateful; and whoever is grateful, he is grateful only for his own soul, and whoever is ungrateful, then surely my Lord is Self-sufficient, Honoured'.*"

they advised the *walīy* to hide his *karāmāt*, to downplay their value as much as possible and to consider them a test rather than a gift from God, while the prophet's duty is to show the miracles and inform his people about them as a proof of his prophethood.

In practice, however, the *karāmāt* of the *awliyā*ᵓ, as reported in the written and oral literature, have not, at any time, been inferior to the miracles of the prophets, as the following examples from *Kashf al-maḥjūb* by al-Hujwirī demonstrate:

Mālik b. Dīnār,[14] attained such high stature that one time, while he was on a ship with a group of people, he was accused of stealing a jewel that went missing. No sooner had he lifted his head towards the heavens to lament his state, than all the fish in the sea surfaced, each with a jewel in its mouth. Mālik only took one single jewel and gave it to his fellow passengers. He then stepped out on the water and walked with ease all the way to the shore.

Dhūl-Nūn al-Miṣrī was a man who perplexed the Egyptians. They denied his abilities during his lifetime and only realised the beauty of his powers as he lay dying. That night, seventy men saw the Prophet in a dream saying: "*Ḥabīb Allah (Beloved of God), Dhūl-Nūn, is preparing to come, and I have come to welcome him.*" When he died, some writing appeared on his forehead saying: "This is the beloved of God, he died in the love of God, a martyr of God." During his funeral, birds gathered in the sky and shadowed the procession. The Egyptians were amazed and regretted the harsh treatment they meted out to him.

Muḥammad b. ᶜUmar al-Warrāq[15] is said to have given one of his students a notebook, telling him: "Throw it into the sea." His pupil went home and hid it there, then returned to him saying: "I did." Al-Warrāq asked him: "What did you see?" The pupil replied that he saw nothing. Al-Warrāq said: "Then you have not done what you were told. Go back and throw it into the sea." The student complied

---

14 Abū Yaḥya Mālik b. Dīnār al-Baṣrī (d. 130 AH/748 AD) was one of the prominent *tābiᶜūn* (successors), one of the notable early Qur'an calligraphers, a Sufi ascetic and preacher. He was the disciple of al-Ḥasan al-Basri.

15 Abū Bakr Muḥammad b. ᶜUmar al-Warrāq al-Tirmidhī, also known as al-Ḥakīm (d. *c.* 240 AH/878/9 AD), was one of the prominent Sufis of the third/ninth century.

and threw the notebook into the sea. As soon as he did, the waters divided and an open casket emerged. When the notebook fell into the casket, the lid closed and the casket submerged into the waters. The student returned to his master, recounting the events and asking him about their meaning. His master said: "I had written a book about the *uṣūl* (foundations) and *al-taḥqīq* (proofs), but it was too difficult to understand. My brother al-Khiḍr,[16] blessings upon him, asked me for it. God commanded the waters to take it to him."

It was narrated that Abū-l-ᶜAbbās al-Qaṣṣāb[17] "saw a boy holding the reins of a camel carrying a heavy load. The camel had stumbled and fallen, breaking its leg. The boy yelled for help and the people gathered around him. Al-Qaṣṣāb passed this scene and was told of what had transpired. He picked up the reins, raised his head towards the heavens, and said: 'O God, heal this camel, for if you do not find it in you to heal him, why did you break my heart with the tears of this boy?' The camel got up immediately, and walked away in the best of health."

Reinterpreting Pagan Beliefs in an Islamic Context

As soon as the concept of the sanctification of the *awliyāᵓ* was established in Islam, people rushed to re-interpret aspects of the old pagan religions which they wanted to retain in an "Islamic manner". The authorities and jurists soon realised the futility of resisting the masses. If they wanted Islam to spread, they had to be more amenable and to accept some local pagan elements, provided these were "Islamised" first. The populations of the countries conquered by the Arabs thus succeeded in retaining their customs and traditions originating in their pagan past by re-interpreting them in an Islamic context. Persians, for example, continued to celebrate Nowruz (festival of spring and the start of the New Year), claiming that it marks the day the Prophet chose ᶜAlī as his successor. When Caliph al-Manṣūr wanted to use stones from the ruins of the ancient Persian capital of Persepolis

16 Al-Khiḍr, is a pious righteous servant of God with great wisdom and mystic knowledge, who is described in the Qur'an in Q. 18:65–82.

17 Abū-l-ᶜAbbas Aḥmad b. Muḥammad al-Qaṣṣāb was one of the greatest Sufi masters in Transoxania in the second half of the fourth/tenth century.

(known as Takht-e-Jamshid)[18] for the construction of a new capital, his Persian vizier, Khālid b. Barmak, protested that it served as a prayer space for ᶜAlī b. Abū Ṭālib. Persian mythology (much like Greek mythology) explained the red skies at sunset as the blood of one of the gods who had been wounded, and so the Muslim Persians explained it as the blood of the martyr al-Ḥusayn b. ᶜAlī, going further by claiming that before his martyrdom, sunsets did not colour the skies red!

The Arabs in *Jahiliyya* revered their heroes and men of courage, preserving their stories and traces of what they left behind. With the advent of Islam, they directed this reverence to the personal effects of the Prophet, then after that to the personal effects of the *awliyā'*, which they believed to bestow blessings. History tells us that Khālid b. al-Walīd used to place some hairs from the Prophet's forehead into his *qalansuwa* (head-covering) every time he went to war. Al-Wāqidī wrote: "Khālid never fought anyone without being victorious, with the grace of God. During the Battle of Yarmūk, his *qalansuwa* fell and he kept screaming: '*Al-qalansuwa*! *Al-qalansuwa*!' Afterwards he was asked: 'O Abū Sulaymān, why did you scream for your *qalansuwa* in the midst of a cut-throat fight?' He replied: 'It contained some of the Prophet's hairs. I never fought anyone, while wearing it, without defeating him.' Likewise, Anas b. Mālik, while on his deathbed, asked his family to place some of the Prophet's hair under his tongue, and Muᶜāwiya b. Abū Sufyān asked that one of the Prophet's garments, which Muḥammad had gifted him, be used as his shroud and that some of the Prophet's hairs be placed in his mouth, ears and nostrils. He believed they would alleviate the severity of his judgement on Resurrection Day. The Prophet's mantle and his staff would later become the symbol of the caliphate."

With the passage of time, reverence for these personal effects increased, and with it their numbers increased and people continually "discovered" new ones, claiming this thing or that happened thanks to them. ᶜAbd al-Ghanī al-Nablusī[19] mentioned that when in India, he met an Indian scholar, who told him that in India there were numerous hairs from the Prophet's head. He also told him that these hairs move and multiply of their own accord!

---

18 The ceremonial capital of the Achaemenid Empire (*c.* 550–330 BC).

19 ᶜAbd al-Ghanī b. Ismāᶜīl al-Nablusī (1050–1143 AH/1641–1731 AD) was an eminent Muslim scholar, litterateur, poet, Sufi, teacher and traveller.

The Continued Reverence for Ancient Shrines

Even at the dawn of Islam, an aura of sanctity was bestowed on certain places, such as the tree under which *bayᶜat al-riḍwān* took place.[20] However, it was during the ᶜAbbāsid dynasty that matters reached significant proportions. The house where the Prophet was born, for example, which had remained an ordinary house throughout the Umayyad era, was turned into a mosque only after it was bought by al-Khayzurān (Hārūn al-Rashīd's mother). In the ᶜAbbāsid era, when at first the Persians, then the Turks, had the upper hand, there was an increased reverence for certain places, such as the graves of the righteous, to which the people flocked. Yet many of these shrines bore no connection to the Prophet or his family. In fact, these sites, as well as the graves claimed to be burial sites of the *awliyāʾ*, were spots where pagans and other ancients performed their rituals and worship rites before the advent of Islam.

Ancient holy shrines, which would otherwise have been demolished or forgotten, were thus preserved after the spread of Islam by being given an "Islamic" character, or attributed to some Islamic religious event or one of the Muslim *awliyāʾ*. Examples of these include:

- a shrine near Damascus, where people used to worship the moon, which people claim is the tomb of a holy man whom they call "Shaykh Hilāl" (crescent)!;
- a monastery at the foot of Mount Jawshan, overlooking Aleppo, which is mentioned in Yāqūt al-Ḥamawī's *Muᶜjam al-Buldān* and was inhabited by male and female hermits and whose ruins were revered by the Christians until the Muslims built an "Islamic" shrine there, claiming that al-Ḥusayn was seen praying there;
- a grave site near the city of Tyre attributed to Shaykh Maᶜshūq (Loved or Lover), which is undoubtedly a relic of the Phoenician legend of Adonis, Aphrodite's lover;
- a sacred stone column in Nablus which was, after Islam, named the grave of Shaykh al-ᶜAmūd (column)!;

20 *Bayᶜat al-riḍwān* is a pledge of allegiance to the Prophet by his Companions prior to the Treaty of Ḥudaybiyya (6 AH/628 AD), also known as the Pledge of the Tree. Those who took the pledge were also known as *aṣḥāb ash-shajarah* (the People of the Tree).

- shrines in India that included bones or personal effects and relics of Buddhist reverence, which were soon "Islamised" and said to contain the bones of ᶜAlī b. Abū Ṭālib or one of his descendants.

The practice of tree worship, which had been known since time immemorial, continued after the advent of Islam, but not before the respective tree was attributed to one of the *awliyāʾ*, by either claiming that it stood next to the *walīy*'s tomb or that it harboured the spirit of one. Often, the cutting down of trees was prohibited on account of them surrounding the grave of a *walīy*. Whoever cut down such trees or damaged them was threatened with shame and ill-fate.

In his *al-Khiṭaṭ al-Tawfiqiyya*, Ali Pasha Mubarak included many examples of trees considered holy by the Egyptians, some of which were claimed to be inhabited by spirits of *awliyāʾ* with unknown names or the spirit of a female "saint" called Shaykha Khaḍra (green)!

Similarly, near Damascus there was an ancient sacred olive tree, which people called Sit Zaytūn (Lady Olive). Many people, especially women, performed a pilgrimage to it to ask for a child, or the love of a spouse or harm for the co-wife, while a resident dervish collected alms from the visitors and blessed them.

These *awliyāʾ* in Islam were thus not necessarily real existent historical figures. The myth-makers did not waste much effort putting the events of these so-called *awliyāʾ*'s lives into a reasonable historical context. The common people, who passionately and enthusiastically receive these legends and are always ready for more, are known to have a limited desire to search for real proof. Hence, it was acceptable for some books to claim that al-Ḥusayn's head had been brought to Cairo by the Fatimids, or for the allegation to be made that after it was severed, it rolled all the way from Karbala to Egypt (across the Red Sea)! All it required to "Islamise" a pagan belief was to change the name of a former god to a Muslim name, preceding it by sayyid, shaykh or *walīy*. Sometimes they were named after the town they supposedly lived in or originated from, such as Shaykh Shaṭā or Shaykh al-Ṭanṭāwī.

In his *al-Khiṭaṭ*[21] al-Maqrīzī writes:

21 The book is titled *al-Mawāᶜiz wa al-ʾiᶜtibār bi dhikr al-Khiṭaṭ wa-l-āthār*, but it is known as *al-Khiṭaṭ* or *Khiṭaṭ al-Maqrīzī*.

> In Zuqāq al-Mazār there is a tomb, which the common people and the ignorant claim is the tomb of Yaḥya b. ᶜUqb, the teacher of al-Ḥasan and al-Ḥusayn, sons of ᶜAlī b. Abū Ṭālib. This is a fabricated lie and an absurd claim. They also claim that the grave in Ḥārat Bargawān is that of Jaᶜfar al-Ṣādiq, and that another tomb is that of Abū-l-Turāb al-Nakhshabī, or that the tomb to the left of Bāb al-Ḥadīd, behind Zuwayla, is that of Zāriᶜ al-Nawā, and that he is one of the Prophet's Companions. All these and other such claims are obvious lies. They are but "*anṣāb*",[22] which their demons made them worship so that they should be, to them, a source of strength. (He is referring to Q. 19:81–82)[23]

He then writes:

> Sedition lies in this place (the tomb of Abū Turāb) and the place in Ḥārat Bargawān known as the tomb of the Great Jaᶜfar al-Ṣādiq. They have become like the "*anṣāb*" which the Arab pagans used to worship,[24] a refuge for the fools from the general public and for women (note the link between the fools and the women by both al-Birūnī and al-Maqrīzī). In times of adversity and hardship they go to these two locations to offload their agony and distresses. They pray for what only God may fulfil, as only He is capable of relieving a servant's indebtedness, or realise a wish for a child, or similar requests. They carry their *nudhūr* (offerings)[25] of oil and other such things, believing that this will rescue them from harm, or will bring benefits to them.

22 In the Qur'an "*al-anṣāb*" are sacrifices at altars, idols or entities other than God.

23 Q. 19.81: "*And they have taken gods besides Allah, that they should be to them a source of strength*"; Q. 19.82: "*By no means! They shall soon deny their worshipping them, and they shall be adversaries to them.*"

24 He is referring to Q. 5:90: "*O you who believe! Intoxicants and games of chance and anṣāb* (sacrificing to stones set up) *and azlām* (divination by arrows) *are only an uncleanness, the Shaitan's work; shun it therefore that you may be successful.*"

25 *Nadhr* or *nazr* (pl. *nudhūr* or *nuzūr*) is an Arabic word literally meaning "offering" or "spiritual vow". The concept was developed based on Q. 5:27–31, 3:35 and 19:26. It involves offering something valuable in the hope of receiving something of higher value. The value does not have to be material, it can be a pledge to do something, to refrain or abstain from something.

Nowadays, Abū Turāb's mosque (which may have been called by that name because it was fraught with dust from all sides, according to al-Maqrīzī) is known as Shaykh al-Atribī's (dusty) mosque!

The Pious Awliyāʾ *in Egypt*

Egyptians, in particular, have gone to great lengths in the veneration of their *awliyāʾ*. Historians of Ancient Egypt and the Coptic age noticed how the ancient Egyptian gods were transformed into Coptic saints in the Christian era, and then to *awliyāʾ* under Islam. This happened without any change in the places of worship and sanctification, and sometimes even without a change in the rituals. This fits perfectly with Ernest Renan's[26] observation that mankind has always, from the dawn of time, worshiped in the same places.

Maspero,[27] for example, tells us about a celebration of the *Mawlid* (birthday) of one of the *awliyāʾ* in Akhmim in Upper Egypt, and notes very similar rituals to those practised by the ancient Egyptians in Akhmim itself.

European travellers also wrote about the similarities between the practices of women visitors at the tomb of al-Sayyid al-Badawī in Tanta during the celebration of his *Mawlid*, and the Egyptian women's procession to Bubastis (Tal Basta in the Delta), as described by Herodotus. This included some shocking habits inherited from the ancient Egyptian religions. In the *Mawlid*, a donkey would be brought by some Dervish of al-Ṭariqah al-Shinnāwiyya to al-Sayyid al-Badawī's tomb, and they would race to pluck out some of the donkey's hairs to put them into amulets, which is exactly what the ancient Egyptians did to this poor animal.

There is a possible link between the Egyptians' pilgrimage to the shrines in Tanta, their ancient ancestors' pilgrimage to "Bubastis" and the Copts' pilgrimages in the past to the tomb of their saint there. It is known that the goddess of Bubastis, called "Bastet", was depicted as a woman with the head of a cat, carrying a small pouch on her left arm. Traditionally, and until recently, Egyptian

26 Joseph Ernest Renan (1823–1892) was a French philologue, philosopher, historian, orientalist and writer.

27 Gaston Camille Charles Maspero (1846–1916) was a renowned French Egyptologist and director-general of excavations and of the antiquities of Egypt.

Muslims would take a large number of cats on the *Maḥmal* procession[28] heading to Mecca before the pilgrimage. A man, hired particularly for that purpose, took care of the cats and fed them. He was known by the general public as Abū-l-Qiṭṭat (Father of the Cats). Note how many Egyptians still call cats "Bissa", a name derived from the Ancient Egyptian. In order for the public to justify the continuation of this practice after Islam, they claimed that the Prophet loved cats, and even mentioned a certain cat whom he showered with tenderness and who gave birth to her litter in his lap.

The ancient Egyptians also performed a pilgrimage to shrines in the village of Shata, near Damietta. After Islam, an annual *Mawlid* was held there for a local saint whom they called Shaykh Shaṭa.

Before the Arab conquests, the Copts used to congregate at the site of the Sphinx as the sun entered the sign of Capricorn, where they burned incense, dried plants and herbs, and chanted a traditional phrase thirty-three times, followed by prayers to God to respond to their wishes. For at least another century, after the advent of Islam, Egyptians kept up the tradition of collecting plants or aromatic herbs while chanting ritual phrases, and preserving these plants in brightly coloured boxes, believing they bring them prosperity and blessings.

Traces of snake worship, formerly practised in Thebes, persisted in the rituals of the *awliyā᾽* veneration in Islamic Egypt. Paul Lucas[29] wrote that during his visit to Upper Egypt in 1699, he found people revering a snake to which they attributed certain miracles. Richard Pococke[30] wrote that he visited a village near Girga in 1752, where people revered a "holy snake" at a mosque which houses the tomb of a saint (Shaykh Harīdī), and where it was believed to have resided since the time of the Prophet. They offered sacrifices to the snake, which they claimed was the source of blessings and healing from all diseases. Pococke himself saw traces of blood, entrails and intestines of the sacrificial animals at the door of the mosque. Concerning

28 The *Maḥmal* was the ceremonial embroidered palanquin, carried on a camel, which was the centrepiece of the pilgrim caravan from Cairo to Mecca. The Ḥajj *Maḥmal* was normally covered in a silk cloth that was embroidered in silver and gold-plated silver wire, with arabesque designs and inscriptions from the Qur'an.

29 Paul Lucas (1664–1737) was a French merchant, naturalist, physician, antiquarian and traveller. He travelled to Egypt in three major voyages, 1699–1703, 1704–1708 and 1714–1717.

30 Richard Pococke (1704–1765) was an English prelate and anthropologist. He was the Bishop of Ossory (1756–1765) and Meath (1765), and is best known for his travel writings and diaries.

this particular practice, Ali Pasha Mubarak wrote that large groups flock to the tomb of Shaykh Harīdī on the Thursdays of the month of Abīb (Epip)[31] to sacrifice animals to a saint claimed to be one of the benevolent Jinn.

Al-Sayyid al-Badawī

There is no doubt that al-Sayyid al-Badawī,[32] closely followed by al-Sayyid Ibrāhīm al-Disūqī,[33] is the most popular Sufi saint in Egypt. In his *ᶜAjāʾib al-athār fi-l-tarājim wa-l-akhbār* (translated as *The Marvellous Chronicles, Biographies and Events*), al-Jabartī writes that the Egyptians believed the end of the world would happen on Friday 24 Dhū-l-Ḥijjah 1147 AH/17 May 1735 AD,[34] and awaited this date with great trepidation. When the date passed and nothing happened, some scholars said that God had postponed the Day of Resurrection at the last minute in response to al-Sayyid al-Badawī's intercession. Some people, having performed their regular prayers, used to turn in the direction of al-Badawī's Mosque, then, using it as a *qibla,* they would pray another two *rakᶜas*[35] and utter *duᶜās.*

A column near the pulpit in al-Husayn mosque in Cairo is named after al-Sayyid al-Badawī, as it is believed that during his many visits to the mosque he used to stand, sit at or pray next to it. This column is still held in special reverence by the mosque's visitors, who kiss it, read the *Fātiḥah*[36] there and pray next to it.

---

31 Abīb or Epip is the eleventh month of the Coptic calendar, also called the Alexandrian calendar, which is still used by the Coptic Orthodox Church in Egypt. The name originates from Apida, the serpent that Horus, son of Osiris, killed.

32 Aḥmad b. ᶜAlī b. Yaḥya, also known as al-Badawī (596–675 AH/675–1276 AD), was a Moroccan Sunni Sufi who immigrated to and settled in Tanta, Egypt. He founded a Sufi order named after him, al-Ṭarīqah al-Badawiyya. He was named al-Badawī (the Bedouin) because he used to cover his face like the Tuaregs.

33 Ibrāhīm b. ᶜAbd-El-ᶜAzīz Abū-l-Majd, better known as al-Disūqī because he was born and lived in Desouk in the Nile Delta (653–696 AH/1255–1296 AD), was an Egyptian Sufi and imam. He founded a Sufi order named after him. His feast is celebrated twice a year, in April and in October.

34 Dhū-l-Ḥijjah is the last month of the Islamic calendar, during which Muslim pilgrims congregate at Mecca to perform the pilgrimage on the eighth, ninth and the tenth of the month. Eid al-Adha, the "Festival of the Sacrifice", begins on the tenth day and ends on sunset of the twelfth.

35 A *rakᶜa* is the basic unit of Muslim prayers and consists of the prescribed movements, involving standing, bowing and prostrating in a predefined sequence.

36 *Al-Fātiḥah* is the first chapter of the Qur'an.

Despite the fact that al-Sayyid al-Badawī is of Moroccan origin, the belief common among ordinary Egyptians is that he is the *walīy* who protects their homes. They call him *Walīy Allah* (Friend of God) and *Gayth al-Quṭr* (Saviour of the Nation).

One story tells of a Muslim named Sālim[37] who was captured by the Franks. When one of his captors heard him repeat calls of distress directed at al-Sayyid al-Badawī, he threatened him with torture if he was to call on al-Badawī once again. The Frank placed Sālim in a big box to prevent him from escaping with the help of al-Badawī, and slept on top of the box overnight for increased vigilance. One night, Sālim shouted from inside his box: "Oh *Walīy Allah* Aḥmad, save me from the yokes of this Christian." No sooner had he finished, than his prayers were answered and the box flew away with the Frank on top of it, until it reached the city of Qayrawan (Kairouan) in Tunisia. In the morning, the people opened the box, released its prisoner and untied him in front of his captor. The Frank is said to have converted to Islam and rushed to Tanta for the pilgrimage to the tomb of al-Sayyid al-Badawī.

The jurists, whose doctrines were completely disconnected from the beliefs of the masses, succeeded in persuading al-Malik al-Zahir Jaqmaq[38] in 852 AH/1448 AD to issue a decree halting the celebrations of al-Sayyid al-Badawī's Mawlid in Tanta. However, his decree had no impact whatsoever, and people continued the celebrations. Rumours spread like wildfire among the public that many of those who signed the *fatwa* were afflicted with disasters, affecting their wealth, their children and their health. These disasters, they argued, were divine retribution for their insolence in opposing the veneration of the great *walīy* of Egypt.

Paganism or Islam?

The opinions of scholars and jurists across different countries often agree, and where they diverge it is hardly due to a reason related to the countries in question. Popular religions, however, differ widely across different countries,

37 An Arabic name that literally means safe or undamaged.

38 Sultan al-Malik al-Ẓāhir Abū Saᶜīd Muḥammad al-ᶜAlā᾽ī (d. 857 AH/1453 AD) was a Circassian Mamluk sultan who ruled Egypt 841–857 AH/1438–1453 AD. He was originally a mamluk of Sultan Barqūq, who established the Mamluk Burji dynasty, which ruled Egypt from 783 to 923 AH/1382 to 1517 AD, and was characterised as a turbulent period with short-lived sultans.

even if the official religion in all of them is the same. The general public neither read nor are they affected by the books and the writings of scholars and jurists. They are often able to exceed the limits set by religion without punishment or censure. Furthermore, it is always possible to identify remnants of ancient religions, rituals and beliefs in a certain society by studying religious practices exclusive to rural communities or local popular celebrations particular to that society, all the more so if the followers of other religions are involved and participate in these celebrations and festivals, such as the feast of Sham al-Nessim (Egyptian Easter/Spring Celebration) and the Nile Flood Festival known as *Wafāʾ al-Nīl*.

If we bear in mind that a portion of the public in Upper Egypt believe that circumambulating the grave of Shaykh al-Qināwī in Qena seven times (which is a ritual many perform upon arrival in that city) replaces the exhausting pilgrimage to God's Sacred House in Mecca, and if we consider that a number of scholars have endorsed this opinion, so as to save some people from impoverishment due to the Ḥajj expenses to Mecca, and, finally, if we assume that this shaykh is merely a legend, and that his grave was built on top of the ruins of an Ancient Egyptian temple dedicated to one of their gods, we can conclude that the general public has replaced one of the five pillars of Islam with a pagan ritual dating back to the time of the Pharaohs!

The populations of the conquered countries thus succeeded in deceiving their conquerors. To avoid paying the *jizya*, [39] which the conqueror imposed on anyone choosing to adhere to their old beliefs, and to access the high-ranking positions, which they would otherwise be barred from, their solution was to embrace the new religion and adapt it to include their own, much older beliefs. The rulers were appeased with this arrangement, the jurists acquiesced and the subjects were content. They succeeded – or thought they did – in attaining the worldly pleasures and the rewards of the afterlife.

39 *Jizya* (sometimes also spelled as *jizyah*) is an annual tax levied by Islamic states on their non-Muslim subjects, provided they resided there permanently and were free, adult, sane males. Women, children, elderly people, monks, hermits and slaves were exempted, as well as non-Muslims who only reside temporarily in these Muslim lands.

7
Political and Social Roots of Islamic Sects

The heart is like water, its passions afloat on it like foam over waves.

Abū-l-ᶜAlāᵓ al-Maᶜarrī

If people knew how many whims are included within ᶜilm al-kalam (scholastic theology) they would flee from it like they would from a lion.

Imam al-Shāfiᶜī

There is no greater indication of the impact of the Islamic *Daᶜwah* in the hearts of the Prophet's contemporaries, and the radical changes his message brought about in concepts and values, political, social and otherwise, than the fact that even those who apostated from Islam shortly before his death and after, and refused to recognise the Medinan caliph's authority over the entire Arabian Peninsula, still saw it as necessary to give a religious tinge to their *Daᶜwah*. Their leaders ascribed prophethood to themselves, and portrayed their insurgencies or revolutions as divinely inspired by God, even if the motives for these revolutions are known to have been purely political, social or economic.

In its original form, Islam did not distinguish between civilian and religious authorities, or between civil and religious legislation. Religious community and state were one, the latter only existing to serve the former. The Prophet had been at the helm of both, and was followed by his successor, then his successor's successor and so forth.

The foundational principle of succession (*khilāfa*) was to protect the *Sharīᶜa*. The purpose of the *Sharīᶜa* was to regulate all aspects of human life, those that related to the community and communal life, as well as those that related to individuals in their private life. The relationship between the imam and his subjects was a religious relationship, which bears no resemblance to the political or social relationships as we know them today.

One of the most prominent features of Islamic history was the fact that all revolutionary movements that started in *Dār al-Islām* (Abode of Islam, i.e., Muslim lands) due to social considerations, and thus became politicised, were, from the time of their inception, closely tied to some religious thought. For the followers of such movements, it would have been inconceivable to protest against the ruling power from non-religious motives, or to do so other than against a ruling power that God was not pleased with, to return the nation to the path of the true faith.

Therefore, for Muslims in the Middle Ages any expression of opposition or support for this or that existing government system was a chiefly religious expression. Any government under which a social category lost its privileges, or felt its interests to be threatened or the pillars of its existence to be shaken, had to be an infidel government. Paradise was reserved for those who died in order to bring it down:

> If a person was unable – within a state – to find beauty or wealth, he longs for transition
> Not out of hatred, but out of hope for another, he wishes for its demise and fission[1]

Any dispute, which taken at face value, may seem like a dispute over a purely religious issue, such as the *Miḥna* surrounding the issue of whether the Qur'an was the created or the eternal word of God, allows us to discern the underlying raging political or social conflict of which even the conflicted parties themselves may not have been aware. Examples for such disputes are illustrated below.

The Kharijites

The Kharijites were members of a group that defected from ᶜAlī b. Abū Ṭālib's army in protest against some of his stances, such as his acceptance

1 These verses are attributed to an unnamed poet.

of the principle of arbitration in the dispute between him and Muᶜāwiya. Their movement focused its call on the notion that the nation's affairs should be governed only on the basis of a strict adherence to the provisions of the Qur'an. They took the phrase "No rule except the rule of God" as their slogan. The fanatics among them went as far as claiming that they alone were truly Muslims, and that everyone who opposed them would end up in hellfire. They believed that it was no sin to kill or rob these unbelievers. Their movement was composed of small dispersed groups, each one ranging in number between thirty and five hundred members. They lived in camps near the cities or along trade routes, making their livelihood from looted goods, which they stole either from the cities or from passing caravans, sowing panic and fear in the hearts of the people of the region.

There is nothing in the extant sources to suggest that this particular group suffered from economic grievances that prompted it to that type of behaviour. However, the same sources point to a very important fact, namely, that its members belonged to tribes of nomadic Bedouin origin (especially the tribe of Tamīm), which, even before Islam, used to raid the convoys and caravans of other tribes and live on the spoils obtained. With the advent of Islam, the concept of brotherhood within religion replaced tribal ties and prohibited Muslims from shedding Muslim blood. Yet, at the same time, Islam created a legitimate outlet for the Bedouins' passion for strikes and raids in the Islamic conquests of countries outside the Arabian Peninsula. Some Bedouins were satisfied with this outlet, which allowed them to express both the sincerity of their faith and their love of pillaging at the same time. Others, however, disliked this new, strict and unfamiliar system, and the restrictions it imposed on their freedom. After each invasion or battle, they resented having to return not to the desert they loved, but to camps or cities like Basra, where they felt trapped.

The entry about the Tamīm tribe in *Dāʾirat al-maᶜārif al-Islamiyya* states that:

> The Tamīm related to the cities like the Bedouins to urban settlements. They harassed the cities' populations and abducted their inhabitants for ransom. With the advent of Islam, Tamīm – like other Arab tribes of the Eastern Arabian Peninsula – stayed far from its direct dominion. They were not interested in an alliance with the Muslims, which they saw no benefit from. However, in the eighth year after Hijra, after the

> Prophet's victory over their neighbouring tribes, the tribe sent a delegation to Medina to sign a treaty with the Prophet. It seems that they did not convert willingly to Islam, and they were therefore the first to apostate after the Prophet's death. Tamīm played quite a significant role in *Ḥurūb al-Ridda* (Wars of Apostasy)[2] because of the actions of Sajāḥ.[3] Khālid b. al-Walīd's campaigns were victorious and succeeded in returning the apostating tribes and Tamīm back into the folds of Islam, and the Islamic conquests catered to their predilection for fighting. There is no doubt that the members of the tribe of Tamīm, who were pure nomads, were not used to obeying orders from authorities. They played a big role in all rebellions that broke out during the reign of the Umayyads, and they were the greatest supporters of the Kharijites. The most fanatic *ghulāt* of the Kharijites were from Tamīm, such as Qaṭarī b. al-Fujāʿa,[4] who led the Azāriq faction of the Kharijites, whose followers were mainly from Tamīm.

These people thus felt an overwhelming need to return to their previous lifestyle of a small, close-knit group, a pattern they had experienced before Islam in their life in the desert. The majority of these were members of tribes that had a deep sense of the individual's dependence on his tribe, a belief in the sanctity of that small group, and a sense of belonging that was enough to confer meaning on an individual's life. However, it became necessary for them to find some religious basis from within Islam to legitimise this need. Hence, and to convince themselves that in satisfying their need they were but complying with the provisions of their religion, even if it should lead to martyrdom for its sake, they revolted against the heavy-handed authorities

2 The Wars of Apostasy were a series of military campaigns launched by Caliph Abū Bakr against rebel Arabian tribes after the Prophet's death. The tribes rebelled against paying the *zakāt* to Abū Bakr, arguing that they had submitted to Muḥammad as the prophet of God, but not to Abū Bakr. Most of the tribes were defeated and reintegrated into the caliphate.

3 Sajāḥ bint al-Ḥārith b. Suwayd b. ʿAqfān was a woman from the tribe of Tamīm who, after the Prophet's death, declared herself a prophetess, similar to Musaylima and Ṭulayḥa. She gathered troops to fight Medina. Before her claim to prophethood, she was known for soothsaying. She was immortalised in Arabic proverbs and sayings, such as "more of a liar than Sajāḥ".

4 Qaṭarī b. al-Fujāʿa (d. 78 or 79 AH/697 AD) was a poet and one of the Kharijite leaders, ruling the Azāriq faction for over a decade. He led the uprising against the Umayyad caliphate for over two decades.

and accused them of heresy, abandoned the cities they loathed, labelling them *Dār al-Ḥarb* (Abode of War), and resumed their raids as in *Jahiliyya* for the purpose of looting and acquiring booty, all the while deluding themselves that this was *jihad*. The members of these small, close-knit groups called themselves *ahl al-janna* (People of Paradise).

The Shiʿites

The Shiʿites are, in many ways, the complete opposite of the Kharijites. Their doctrine is based on the belief that the Prophet's descendants from among the Hashemites possess divine powers, which manifested themselves in his person and then moved from him to the next generations of his descendants. For them, the *Imāma*[5] – which is only found among the Prophet's descendants – is surrounded with an aura of sanctity only infidels would dispute. The descendants' command is but an order from God, their will is God's will and may not be denied.

If we trace the beginnings of the Shiʿite *Daᶜwah*, it appears that it did not originate in Persia, as assumed by the Dutch orientalist Reinhart Dozy,[6] but that it started among Arab tribesmen in the southern Arabian Peninsula (the clans of Nahd, Khārif, Thawr, Shākir and Shibām). From there, the *Daᶜwah* spread to the *mawālī*. We know from studying the history of these tribes in *Jahiliyya* that for long centuries prior to Islam, they sanctified their kings, regarded them as descendants of the gods, and established a connection between their faith in their kings and their nation's salvation and glory. The principle of choosing a ruler or prince was both undesirable and alien to them, as they had never known anything other than hereditary rule. Therefore, and as Muḥammad did not leave a son to be his heir, they believed that ᶜAlī, his son in-law and father of the Prophet's grandchildren, should have been his successor and that the *khilāfa* (caliphate) should have become hereditary, remaining in ᶜAlī's family. Hence, all the caliphs except ᶜAlī were considered by them to be usurpers of power and no obedience was owed to them.

---

5 The *Imāma* is a Shiʿite doctrine that believes the imams to be infallible, possess divine knowledge and authority. The imams are the means through which the followers receive knowledge of the Qur'an as well as divine grace.

6 Reinhart Pieter Anne Dozy (1820–1883) was a Dutch orientalist, specialising in the Arabic language, history and literature.

The Kharijites believed that the Muslim community cannot agree on anything that was unsound, while the imam may well deviate from the right path. By contrast, the Shiʿites believed that the imam, who is a descendant of the Prophet, received the spirit of God and hence was infallible. On the other hand, the community – no matter how large – could make mistakes and be misguided, as it is made up of individuals who were not privileged by the Merciful as the imams were, and whose rule could therefore only lead to disaster. For them, the imam is everything, and absolute obedience to him is, in their view, a paramount duty. If anyone performed this duty, he may – with a clear conscience – interpret all other duties and obligations beyond that as symbolic, and may ignore or neglect them.

The Persians enthusiastically embraced this doctrine from the *mawālī*. It resonated with them on two levels: first, they had a centuries-long habit of revering their kings, and a contempt for the people's ability to govern themselves. They believed that the *Shahanshah* (King of Kings) was the embodiment of God's spirit, which was passed on from father to son. Secondly, they had suffered from Arab arrogance and *ʿaṣabiyya*[7] during the rule of the Umayyads, who despised and discriminated against the *mawālī,* in spite of the teachings of equality between Muslims contained in the Qur'an and the *ḥadīth*: in principle there is no preference for an Arab over a non-Arab except in terms of piety. In ʿAlī, the Persians saw – or thought they saw – the embodiment of this principle. As ʿAlī's son al-Ḥusayn is said to have fathered a son with the daughter[8] of their former king Yazdegerd, they therefore believed that the blood circulating in his descendants' veins was a mix of Arab and Persian blood. This deepened their conviction of Shiʿite theories

7 The term *ʿaṣabiyya* in Arabic historical texts refers to the internal loyalty of a group (normally a tribe), or the loyalty of an individual to that group. In the narrowest and most familiar sense, it is the bond of cohesion among the members of that primitive political grouping, the tribe. It is akin to social solidarity with an emphasis on unity, group consciousness and a sense of shared purpose, and social cohesion. According to Ibn Khaldūn, there are different forms of *ʿaṣabiyya*: in primitive cultures, like the nomads and Bedouins, it emanated from blood ties, alliances and clientship; while in civilised and urban cultures, the *ʿaṣabiyya* emanated from reciprocal interactions and dependencies other than "tribalism" or "clannism". In modern times, the term is equated to solidarity. However, it is often negatively associated with it, because it can sometimes suggest loyalty to one's group regardless of circumstances or partisanship at the expense of others.

8 Shahrbānū was a Sassanid princess and daughter of Yazdegerd III, the last Emperor of the Sassanid dynasty.

and doctrines, and they became the most loyal supporters of the concept of the imamate.

Arabs, during *Jahiliyya* and after, believed that certain noble qualities and outstanding talents were hereditary, reserved for specific bloodlines, and that any member of that particular bloodline or clan possessed these talents and traits, or was at least predisposed to possessing them. However, in the interest of the king or the imam, it became necessary to qualify this notion to prevent clan members from disputing the king's or the imam's entitlement. Thus emerged the Shi'ite theory stating that these extraordinary divine gifts were possessed by only one individual in the whole clan at any one time, and that this extraordinary individual, or "imam", would transfer these gifts to his chosen successor to the exclusion of everyone else. This, according to their beliefs, is what Muḥammad did when he chose ᶜAlī as his successor, and what ᶜAlī did when he chose his son al-Ḥasan, and so on.

The Twelver Shi'ites

During the reign of the Umayyads and ᶜAbbāsids, the Shi'ites endured a series of successive calamities. The failed rebellion of Mukhtār al-Thaqafī,[9] the death of Muḥammad Ibn al-Ḥanafiyyah,[10] their bitter disappointment when the ᶜAbbāsids assumed power and they were sidelined, the advocacy of the Sunni creed by Caliph al-Mutawakkil and his successors, and the continued persecution of Shi'ites and the incarceration and killing of their imams, all contributed to their low morale and diminished hope of ever gaining power. As a result, they became increasingly resigned to living within the existing system, and to creating a religious framework that would make it easier for them to adapt to such an arrangement without any psychological suffering, and one that would protect their beliefs from dilution by the overwhelming Sunni presence surrounding them.

In 260 AH/874 AD, or shortly thereafter, some of their leaders took a decisive step in that direction. In January of that year, the Eleventh Imam,

9 al-Mukhtār b. Abū ᶜUbaydah al-Thaqafī (*c.* 1–67 AH/*c.* 622–687 AD) led a rebellion against the Umayyad caliphate to avenge the murder of al-Ḥusayn in Karbala in the name of Muḥammad Ibn al-Ḥanafiyyah.

10 Muḥammad b. ᶜAli b. Abū Ṭālib, was also known as Muḥammad Ibn al-Ḥanafiyyah after his mother (*c.* 15–81 AH/*c.* 636–700 AD).

al-Ḥasan al-ᶜAskarī, died, and was succeeded by his son Muḥammad, who disappeared shortly after his father's death in mysterious circumstances. Although it would have been easy to choose a successor to him, it is likely that the Shiʿite leaders thought the time was appropriate to reconcile with the ruling powers and the Sunni community in which they lived. They decided to refrain from choosing a new imam who would continue to dictate his will to them and to pursue the goal to rule, thereby subjecting his followers to continued persecution by the caliphs. Instead, they announced to the Shiʿite followers that the Twelfth Imam, Muḥammad b. al-Ḥasan al-ᶜAskarī, did not die, but was in "occultation", and would return at the appropriate time in the form of the Mahdi, to lead them to victory, and fill the world with equity and justice as it was filled with oppression and tyranny.

The Jabrites and Qadarites (Advocates of Predestination and Free Will)

Another conflict of a religious nature erupted between two Muslim theological movements: one that believed that a human is powerless and that everything is predetermined by God (Jabrites); and another that believed the human will to be free (Qadarites). The controversy between these two movements focused on the question of whether the ability to influence the course of events is reserved for the Creator alone or whether it is possible for humans to play a role in it.

Arabs in *Jahiliyya* firmly believed that key aspects of their lives were governed by forces beyond their control, which humans were powerless against and which they called *al-dahr* (eternity). It was only natural that such a belief proliferated among the desert populations, who relied primarily on natural phenomena over which they had no control, such as rain and wind, and the availability of water and pasture. These phenomena dictated the places and durations of their residence and travels, as well as their wealth and destitution. While the Meccan merchants' wealth, resulting from their business and trade, emboldened them to discard the thought of *al-dahr*, the Qur'an deprecated their arrogance and over-confidence in themselves and in their strength, stressing that they are powerless, but that it is only God, Lord of the worlds, who wills.

This same concept continued to exist in Islam, and the idea of "God" replaced that of "*al-dahr*". The early Muslims were careful not to exaggerate their perception of the human will. However, the spread of Islam in Iraq, Persia, Egypt and Syria, and the conversion to Islam of large Christian and other communities who were clearly affected by Greek thought emphasising human abilities and achievements, resulted in echoes of this Greek concept reverberating in Islamic thought. Some theologians and *mutakallimūn* (scholastic theologians) argued for free will and the ability of the individual to form his life and influence its events.

If we look beyond the veneer of religious controversy, however, we will see important political tribulations, which were undoubtedly the major cause of this controversy. The Umayyad caliphs were well aware of the strength of the opposition to their rule and the multiplicity of factions that sought to undermine its foundations. Their response to those was to assert that the Umayyad caliphate ruled by the will of God, and that any revolution or rebellion against their authority amounted to disobeying God and was a defiance of His will. Everything was thus predetermined and the Islamic state would continue on the path that God's infinite wisdom envisaged for it, even if Muslims "disliked it, while it was good for them".[11]

Therefore, it was up to their opponents to find a religious justification for their political enmity. This resulted in the spread of the theory that argued for the ability of humankind to fashion their own destiny, and that mankind is not obliged to obey a ruler who disobeyed God's orders and deviated from the right path. Furthermore, it was the duty of a Muslim to change this situation using his own hand, his tongue and his heart.[12] Hence, overthrowing such a rule was obligatory.

*The Mu*ᶜ*tazilites and the* Miḥna

No sooner had the controversy between the Jabrites and Qadarites diminished with the fall of the Umayyad and the rise of the ᶜAbbāsid dynasty, than a new and much graver controversy arose between those who argued that

11 This relates to the second half of Q. 2:216: "... *and it may be that you dislike a thing while it is good for you, and it may be that you love a thing while it is evil for you, and Allah knows, while you do not know.*"

12 This relates to a tradition ascribed to the Prophet which says: "The Prophet said: 'Whosoever of you sees an evil, let him change it with his hand; and if he is not able to do so, then [let him change it] with his tongue; and if he is not able to do so, then with his heart – and that is the weakest of faith'." (recorded in *Ṣaḥīḥ Muslim*).

the Qur'an was created and those who argued that it was eternal. This controversy led to a severe ordeal, akin to the Inquisition in Christian Europe. One might wonder, in our time, how disagreement on such a purely theoretical subject with no obvious scientific significance could have led to such violence, bitterness, hatred and even killing. However, these consequences themselves are the best evidence that the conflict between those who adhered to the Muᶜtazilites' view of the "createdness" of the Qur'an and their Ḥanbalī opponents who espoused the view that the Qur'an was eternal, was not at all a purely theoretical dispute, but that its real causes were non-religious considerations.

Arguing that the Qur'an is eternal and uncreated is difficult for any human to comprehend, given what we know of its revelation in portions over twenty-three years, and the fact that the Qur'an contains many references to certain events that occurred in the time of the Prophet (e.g., the Battle of Badr or his marriage to Zaynab bint Jaḥsh), and given what we know about the verses that were "abrogated or which God caused to be forgotten and [which] were replaced by some better or like them".[13] What then drove a group of Muslims to insist that the Qur'an is not created?

Some orientalists maintained that this group was influenced by the Christian theory that Christ is the uncreated Word of God, and, indeed, this theory may have had some impact on the teachings of some scholars who embraced the doctrine of the Qur'an being eternal. Yet this influence does not explain the violent confrontations that took place between the two opposing camps and the resulting tragedies. These can be understood only within the political context of the time: the ᶜAbbāsid state had led to the emergence of a social class of ministers, governors and professional administrators, mostly from the Persian *mawālī*. These positions were commonly passed on from father to son, and were often held by descendants of the administrators of the affairs of the Persian Empire before the Arab conquests. Given that these had converted to Islam in order to retain their positions, it is easy to deduce that at least the faith of many of them was not particularly strong or sincere. The main aim of the members of this class was to boost the caliph's powers, at least in theory, which would in turn give

13 This sentence alludes to Q. 2:106: "*Whatever communications We abrogate or cause to be forgotten, We bring one better than it or like it. Do you not know that Allah has power over all things?*"

them greater freedom in managing their administrative affairs. One of their main methods to achieve this goal was to free the caliph from the yoke of complying with the provisions of the *Sharīᶜa*, thus giving them the freedom to wield their own power without the constant control of their rivals, namely, the jurists and religious scholars.

This direction taken by the class of ministers and administrators was supported by many Persians and moderate Shiʿites. On the other hand, the position of the scholars and jurists, who opposed them and insisted on the need for the caliph, as well as his ministers, governors and administrators, to commit to the provisions of *Sharīᶜa*, resonated with those Arabs with a democratic and egalitarian predisposition. Thus, during the first years of the ᶜAbbāsid era, two opposing fronts appeared: the first, which could be called the autocratic front, was made up of Persian administrators; while the second, which could be called the constitutional front, and was made up of the Arab jurists and scholars.

It should be stated to the credit of the first ᶜAbbāsid caliphs that they strove to ease the tensions between the two opposing groups, and to find some middle ground in order to win the loyalty of both sides. This came to an end, however, when al-Maᵓmūn came to power with the help of the Persians, having eliminated his brother al-Amīn and his Arab supporters. This caliph, with known Shiʿite leanings, supported the "autocratic front", which was interested in strengthening his power (as well as theirs) and diminishing the power of the Arabs and their enemies from among the scholars. Al-Maᵓmūn found one of the Muᶜtazilite theories, that of the Qur'an's createdness, particularly useful in helping him to achieve his goal. Arguing that the Qur'an was not created but that it is eternal and as old as God, means that it is equal to Him in value and a full expression of the Truth. On the other hand, saying that the Qur'an is created puts it on equal footing with the rest of creation, like people, cattle, mountains and rocks. Hence, it does not rise to the stature envisioned by the scholars and jurists, and a caliph might, accordingly, follow its provisions or ignore them as he wishes. Arguing for the createdness of the Qur'an weakens the foundation of the "constitutional front", which sees the Qur'an as the constitution governing the community and the political system of the state, and places the imam above the *Sharīᶜa*.

Caliph al-Maᵓmūn, followed by al-Muᶜtaṣṣim and then al-Wāthiq, resorted to testing jurists, judges and governors on the issue of the createdness of the Qur'an. Some of those who insisted on the Qur'an being eternal were killed, others were incarcerated and flogged, and yet others were removed from office. Therefore, many succumbed to this immense torture and pressure, and declared their acceptance of the caliph's view. Only very few stood by their convictions and refused to concede, most notably Aḥmad Ibn Ḥanbal, who was flogged, imprisoned and prevented from teaching or participating in any public activity. The caliph was unable to sentence him to be executed due to the strong public support he enjoyed in Baghdad.

However, in spite of the submission by the majority of scholars to the ruling powers, the caliphs and Muᶜtazila did not attain the success they were hoping for, and their policies only succeeded in incurring the wrath of the public, the scholars and the Sunnis. Thus, the government of al-Mutawakkil decided to abandon this policy and put an end to the *Miḥna*, seeking to appease the constitutional front and win its support. Thereafter, the Sunnis had the upper hand in the ᶜAbbāsid state.

The Zaydis and the Druze

At times, certain nations or groups embrace a particular religion or doctrine, or even a political or economic principle that is unique to them, setting them apart from their surroundings. In adopting this doctrine, they strive to remain distinct from their neighbours, who threaten their existence and composition. They emphasise the strong unity and solidarity among its members, thus protecting themselves from being subsumed into their much stronger and more numerous neighbours. The more jealously they guard their freedom, independence and individuality, the more their leaders are prone to introduce strange theories or distinct rituals into their beliefs. They do so in order to completely rule out any possibility of a common ground between them and their neighbours, to ensure their complete isolation and increase their need for solidarity, unity and dependence on each other.

Such practice is found mainly among the residents of mountainous areas, like the Zaydis in Yemen and the Druze in the Levant. The inhabitants of the mountains are usually very different in manners, customs and nature from their neighbours living in the plains, who far outnumber them. They are extremely careful not to allow the relationships with their neighbours to erode their distinct traditions. To achieve this purpose, residents of some mountainous areas in the Levant found it appropriate to adopt the Druze doctrine that deifies the Fatimid Caliph al-Ḥākim, and which maintains that he did not die, but disappeared at the Great Wall of China and would return to establish justice on earth. In doing so, they achieved a success that amazes us to this day, in creating a spirit of strong solidarity among the members of their community in the face of the outside world.

8
The Decline in the Position of the Clergy in the Eyes of Muslims

Previously, greater knowledge would increase a scholar's contempt for the world and his inclination towards renouncing it, but nowadays, it only increases his attachment to the world. Previously, a man would spend his wealth on acquiring knowledge, but nowadays, this knowledge helps men acquire wealth. Previously, knowledge would help a scholar grow inwardly and outwardly, yet nowadays the inward and outward corruption shows on him.

Dhū-l-Nūn al-Misri

A scholar enters between God and his creations; let him be careful how he enters!

Ibn al-Munkadir

Al-Khaṭīb al-Baghdādī (in *Tārīkh Baghdad*) and Tāj al-Dīn Al-Subkī (in *Ṭabaqāt al-Shāfiᶜiyya al-kubra*) list countless examples of the reverence enjoyed by religious scholars in the Middle Ages. The latter writes that when a religious scholar visited Khorasan once, the entire population, including women and children, came out to touch his robes and collect the dust off his shoes to use it as medicine to heal themselves. Merchants brought out their goods of sweets, fruit, garments and furs, scattering them above people's heads. The Sufi women of that town threw their rosaries at him, hoping these would touch him and that they would therefore receive his *barakāt* (blessings).

Ibn al-Jawzī describes the crowd attending Aḥmad Ibn Ḥanbal's funeral, saying:

> A thousand thousand [i.e., a million] people gathered, the likes of which had never been seen before, neither in *Jahiliyya* nor in Islam. They estimated that about sixty thousand women gathered next to the wall. Some people spent the night by the tomb. There was no household untouched by grief, except the houses of evil. The day he died, twenty thousand Jews, Christians and Magi converted to Islam.

Centuries later, Ahmad Amin wrote in his autobiography *Ḥayātī* (*My Life*) that when he sought marriage:

> . . . the turban became a stumbling block in the way. When I approached some of the homes of families with girls of marriageable age, they accepted my youth, my degree, and my salary, but they did not accept my turban. A turban denoted religiosity, which in their view implied radicalism and lack of civility, and was synonymous with backwardness, avarice and other such repulsive meanings. I was told they have no place for a turban. On one occasion, a family first accepted me as a suitor and said they wanted to see me. I understood that they liked me and agreed in principle, but then I was told that the bride saw me from the window as I was leaving and saw my turban, *jibba* [robe] and caftan and was horrified. She categorically rejected to marry me despite her family urging her to accept.

Ahmad Amin then writes about discarding his clerical garments:

> What encouraged me to do so were the troubles I faced when wearing the turban. Most people in Egypt – especially in the cities – revere the turban outwardly, while disrespecting it inwardly . . . a preconceived notion permeates their thoughts: that a man wearing a fez is respectable unless proven otherwise, and one wearing a turban is despised unless proven otherwise. Many incidents happened to me which led me to hate the turban: once I went to a hotel whose owner told me that he did not have any vacancies. A man wearing a fez came in after me and a vacancy was found for him. Another time I went to the

post office and a man wearing a fez stood in line behind me, yet the employee served him first. And once I rode in the first-class carriage of the tram, and the conductor called me saying: "Come here – pointing me to the second-class carriage – this one is first class . . ."

What could have happened during those centuries which caused the prestige of the clergy to dwindle in the hearts of the public?

In the early days of Islam, the clerical system was unknown. There was no discrete class of clerics in the state, nor was there a distinction between religious and worldly issues. God's words decided all community functions and institutions. Judiciary and war were as sanctified as prayer. Mosques were as much a place for prayer as for public meetings, and they were even used as a ground for military training. Members of the community were the army; their imam at prayer was their leader in the time of war.

However, the Umayyad caliphate saw the emergence of a political opposition which mobilised "religion" in the fight against the Umayyads. Citing Q. 3:104: "*And from among you there should be a party who invite to good and enjoin what is right and forbid the wrong . . .*", they argued that it was every Muslim's duty to enjoin what is good and forbid what is evil, using his tongue and his hand, and that it was not sufficient to merely comply with the will of God, but that a Muslim had to ensure that God's will reigns supreme in society. Hence, there was no place for silent acceptance of corruption in the state, because religion required the individual to intervene in public life and politics. In fact, politics was for them nothing but an arena for religious activity.

The Umayyads, for their part, were also able to use religion to support the existing system and their rule, to exhort people to obey their rulers and those in "*authority from among them*"[1] and to safeguard and maintain the unity of the community.

Meanwhile, a third group emerged among the pious, who avoided politics and its perils, considering it to be *fitna*,[2] and who trusted neither the religious claims of the Umayyads nor of their opponents. Many of these

1 This relates to Q. 4:59: "*O you who believe! obey Allah and obey the Apostle and those in authority from among you; then if you quarrel about anything, refer it to Allah and the Apostle, if you believe in Allah and the last day; this is better and very good in the end.*"

2 *Fitna* literally means strife, but is usually used to denote temptation, sedition, civil strife, affliction and distress.

abandoned politics and immersed themselves in the study and interpretation of the Qur'an. In addition, they collected and carefully studied the Prophet's sayings as well as the events of the time of the Prophet and the Rightfully Guided Caliphs. If one of them became known for his knowledge and piety, he would find a place in the mosque, where those wishing to learn from him would surround him to study the Qur'an's exegesis, jurisprudence and history. The *madrassa*[3] system was most likely not yet established at that time.

Nevertheless, most scholars were on the side of the political opposition to the Umayyad caliphate. They objected to their form of governance of the Islamic community, and believed the Umayyads to be unfit to rule the nation. In their view, the Umayyads were the Prophet's most dangerous enemies during his lifetime, most of whom unwillingly embraced Islam after the conquest of Mecca, then knew how to reap for themselves the fruits of the expansion, conquests and rising power of Islam. The Umayyads, these scholars believed, initially exploited ᶜUthmān's weakness and nepotism to acquire wealth, then took advantage of his murder to claim the rule. Hence, they were seen as usurpers of power, relying only on brute force, without any legitimate claim to the caliphate.

Several of these scholars sided with the ᶜAbbāsids in the late Umayyad era, and supported their claim to the succession. Once in power, the ᶜAbbāsids returned the favour, keeping these scholars close to the court, raising their status, inviting them to their councils and entrusting them with raising their children. Slowly but surely, they also appointed some of them as judges, until all judges in the state were from among them.

When and how did the distinction between religious scholars and the general public appear? Even though the *madrassa* system was still unknown in ᶜAbbāsid times, there existed some *katātīb*[4] for boys. The mosques continued to be the place for learning the Qur'an, the *ḥadīth* and *fiqh* (jurisprudence),

---

3 *Madrassa* literally means school, whether secular or religious, private or public. However, it is used in English to denote Islamic religious schools.

4 A *kuttāb* (pl. *kattātīb*) was a designated place for instruction, usually in a section of the mosque or a room in a private home or a religiously endowed building (*waqf*). It did not follow a fixed curriculum, but the pupils learned rudimentary writing and arithmetic. However, its main purpose was to commit some or all of the Qur'an to memory and receive instruction in *adab* (codes of ethical conduct and moral behaviour). Generally, boys made up the majority of pupils in a *kuttāb*, though there were a few reserved for girls, usually in the home of a female teacher.

with the learning circles covering subjects as diverse as the sciences in that era. No degrees were awarded upon passing a final exam at the end of the studies. Instead, the opinion of fellow scholars and students was the ultimate test. Whoever perceived in himself the ability to run a religious teaching circle, like the *ᶜulamāʾ*,[5] was inevitably subjected to debates with the scholars. This in itself was enough to protect the *ᶜulamāʾ* from intruders and ignorant laymen. Over time, religious education in the ᶜAbbāsid era became more organised, with structured curricula allowing for specialisation. If a student excelled in these curricula, he was considered a scholar. The jurists had the most students, as *fiqh* (jurisprudence) qualified and enabled students to assume profitable official positions. This was especially the case when princes and notables from the elite consistently appointed such scholars as tutors for their children.

The close proximity between scholars and the caliphs and emirs had some benefit. It showed the general public the importance of the sciences and encouraged many of them to study jurisprudence. It further allowed the scholars to aspire to assume the upper hand in the affairs of the state, above the administrators and ministers. They sought to oblige the ruler to commit to all the provisions of the *Sharīᶜa*, which was all that interested them since they were the only ones qualified to confidently determine what constituted *Sharīᶜa*.

What actually happened, however, was contrary to what they expected. While clerics did receive a great deal of recognition from their rulers and had become a distinct class within the nation, their position and status were weakened. This was due to the fact that their life, livelihood and aspirations fell into the hands of those who had the power to appoint them to the positions available to the scholars and jurists, namely, the caliphs, ministers, princes, governors and the powerful elite. The only way for them to access the positions to which they aspired, and which they were qualified to fill due to their knowledge and proficiency, was by gaining the benevolence of their rulers. The only way to secure a promotion within the administration was by nurturing good relations with the rulers.

The *Miḥna*, started by al-Maʾmūn and continued during the rules of al-Muᶜtaṣṣim and al-Wāthiq, is evidence of the fact that the class of jurists

5 *ᶜUlamāʾ* (sing. *ᶜālim*, English ulema) are Muslim scholars who are recognised as having specialist knowledge of Islamic law and theology.

and scholars were powerless to resist the rulers. With only two or three exceptions, they completely bowed to the will of the rulers, crowding around them, flattering them and catering to their desires. This led to antagonism between the various scholars fighting over the available positions. If one scholar openly placed God's satisfaction above that of the ruler, they disparaged, criticised and shunned him in the hope that the ruler would discard him and put another one from their midst in his place. If on some occasions circumstances allowed scholars and jurists to take collective action against the authority, or for a particularly courageous jurist to appear in the Muslim world, such as, for example, Aḥmad Ibn Ḥanbal or Ibn Taymiyyah, this was the exception to the rule.

In his *Talbīs Iblīs* (*The Devil's Deception*) Ibn al-Jawzī wrote:

> It is the devil's deception that causes the jurists to attach themselves to princes and sultans and to ingratiate themselves with them. It forbids them from denouncing the wrongdoings of the ruling elite, in spite of their ability to do so, and may lead them to legitimise issues that are prohibited in order to receive worldly rewards. As a result, corruption occurs on three levels: firstly, the prince thinks: "If I was not right, the jurist would have denied me this ruling. But how can I not be right if his livelihood depends on what I pay him?" Then the common man thinks: "There is nothing wrong with this prince nor his money or actions, because such and such jurist associates with him." And finally, it is the jurists themselves, who corrupt their own beliefs.

In general, being too close to the sultans was extremely dangerous: at the beginning, the intention might be good, but it soon changes due the sultan's generosity or the jurist's greed. Consequently, the jurist complies and never denounces any of their actions. The early scholars avoided the princes for their injustice. Princes would call for them when they needed their *fatwa*s or endorsement. A class of people therefore arose, who were strongly attached to worldly things and who learned the sciences that would benefit the princes, bringing it to them to attain worldly riches. This is evidenced by the fact that in older times, princes were keen on hearing discussions on the foundational texts, so the scholars devised *ᶜIlm al-Kalām* (Islamic scholastic theology, lit. science of discourse). When they grew tired of it and became interested in juristic discussions, the scholars devised the polemics. When the princes then became interested in sermons, many scholars turned their attention to these.

Ibn Aqil[6] said:

> I saw a jurist from Khorasan wearing silk and gold rings. I asked him: "What is this?" He said: "blessings from the Sultan and spite to my enemies". I replied: "in fact, your enemies should delight at your misfortune, if you are Muslim! The Sultan gave you his blessings and you left your faith. May God punish you with humiliation for belittling His commandments!"

Sufyān al-Thawrī[7] used to say: "I am not afraid of the princes insulting me, but I am afraid my heart might be swayed by them if they treat me with generosity." Perhaps one of the first and most famous stories on this matter is the one about the judge Abū Yūsuf, one of the founders of the Ḥanafī doctrine. People thought of him as the primary example of the jurist who is not bound by a particular principle and who is able to find a way out of any doctrinal problem to satisfy his clients. Abū Yūsuf succeeded in making himself indispensable to Hārun al-Rashīd thanks to what his supporters called his utmost flexibility and pragmatism. He has been quoted as saying the following words, which represent him perfectly: "The biggest blessings are three: the first is the blessing of Islam, without which no other blessings are possible, the second is the blessing of wellness and health, without which life is not agreeable, and the third is wealth, without which life is incomplete." In his youth, Abū Yūsuf was very poor and shabby. His teacher Abū Ḥanīfa used to try and raise his morale by telling him: "you must not despair, if you are granted a long life, you will be eating *Lawzīnaj*[8] with peeled pistachio in exchange for your *fiqh*!" And so it happened.

6 Abū-l-Wafa ᶜAlī b. ᶜAqīl b. Aḥmad al-Baghdādī (431–513 AH/1039–1120 AD) was a Ḥanbalī theologian.

7 Abū ᶜAbd Allah Sufyān b. Saᶜīd b. Masrūq al-Thawrī (97–161 AH/716–778 AD) was a Kufan jurist, ascetic, traditionist and founder of the Thawrī doctrine of jurisprudence, which died out around the seventh/thirteenth century.

8 *Lawzīnaj* is a dessert, a sweet dish made with pastry filled with almonds (*lawz*).

Al-Tanūkhī,[9] in his *Nishwār al-Muḥāḍarah wa akhbār al-mudhākara*[10] writes about the reason for Abū Yūsuf's affiliation with Hārun al-Rashīd:

> He came to Baghdad after Abū Ḥanīfa's death. There, he was taken to a general who needed to consult a jurist on an oath that he had reneged on. Abū Yūsuf issued a *fatwa* that he had not reneged on his oath. The general gave him a sum of dinars, bought him a house near his own and frequently called on him. One day the general went to the court of Hārun al-Rashīd and found him distressed. When he asked him about the reason for his chagrin, Hārun al-Rashīd replied: "It is something of a religious nature; find me a jurist whom I can ask for a *fatwa*." The general brought Abū Yūsuf to him. On his way in, Abū Yūsuf saw Hārun al-Rashīd's son locked up in a room, signalling him with his finger for help. Abū Yūsuf did not understand what he wanted. He then went to the caliph and greeted him. Hārun al-Rashīd asked: "what do you say about an imam who saw a man committing *zina* (adultery), does he have to apply the *ḥadd* punishment?"[11] Abū Yūsuf immediately understood that the adulterer was the caliph's son, and that the caliph was loath to apply the *ḥadd* punishment. Abū Yūsuf replied: "No *ḥadd* punishment is to be applied, as the Prophet said: '*idra'ū-l-ḥudūd bi-l-shubuhāt*'."[12] The caliph asked: "what suspicion can there be when the fact has been witnessed?" Abū Yūsuf answered:

9 Abū ᶜAlī al-Muḥassin al-Tanūkhī (327–384 AH/940–994 AD) was an Iraqi traditionist, jurist, writer, poet and judge.

10 Parts of this book were translated as *The Table-talk of a Mesopotamian Judge* by D. S. Margoliouth in 1922.

11 *Ḥudūd* (sing. *ḥadd*) laws or *ḥudūd* ordinances are Islamic punishments that are mandated and specified in the Qur'an. They are called *ḥudūd* (lit. limits) as they are defined as a violation against God's set limits. They are applied to crimes of adultery, fornication, the slander of illicit sex, apostasy, intoxicant consumption, robbery and theft. However, in spite of the grave punishments, which include flogging, amputation of the hand or crucifixion, they can be overturned by the slightest of doubts or suspicions and were rarely applied.

12 *Darᶜu-l ḥudūd bi-l-shubuhāt* (lit. fending off the *ḥudūd* by suspicions and technicalities) is a known legal principle that recommends the slightest doubt to be interpreted to the benefit of the accused. Out of compassion and mercy, the Prophet used this principle to lessen the harsh corporal punishments. A tradition is ascribed to the Prophet as saying: "Fend off the *ḥudūd* as much as you can. If you can find a way out of them, then let them go. That is because it is better for the Imam to err in forgiveness than to err in punishment."

> "witnessing is no more significant than knowing what happened, and the application of the *ḥudūd* punishments is not based on knowing that something happened. For the *ḥudūd* are God's right, and the imam is enjoined to apply the *ḥudūd* laws, hence they become one of his rights, and nobody can take his rights through knowledge, but rather the *ḥadd* is to be applied after confession and proof." Hārun al-Rashīd prostrated, thanking God, he ordered a large sum of money to be paid out to Abū Yūsuf, and asked him to move into the palace. As soon as he left, Abū Yūsuf received another gift from the adulterous son, followed by yet another generous gift from his mother. His position at Hārun al-Rashīd's court continued to strengthen until the caliph appointed him as *Qāḍī al-Quḍā* (Chief Justice).

Thus, the primary concern of most jurists became the hunt for opportunities for promotions to higher office. To do that they sought the proximity of the ruling elite, and ingratiated themselves with them by issuing *fatāwa* (sing. *fatwa*) for them and for the princes whenever these wanted to circumvent a provision of the law, or to implement a policy that was not acceptable to their subjects, or to insult an enemy at home or abroad who was threatening their power.

Al-Ṣūlī,[13] in his book *al-Awrāq*, recounted how Caliph al-Rāḍī refrained from drinking wine for about two years, while his companions used to drink in his presence. When they wanted to seduce him to follow suit, he said: "I swore an oath to God that I would never touch it." They called the jurists to his court to find a way to exempt him from his obligation. The jurists quickly found a way out and advised him to distribute 1,000 dinars in charity after returning to drink. He resumed his drinking habit and was very grateful and pleased.

Therefore, it was not at all surprising that the majority of the jurists in the Muslim world neglected an essential and serious duty they were supposed to assume, namely, to develop the doctrinal and intellectual basis of religion so that it may respond to the needs and problems of their contemporaries.

---

13 Abū Bakr Muḥammad b. Yaḥya al-Ṣūlī (266 or 267–335 AH/880–946 AD) was a poet, scholar, historian and litterateur with Shi'ite leanings. He was also known for his impressive chess-playing skills, which granted him the title al-Shaṭaranjī (the chess player).

Indeed, where they had any energy left after their struggle for positions, they did the exact opposite of this duty. They took advantage of the inherent aversion felt by Arabs towards innovation to denounce and fight everything new, given that most of the innovations were not to the liking of the rulers and people in power, who were conservative by nature. Thus, for nearly one thousand years they confined their intellectual activity to the fight against new developments on the pretext that they were innovations amounting to heresy and misguidance, which would ultimately lead to hellfire,[14] or to discussing the ramifications of purely theoretical religious minutiae, unrelated to practical applications, merely to show off their prowess in debate and deliberations.

The jurists thus lost touch with the ordinary daily life of the masses, and lived in a world of their own which they only shared with their peers. Their public image and prestige waned as a result, and the public turned to the Sufi shaykhs, seeking their guidance, counsel and *barakāt*. All the more so, since these Sufi shaykhs – at least initially – renounced the world, boldly spoke up to the rulers and celebrated the essence of religion, significantly more than the jurists and scholars did. When the rulers noticed the deterioration of the status of jurists and religious scholars in the hearts of their subjects, they too lost interest in them and lessened their dependence on them in order to guarantee the loyalty of their subjects, while at the same time starting to court the Sufis to achieve the same purpose.

This was the situation, when "*Allah's curse and His wrath for their revolt against His commandments, overtook them, while they were powerless.*"[15]

When Muhammad Ali became the ruler of Egypt, he yielded, heart and soul, to Western influence. Islam was of little avail to him. He was overcome by a need for a strong army that would help him achieve his far-reaching ambitions. To that end, he put all the state's institutions and resources at the service of the military. He believed that to build a strong army, officers needed to receive Western-style education and training, and he therefore started to establish an education system that was radically different from traditional

14 This is based on a tradition ascribed to the Prophet that says: "The most evil matters are those that are newly invented, for every newly invented matter is an innovation and every innovation is misguidance and every misguidance is in the Hellfire."

15 The wording here refers to Q. 51:44: "*But they revolted against the commandment of their Lord, so the rumbling overtook them while they saw.*"

Islamic education. Naturally, clerics were not integrated into such a system, but were completely side-lined and their class neglected. Thus, for the first time in Egypt, followed by one Islamic country after the other, two entirely distinct education systems began to develop alongside each other, splitting intellectual life into two discrete paths. While the old, traditional system started with the *kuttāb* in the village and ended at al-Azhar in Cairo, or any equivalent religious institution in Egypt or another Islamic country, under the new system primary and secondary schools and universities were established and curricula developed along the lines of European educational institutions. These institutions omitted the teaching of religion and its sciences, with the exception of a few lessons, which, out of hypocrisy, were forced onto the curricula and were very different in spirit from the other subjects. Everyone was aware of this hypocrisy and hence neglected these lessons, which neither affected students' grades nor their degrees. The material taught was not sufficient to give the students any grounding in the religious sciences.

If we assume the good faith of those in charge of these educational institutions, we can say that they did not have the slightest idea of how to reconcile Islamic education with the purely Western-style curricula implemented in these types of schools. If we ascribe an ulterior motive to them, we can say that the foreign colonisers, who devoted a great deal of attention to the education system, aimed to destroy Islam in the hearts of the youth and to educate generation after generation of pupils who were devoid of anything that might tie them to their past, their religion and traditions.

Be that as it may, this was exactly what happened. The graduates of these schools and universities lost all interest in religion. If they did not, this was mainly due to either personal reasons or due to a family environment that was dominated by religion, but not to the nature of their education. In any case, they were not interested in convincing those around them or were incapable of doing so. What made matters worse was the unforgivable neglect of Arabic-language education, which led to a glaring deterioration of Arabic-language skills among the graduates of these schools. The result was an almost complete severance of the link between them and their religious and cultural heritage, whose intellectual output they referred to as "yellow books".[16]

16 "Yellow books" is not only an expression to denote old or ancient works, as in the term "yellowing pages", but is also used to refer to books that are not well researched, include exaggerations and are generally not trustworthy.

Thus, as of the early nineteenth century, a huge gulf emerged in the Islamic world, in a manner and scope never witnessed before, between religious and secular education, and therefore also between the clergy and the general public. The undoubted fact is that the increasing detachment of the class of clergy was a reflection of a general decline in the Islamic world – the Islamic world that in the past produced the greatest scholars from among professions such as grocers, tailors or wheat merchants. This detachment is what caused the religious scholars – even more than in the past – to use their religious knowledge to make a living rather than see it as a path leading to God. However, thankfully, it is no longer a path to eating *lawzīnaj* with peeled pistachio – except in rare cases!

On the one hand, we find that the majority of those who studied in secular schools may have, due to their rampant ignorance about religion, come to dispense with what the jurists have to offer and also to despise them. This contempt is reflected in the use the derogatory term "*fiqqī*"[17] to refer to teachers of the *kuttāb* or Qur'an reciters in mosques and at funerals, with all the negative connotations the word evokes. On the other hand, many of the Muslim rulers, starting with the Ottoman officer Muhammad Ali, who were determined to pursue Westernisation without reservations, turned against the clerics and resorted to every means available in order to reduce their influence and play them against one another. Even worse was how they discredited those clerics with the general public, so that the latter would kowtow to the authority without embarrassment or scepticism in the direction that was laid out for them.

The examples from our contemporary history are countless, however, I will quote some of the events recorded by al-Jabartī in his *ᶜAjāʾib al-āthār fiʹl-Tarājim waʹl-Akhbār*[18] He describes an incident that took place in Jumada Al-Awwal 1224 AH/ July 1809. When Muhammad Ali felt threatened by the activities of ᶜUmar Makram,[19] he held a meeting with the clerics of al-Azhar

17 *Fiqh* (lit. deep understanding or full comprehension) is usually translated as Islamic jurisprudence. The jurist or scholar educated in *fiqh* is called a *faqīh*. *Fiqqī* is a corruption of the word *faqīh* and is used to denote the same in a derogatory way, akin to calling priests spell-casters, Bible thumpers, papists or holy rollers.

18 *ᶜAjāʾib al-āthār fiᶜl-Tarājim waᶜl-Akhbār* is known for short as *Tārīkh al-Jabartī*.

19 ᶜUmar Makram (1750–1822) was an Egyptian political and popular leader, and a religious shaykh educated in al-Azhar. He led the public to revolt against the French in 1798 and again in 1800. He also led the revolt against the British in 1807 and was instrumental in supporting Muhammad Ali to be made *Wāli* (viceroy) of Egypt, by forcing the Ottomans to replace Ahmad Khurshid Pasha with Muhammad Ali. Yet when he discovered that Muhammad Ali intended to rule Egypt himself, he objected to a foreign ruler.

in which he reprimanded ᶜUmar Makram for his intransigence and for inciting the public to revolt. He told them: "Your defamatory tactics and your clandestine meetings at al-Azhar do not befit you. It is as if you are trying to scare me with such meetings, agitating the evildoers and inciting the public to revolt, like you did in the time of the Mamluks. I am not scared of this. If anything should happen from the subjects, I have only the sword and revenge." They said: "This will not happen, we do not like revolts and the eruption of strife. We only meet to read al-Bukhārī." However, the meaning of the Pasha's words was clear to them. In fact, each side understood the other's underlying message. Muhammad Ali's words agreed with their hatred of ᶜUmar Makram. Their council adjourned with divided opinions, hypocrisy, hatred and envy abounded. Their discussions continued night and day. The Pasha sent for ᶜUmar Makram, promising to do whatever he asked, as well as a daily *satchel* (bribe), yet Makram declined.

The Pasha, still anxious, had him spied on, examined his activities and his visitors from among the senior military officers. When Muhammad Ali finally exiled ᶜUmar Makram, many of his fellow turbaned shaykhs escorted him, feigning lamentations and grief. That same morning, Shaykh al-Mahdi visited Muhammad Ali Pasha and requested to take over the functions and office of ᶜUmar Makram. He was granted the supervision of the Imam al-Shāfiᶜī *waqf* (endowment) in return for his diligence in betraying ᶜUmar Makram. The clerics then wrote a report, ordered by Muhammad Ali, to be sent to the authorities in which they built a case against ᶜUmar Makram. It cited the cause of his expulsion and exile, listing his flaws and wrongdoings, amongst them that he incited strife amongst the soldiers to depose Muhammad Ali Pasha. When Aḥmad al-Ṭaḥāwī secluded himself in his home and abandoned the clerics, they insulted and degraded him for not joining them in their perjury. Their actions were borne out of envy and resentment of Makram's good fortunes, despite him being the defender of the clerics and the people. After his exile, their status suffered an even sharper decline. According to al-Jabartī, ᶜUmar Makram, however, got part of what he deserved, as helping anyone against injustice is rewarded. "God does not deal unjustly with anyone."[20]

---

20 This statement relates to Q. 18:49: "*And the Book shall be placed, then you will see the guilty fearing from what is in it, and they will say: 'Ah! woe to us! what a book is this! It does not omit a small one nor a great one, but numbers them (all); and what they had done they shall find present (there); and your Lord does not deal unjustly with anyone.'*"

Muhammad Ali resorted to demolishing the prestige of the clerics through a moral massacre akin to the bloody massacre of the Mamluks. He masterminded incidents and exploited others, after which al-Azhar clerics and their associates were charged with crimes such as counterfeiting currency ("so that whoever paid a few Piasters for something they bought was told: 'They are not Azhari Piasters, are they?'"), or stealing people's belongings ("the issue of the robbery of a foreign woman's house in the city resulted in much gossip about the Azharites and reminded them of the counterfeit dirhams") or consorting with pimps and prostitutes ("the senior officials of the state, the army officers, and even the general public made the Azharites and their families the topic of their entertainment and the target of their mockery. After al-Azhar was a beacon of *Sharīᶜa* and religious knowledge, it became the opposite, a den of thieves, counterfeiters and many other hidden things.").

However, in spite of al-Jabartī's sorrow about this deliberate distortion of the reputation of the clergy, and although he considered them deserving of lament rather than accusation, he does not turn a blind eye – as we have seen and as we shall see hereunder – to their misdeeds and their distortion of religion. He writes:

> They were captivated by worldly pursuits and abandoned the study of religious issues and the teaching of science, with the exception of the memorization of the Qur'an. They left their work at the colleges. Their houses resembled those of the former princes, with many servants and helpers. They hired Coptic clerks and couriers, resorted to threats if their demands were delayed, and turned a deaf ear to the complaints of the farmers. They engaged in internal disputes out of envy, hatred and malice. As a result, their situation was reversed; they met only to discuss worldly affairs – allocations, liabilities, governmental shares and surplus. They collaborated with the Copts, inviting their community leaders to their associations and banquets.

Elsewhere he writes:

> The prestige and respect formerly awarded to them vanished. They engaged in worldly exploits and personal fortunes, and listened to the devil's misguidance. They were drawn by the ignorant to immoral behaviour and rushed to attend wedding and funeral banquets, fighting

> over the food like cattle. You see them rushing to all invitations and prostrating in front of the dinner tables, snatching the kebab and roasts and neglecting their advisory duties.

Under the rule of Muhammad Ali there was no room for them or for the likes of ᶜUmar Makram and al-Jabartī, who openly engaged in constructive criticism against his tyranny and despotism or denounced his complete submission to the West and its influence. Al-Jabartī writes describing the orchard of Muhammad Ali's palace (which can be taken as a metaphor):

> and he planted his orchard with strange species of exotic flowers, in various forms . . . which were imported from abroad. These plants were transplanted to Egypt and flourished, but while they looked good, they completely lacked any fragrance.

This in turn broke the ground for a new type of clerics, most notably Rifāᶜa al-Ṭahṭāwī,[21] who owed their livelihood and daily bread (and peeled pistachio!) to the authority, and were therefore more than willing to promote its purposes, and to continuously remind people of the successes of Western civilisation, European urbanisation and architecture, which were worth emulating in the Middle East. This is similar to the conduct of the clergy in Russia during the rule of the despicable Tsar Peter, called "The Great".

It is not surprising to note that this new type of religious scholar, who enjoyed the patronage of Muhammad Ali and the rulers of other Islamic countries, failed to produce one single leading intellectual figure who may have taken it upon himself to guide Muslims educated in the Westernised schools, to train them to take a positive stand for their religion, to confront the continuous organised campaigns and successive attacks on Islam by European writers whose books they read, or the missionaries working in their midst. Even ᶜAbd al-Raḥmān al-Kawākibī,[22] the "thinker" who is persistently described by Muslims as progressive, drew the bulk of his views on reform, as found in his books *Umm al-Qurā* (*Mother of the Villages*) and

---

21 Rifāᶜa al-Ṭahṭāwī (1801–1873) was an Egyptian cleric, writer, teacher, intellectual and Egyptologist. He was the first to attempt reconciliation between Islamic and modern Western civilisations.

22 ᶜAbd al-Raḥmān al-Kawākibī (1854/55–1902) was a Syrian author from Aleppo and an avid supporter of pan-Islamic Arab solidarity. His two most influential books *Umm al-Qurā* and *Ṭabāʾiᶜ al-istibdād* set the basis for pan-Arab nationalism.

Ṭabā'iʿ al-istibdād (*The Nature of Despotism*), from the books of two European intellectuals, namely, *The Future of Islam* by Wilfrid Blunt[23] and *Of Tyranny* by Vittorio Alfieri,[24] respectively. He was the first to introduce to Muslims the malicious, destructive idea of replacing the concept of Islamic nationalism with Arab nationalism, which resulted in the fragmentation of solidarity and unity among the residents of *Dār al-Islām* until the present day. It was the first stage of the plan laid out for us by the West, and it was followed by further rifts and fragmentation between the Arab nations, leading to doubts over the feasibility of the idea of Arab nationalism itself.

The first person in the Islamic world to attempt a serious reconciliation between the teachings of Islam and the requirements of the modern era – without a humiliating deference to Western civilisation – was a man from its furthest corners, Shaykh Jamāl al-Dīn al-Afghānī.[25] He was followed by his Egyptian student, Shaykh Muḥammad ʿAbduh,[26] author of *Risālat al-tawḥīd* (*Treatise on the Oneness of God*, often translated as *The Theology of Unity*). These two presented Muslim clerics with a golden opportunity, which they should have taken had they been wise enough. This opportunity would have rectified their situation, restored their place in the hearts of the people, and contributed to their resurgence and their reinstatement by the rulers. At the time when al-Afghānī and his student's call resonated loudly in the hearts of the public and the political parties in the East, the scholars mistakenly thought that they could win back the favour of the ruler by fighting this call and standing against the two men who wanted to reopen the door of *ijtihād* after it had been said to have been closed for a thousand years.

The clerics were at a loss, which in turn affected successive generations of Muslims, who – as a result of the relentless influence of Western civilisation – were in dire need of scholars who could lead them out of their confusion. The

23 Wilfrid Scawen Blunt (1840–1922) was an English writer and poet, who travelled extensively in the Middle East, especially in Algeria, Egypt and Syria, and was well known for his views against imperialism.

24 Count Vittorio Alfieri (1749–1803) was an Italian dramatist and poet. Most of the main characters in his works were tragic "heroes of freedom", whose ambition and need of revolution pushed them to fight tyranny and oppression wherever they existed.

25 Sayyid Jamāl al-Dīn al-Afghānī (1838/39–1897) was a political activist and one of the founders of Islamic Modernism and an advocate of pan-Islamic unity.

26 Muḥammad ʿAbduh (1849–1905) was an Egyptian Islamic jurist, religious scholar and liberal reformer. He was also Grand Mufti of Egypt.

clerics claimed that inspiration in religious matters had ceased ten centuries ago and forever more. This is akin to claiming that God Almighty has retired from "work" a thousand years ago, and that his voice has not been heard since. It is our claim that those who do not believe that inspiration is a constant requirement, in order to address the changing needs of human beings, cannot be faithful to divine inspiration and revelation, which we see as a heresy beyond which there is none.

Another consequence was that many contemporary Muslims, who had despaired of having the clerics lend them a guiding hand, ended up throwing out the baby with the bathwater, renouncing Islam in its entirety, while a minority refused to keep pace with the times and its requirements and completely closed their doors to modernity. Those who did not accept either scenario, in their quest for enlightenment and guidance, turned away from the so-called *fiqqī* (whose role, according to them, was limited to blessing the authorities' actions even if they contradicted one another, denouncing their enemies even if they had good intentions, and censoring books and preventing the airing of a film about the Prophet or a play about al-Ḥusayn), and instead sought guidance on religious affairs from well-informed non-clerical intellectuals, even if relatively weak in their knowledge of theology and jurisprudence. These are well on their way to becoming, in our humble opinion, the real clerics of our time.

There was a time when a Prophet's biography by Dr Haykal, or a play about the Prophet by Tawfiq al-Hakim[27] would have provoked the outraged clerics to denounce the audacity of men other than themselves to address issues that are at the core of their specialty. However, we believe that this may be a thing of the past, and that we may now be seeing a return to the situation known in early Islam, when the most eminent jurists emerged from among grocers, tailors or wheat traders.

27 Tawfiq al-Hakim (1898–1987) was a prominent Egyptian writer and author.

9
The Chances of Successfully Establishing a Society Based on Islamic Principles

If He wills, He can do away with you, O people, and bring others [in your place]. And Allah has the power to do this.

Qur'an 4:133

European civilisation developed in a mostly seamless and homogeneous manner, without major tremors cutting off one generation from the traditions of those preceding it. While there were three notable exceptions in the continent's political and social history, namely, the French Revolution, the Industrial Revolution and the Bolshevik Revolution, the fruits of its intellectual and scientific development followed one another calmly and methodically, each complementing the other and building on what was already there.

And so the ox-drawn cart made way for the horse-drawn carriage, and the latter was replaced by the steam engine, followed by the car and then the plane. These appeared at intervals without making sudden breaks with traditions or causing violent tremors that destroyed existing lifestyles. Similarly, philosophical thought evolved gradually, connecting Greek philosophers, the Scholastics, Thomas Aquinas, Descartes, Hume, Kant, Hegel, Husserl and the Existentialists. Each read the output of his predecessors, added to it, modified it or corrected their mistakes, using the same or similar terminology.

Ordinary readers did not struggle or feel any shock as they moved from Plato to Sartre, or from Wittgenstein to St Augustine.

Nevertheless, and despite the fact that all the constitutional, political, social and economic institutions and systems in Europe gradually crystallised out of existing needs and circumstances, over the course of history there were always certain people who were incapable of adapting, or who rejected the new values, because they left them confused or anxious, or powerless to keep up. Some of these people found a solution to their problem either with a priest in the village, or a psychiatrist in the city, or through socialising or by finding among the multitude of political parties available one whose principles agreed with their own. Others, who could not cope with the fast pace of change, resorted to tranquillisers, alcohol, drugs or violence.

From the Camel to the Plane

If this was the case for large numbers in the West, where evolution took place at a relatively calm, naturally sequenced pace, what of Islamic societies, where we can say without much exaggeration that their members were catapulted, almost instantaneously, from riding a camel to riding in cars and planes? What about the intelligentsia who went from reading *al-Nazarāt wa-l ᶜabarāt* by al-Manfalūṭī[1] and *al-Maqāmāt* by al-Yāzijī[2] to reading Russell and Günter Grass? What about their daughters, who were previously forbidden from opening the door lest a stranger should see them, and whose mothers until recently wore the *niqāb* (face veil), who have now started to go to the cinemas showing sexually charged movies? No wonder, then, that we see in the men and women of these Islamic societies much more nervous tension than any witnessed in the West – a tension reaching schizophrenic proportions, and becoming a threat that might topple the two-horse cart described by Arnold Toynbee: the first horse, whose speed increased at an exponential rate, represents reason and technology, while the second horse, whose speed increased only fractionally, represents passion and tradition.

Add to this that everyone who was blessed (or cursed) with some sensitivity recognised their failure to pursue and keep up with this race, to

1 Muṣṭafa Luṭfī al-Manfalūṭī (1876–1924) was a famous Egyptian writer and poet, named after the city of his birth, Manfalout in Upper Egypt.

2 Ibrāhīm al-Yāzijī (1847–1906) was a Lebanese philologist, poet and journalist, well known for his translation of the Bible into Arabic.

fulfil their expected role and to adapt their behaviour to the requirements of modern life. This applies to the general public as much as it does to our intellectuals, who are continually struggling to catch up with the evolution of Western thought and scientific achievements, thus leaving them with barely enough time and energy to be creative or to incorporate what they have learned, to make their own contributions.

In the West, women's emancipation – their sexual freedom, political rights and economic independence – came as a result of long centuries of evolution and struggle. In Islamic societies, it was not the result of original, deep-rooted thought, nor was it a reward for women's vital participation with men in the struggle against the enemy, as in Russia, or for colonising new territory, as in the United States. Rather, emancipation was the result of two or three books published in the early twentieth century, as well as the activities of some wives of high-ranking officials, and the desire of some governments to be seen as enlightened by the West. Is it any surprise, then, that their current status resembles the woman who danced on the stairs,[3] lost and confused, not knowing where she belongs?

Some may argue that it is a matter of time before new patterns become habitual and Western values are soaked up, as every new beginning is difficult. They may boost their argument by comparing a generation that considered a train trip from Cairo to Tanta to be a hazardous, risk-filled journey that only God could protect from, with the next generation of those who are used to travelling by plane every summer vacation to sell newspapers in Vienna, or harvest fruits in France.

However, personally, I do not see any value in such comparisons. I do not consider an Arab youth selling newspapers on the sidewalks of Vienna, or an Arab girl wearing a bikini on the beach, closer to the spirit of Western civilisation than a peasant woman selling cottage cheese in the village market in Monufia,[4] nor do I consider them more likely to have the key to the problem. I do not consider the *sawāris*[5] carts inferior to our imported public

3 This refers to an Egyptian proverb that denotes a useless action: she danced on the stairs, those on the top floors did not see her and those on the bottom floors were also not aware of her.

4 Monufia is one of the governorates of Egypt, located in the North Nile Delta.

5 *Sawāris* are horse-drawn carriages of the Omnibus Company, the first public transport company established in Cairo. Each carriage transported about twenty people at once. They could also be drawn by oxen or mules. They were named after the Suares brothers, a well-known family of Sephardic Jews, who in 1889 also launched Egypt's first suburban railway.

buses, whose passengers far exceed the numbers allowed and can be found standing on their ladders or riding on their roofs, and whose driver stops, with a packed load of passengers, to buy a *fūl*[6] sandwich or a cup of tea for his breakfast.

Strange scenes pervade our society, reflecting a spirit that is neither Eastern nor Western. A government undersecretary or department director who by day is indistinguishable from his peers may spend the night in a *ḥalaqāt dhikr* (circles of *dhikr*) of one of the Sufi orders. Lecture halls in the universities are frequented by bearded male students wearing a *jilbāb*[7] as well as by female students wearing the latest fashions directly from Parisian fashion houses. A diplomat who spent most of his career abroad may resort to the police to force his wife to go into *Bayt al-Ṭāʾa*.[8] So-called "literary giants" and "renaissance leaders" rely in their study of philosophy on a book by Will Durant in which he assembled a series of lectures he gave to semi-literate American workers to introduce them to the concepts of philosophy. Other intellectuals have discarded al-Jabartī, Ibn Rushd (Averroes),[9] al-Ghazālī and Ibn Ṭufayl,[10] and become engrossed in trivial European literature by the likes of Oscar Wilde

6 *Fūl* is a staple food in Egypt, and is a dish of cooked fava beans served with vegetable oil and cumin. Traditionally, it was an Egyptian breakfast and now the fava beans are also the national dish, eaten at all times of the day.

7 The term *jilbāb* refers to any ankle-length, loose-fitting garment with long sleeves, which covers the entire body, except for hands, face and head. It was traditionally worn by Egyptian peasants, both men and women, and is now considered the "Islamic" garb, especially as it is commonly worn in the Arabian Peninsula, Iraq and neighbouring Arab countries.

8 *Bayt al-Ṭāʾa* (lit. "the house of obedience") is the institution of forcing a wife who has left her husband's house and therefore is considered "*nāshiz*" (disobedient, rebellious) to return to it. According to the Egyptian 1897 Ordinance Organising the Sharīʿa Courts and the equivalent 1931 Law, a husband who has been granted an obedience decree by the court may seek the assistance of the police in forcing his rebellious or disobedient wife to return to the conjugal dwelling. Enforced obedience is not mentioned in the Qur'an or *ḥadīth*. The institution of enforced obedience was abolished in 1967, despite the resistance of some religious scholars and judges who refused to abide by the new order.

9 ʿAbū l-Walīd Muḥammad b. ʿAḥmad b. Rushd, known as Ibn Rushd (520–595 AH/1126–1198 AD), was a medieval Andalusian polymath – a logician, philosopher, theologian, grammarian, jurist, geographer, mathematician, physician and astronomer.

10 Abū Bakr Muḥammad b. ʿAbd al-Malik b. Muḥammad b. Ṭufayl al-Qaisī al-Andalusī, known as Ibn Ṭufayl (484–581 AH/1105–1185 AD), was an Arab Andalusian Muslim polymath – a writer, novelist, philosopher, theologian, physician, astronomer, vizier and court official. He is most famous for writing the first philosophical novel, *Ḥayy Ibn Yaqdhān*, also known as *Philosophus Autodidactus*.

and Somerset Maugham, to the extent that one of those "great" writers and storytellers stole the idea of a novel written by Françoise Sagan before she was twenty.

What do we call this?

Real Opportunities for Progress

In our opinion, it is essential to recognise two facts:

First: there is no opportunity for real progress in a society that has dismissed its history and traditions. The indiscriminate and random importation of lifestyle patterns pertaining to other communities ultimately leads to the loss of identity, homogeneity and dignity, without a significant return to compensate for the loss. The result is a society that is bland, characterless and unable to make any unique contribution to human civilisation. If we take an in-depth look at our intellectual output during the last hundred years, we will realise that the best and most enduring of works were written by writers who had a solid foundation in the Arabic heritage, not by Westernised writers without a heritage.

Second: there is no opportunity for us to recover our dignity, serenity and self-confidence and to be free of that nervous tension that is destroying us, which is exacerbated by the ever-increasing gap between the West and the East, despite our breathless attempts to overcome it, other than by pausing and reflecting on the matter as a whole. We need the active contribution of all those who can clarify the link between the nation's heritage and its future, and those who can screen our traditions to select those that can help in this construction. Islamic *Da*ᶜ*wah* will play a key role in this respect.

The chance of success for the call to establish an Islamic society on the basis of purely Islamic tenets today is – in my opinion – no smaller than the chance Islam had when it spread across the Arabian Peninsula in the seventh century. My conviction stems from the fact that in both cases success is based on providing effective solutions to social ills, economic woes and ideological misconceptions prevalent in this society, as well as determining a clear path to enable new and fruitful contributions and reviving the enthusiasm required to achieve this. Islam allowed the disparate, hostile Arab tribes to provide an authentic Arab contribution to human civilisation, thus serving as a gateway for Arabs to enter history. In my opinion, the success of a renewed Islamic effort in our society can achieve the same result; however, only if certain conditions are met. Among these conditions are:

1. Admitting the undeniable fact that our Islamic society is part of a world that is progressing vigorously and on its way to becoming one world, and that this does not allow for isolation, but calls for inclusive, diverse societies. Even if we decide that this isolation might be beneficial, countries with a superior military will not allow us this freedom unless we prove that the particular way of life chosen for our society would not contradict but serve the endeavour to solve common global problems.
2. Being aware that a new society can be built only with a considerable amount of self-confidence, which will come only if we are confident that Islam, Eastern traditions and the Arab intellectual heritage can indeed offer positive values, some of which are superior to those of other civilisations. Confidence in our own values existed in our society until the end of the eighteenth century, when Western influences began to erode our confidence in ourselves, our traditions, heritage and religion. It was this confidence that at one time enabled a healthy borrowing from the heritage of other civilisations (the way al-Jāḥiz,[11] al-Tawḥīdī[12] and Ikhwān al-Ṣafā[13] borrowed from Greek sciences). Without it, any borrowing will lack any compass or criteria. It will be up to the intellectuals and thinkers to present conclusive evidence for the foundations upon which they built their belief, even (or rather, especially) for those whose religious

11 Abū ᶜUthman ᶜAmr ibn Baḥr al-Kinānī al-Baṣrī, known as al-Jāḥiz (159–255 AH/776–868/869 AD), was a famous Arab writer, litterateur and Muᶜtazali theologian.

12 ᶜAlī b. Muḥammad b. al-ᶜAbbās, known as Abū Ḥayyān al-Tawḥīdī (310–414 AH/922–1023 AD), was one of the most influential intellectuals and thinkers of the fourth/tenth century and is described as "the philosopher of litterateurs and the litterateur of philosophers".

13 The Ikhwān al-Ṣafā (Brethren of Purity, also Brethren of Sincerity) were a secret anonymous group of Muslim philosophers around the fourth/tenth century, with a strict hierarchy of four ranks which were determined by age, skills, knowledge and nobility. Their full name was "Ikhwān al-Ṣafāᵓ wa Khillān al-Wafā wa Ahl al-Ḥamd wa abnāᵓ al-Majd" (Brethren of Purity, Loyal Friends, People Worthy of Praise and Sons of Glory). They wrote an encyclopaedia in fifty-two epistles, categorising knowledge including mathematics, natural sciences, psychology, music, magic, theology and logic.

sentiments have waned and who have lost their respect for traditions and heritage.

3. Just as it is possible to deduce the religion of the truly religious by observing their behaviour at home and in their community rather than from their birth certificate, our society will not be Islamic just because the constitution stipulates that Islam is the state religion, nor does the adoption of certain provisions of Islamic *Sharīᶜa* make it Islamic. It becomes an Islamic society when the spirit of Islam permeates all its institutions and all the details of daily life.
4. Some may argue that society cannot be built on a certain concept of divine will. They claim that the development of society is subject to laws of determinism that are barely connected to, or shaped by, ideals and human will – indeed, that the development of society destroys ideals and ideas only to replace them with others. They may support their opinion by saying that the views of the pious and the scholars did not play a major role in the development of Muslim society, but that – just like in any other society – development came about as a result of prevailing economic, political and social conditions.

We respond to them as follows:

The undeniable inevitability of the laws of history – as understood by Muslim historians and as we understand them – are themselves an expression of divine will. It was precisely for the purpose of detecting the essence of this will that Muslim scholars in the Middle Ages studied history and codified it, by studying the evolution and direction of events, just like passengers may observe the route taken by a vehicle in order to deduce its unknown destination chosen by the driver. Hence, there is a divine will, represented by the inevitability of history, but which can be inferred by observing historical trends and currents.

Everyone understands the word "Islam" in the sense of acquiescence and submission to the will of God, acknowledgement of His wisdom and plan and acceptance of His decree, while at the same time ensuring that His will reigns supreme. There is no contradiction between the "acceptance of His decree" and "ensuring His will reigns supreme" through, for example, resistance, revolution or *jihad*. An observant scholar can distinguish between inevitable historical trends that represent God's will that must be accepted, and events and trends that go against the tide of history, counter its inevitability and hamper the fulfilment of its purpose. These are trends that should be resisted and against which *jihad* for Allah should be waged, "until the will of God reigns supreme".[14]

Historical Determinism is God's Will

Accordingly, we can imagine that some so-called Islamist movements in our society may be working against the will of God, and may therefore be un-Islamic, if they ignore the inevitability of history, while some may be truly Islamic – even without realising it themselves – if they are conscious of historical trends, and actively enable these trends to fulfil their purpose.

With every new historical development, these Islamic movements should ask themselves the following questions and seek to answer them:

- Is this development inevitable and should we acquiesce to it, or is it a "foreign" one that needs to be resisted and eradicated?
- Which divine will is reflected by this inevitable development?
- What is the Islamic perception on the submission to this will?

We believe that it is this Islamic perception that will distinguish our responses and reactions to existing challenges and ongoing developments from the responses and reactions of non-Muslims, whose thought processes would lead to the realisation of the same historical laws.

However, in this regard we should note what we consider a very important fact. A Chinese proverb says: "Give a man a fish, and you feed him for a day. Teach a man to fish, and you feed him for a lifetime." In our opinion, this maxim applies to religious truth more than any other field. Having the spirit of Islam permeate one's life, rather than adhering to specific provisions here and there, is enough to serve as a compass to guide us to the right path at any time, in any place and in any circumstance. We will provide an example below to illustrate what we mean:

---

14 The slogan "until the will of God reigns supreme" comes from the writings of Ibn Taymiyyah, who argued that God enjoined every Muslim to promote good and forbid evil until the will of God reigns supreme. This became the slogan for various Islamist groups, who all claim to know God's will and to be working to ensure that it reigns supreme.

The predominant form of ownership in the Arabian Peninsula during *Jahiliyya* and at the time of the Prophet was movable assets rather than real-estate ownership. A Bedouin could load all his possessions on a camel and move with it from one place to another in pursuit of water and pasture. Therefore, an attack on a traveller in the desert, stealing the camel which carries his water, food, tents and weapons, was almost equivalent to killing him. Thus, in such a society, it was very important to legislate a firm and very severe punishment as a deterrent for the crime of such theft. However, with the advent of Islam to communities that had forms of ownership more important than the movable type, and where robbing a man of his water-skin was not seen as so heinous a crime, the community could enforce another punishment for the crime of theft than the one meted out in the Bedouin community, without this being considered a departure from Islam and its spirit. On the contrary, abiding by the spirit of Islam requires us to choose this second punishment, as it would achieve – in the non-Bedouin community – the same desired results envisaged by Islam as the first one did in the Bedouin community.

The poet al-Mutanabbī wrote:

> If you honour a generous man, as his king he will you behold . . .
> but if you honour the mean-spirited man, he will surely revolt![15]

This means that the same treatment in two different situations will inevitably result in two distinct outcomes. Any teacher will know that there are different ways to treat boys with distinctive and contrasting temperaments and educational levels in order to achieve the same result, which is receiving a good education.

The same principle can be extended to the prohibition of pictures and imagery in a society that until recently had worshiped idols. It can also be extended to the *ḥijāb* (veil or head covering) which was imposed in Medina when women were harassed by the youth in the city and experienced offensive sexual advances every time they went out alone to the desert (to relieve themselves). Therefore, Q. 33:59: "*O Prophet! say to your wives and your*

15 S. Stetkevych translates it as: "When you honour a man of honour, you own him; When you honour an ignoble, he's impudent".

daughters and the women of the believers that they should cast their outer garments over their persons this will be more proper, so that they should be known and thus not molested . . ." was revealed, so the youth could distinguish between the chaste and the other women.[16]

What reinforces my opinion is the following:

Certain Qur'anic provisions were abrogated with the revelation of other verses, when the situation of the Muslims changed after their migration, with the spread of Islam and the conquests, and other developments that occurred within less than a quarter of a century. This necessitated the abrogation of some of the earlier provisions. See Q. 2:106: "*Whatever communications We abrogate or cause to be forgotten, We bring one better than it or like it . . .*"[17]

Recognising that it is the spirit of Islam which should inspire our behaviour would inevitably remove the accusation that Islam is incompatible with the requirements of the times and the historical developments

---

16 *Author's footnote*: See, for example, *Asbāb nuzūl al-Qur'ān* by al-Wāḥidī. It is evident from some references in *Kitāb al-Aghānī* by Abū-l-Faraj al-Iṣfahānī that the veil was known in *Jahiliyya*, although only in the cities and not among the Bedouins. The veil was the norm for the tribe of Quraysh in pre-Islamic times, albeit the historian al-Fākihī wrote that the men usually took their daughters and slave girls to perform the circumambulation around the Ka'ba without the veil to attract prospective husbands or buyers. Once the aim was achieved, they returned to donning the veil. The Qur'an referred to this in Q. 33:33: "*And stay in your houses and do not display your finery like the displaying of the ignorance of yore . . .*" Commentators and exegetes disagreed on the interpretations of the verses of the veil and whether it addresses the wives of the Prophet alone or obliges all Muslim women to wear it (see, for example, Chapter 33, verses 32–34 and 53–55). As for what is meant by the word "adornment" or "ornament" in Q. 24:31, some opined that it means that the whole body should be hidden and only the face, hands and feet can be uncovered (although there was disagreement about the foot's dorsum), others said that the whole body should be covered except for one eye, while yet others went as far as saying only the forehead was meant, as it suffices as a sign that the woman is chaste (or married) so men would refrain from harassing her. In any case, Sukayna bint al-Ḥusayn (the Prophet's great-granddaughter) and ᶜĀᵓisha bint Ṭalḥa b. ᶜUbayd Allah were unveiled and uncovered and nobody challenged their piety or chastity. Until the third/ninth century – and perhaps even after that – women were entitled to pray in the mosques together with the men. However, the early commentators and Qur'an exegetes – most of whom were Persians, where a thick veil for women was known and worn several centuries before Islam – demanded more covering from women than stipulated by the Qur'an (see *Ḥawādith al-duhūr fi mada al-ayyām waᵓl-shuhūr*, by Ibn Taghrībirdī, who attributed the origins of the harem system in Islam to the Persians), and imposed on all Muslim women what the Qur'an imposed on the wives of the Prophet and his daughters. Their reasoning was that it is desirable for all to follow their example.

17 Q. 2:106: "*We do not abrogate a verse or cause it to be forgotten except that We bring forth [one] better than it or similar to it. Do you not know that Allah is over all things competent?*"

that occurred since the first/seventh century. Furthermore, the governments and scholars would not need to resort to hypocrisy and sophistry, or to turn a blind eye to conflicting interpretations, for example, when calling for the abolition of slavery which is permitted by Islam, or when replacing the *ḥadd* punishment of amputating the hands of thieves as stipulated by the provisions of *Sharīʿa* with imprisonment.

Adopting this way of thinking will reduce the number of our educated youth who abandon Islam in its entirety, claiming that religions and traditions belong in museums and are only for tourists to marvel at because they do not meet the needs of the times. It will then be easier to convince them that religions and traditions are not an obstacle to progress, but could indeed be a key to it.

Historical Honesty

Our primary duty is historical honesty. The same courage shown by religious people willing to sacrifice their lives for their faith could also be displayed by them in confronting history honestly, regardless of how bitter it may be, and abandoning the romanticism that characterises and deforms their perception of their history. While faith may indeed move mountains, knowledge alone is capable of moving these mountains to their proper place.

Islam taught the early Muslims – and taught them brilliantly at that – how to meet the challenges of the times in which they lived. Any scholar who succeeds in showing us how to meet the challenges of our time in the spirit of Islam is the best Muslim of our time. We will owe him the greatest debt of gratitude.

As for the attempt by some people – such as the philosopher Iqbal[18] – to console themselves by stating that the hope for Muslims is for Europeans to destroy themselves in a global war started by them, this is nothing but a delusion of the feeble-minded that no Muslim who respects himself and his religion can accept.

If we are asked "why Islam?", we reply that it is a religion under whose umbrella members of our society can be both ethical and creative, and that

18 Sir Muhammad Iqbal (1877–1938), was a famous Indian poet, philosopher, politician, academic, barrister and scholar and one of the most important figures of Urdu literature. He is known as the "Spiritual Father of Pakistan".

we therefore have to find Islamic solutions to social and political problems rather than Western solutions. We have seen how those of us who believed the words of the West, "Follow me, and your problems will be solved," have now discovered that the West was not sincere in this claim at any given point in time, and that most of those who followed that call ended up with even bigger problems.

However, we have to realise that the problems of our era cannot be solved by running away from them or ignoring them, otherwise the call for Islam in our society, despite its greatness, would have ended up like Savonarola's call.[19] Islam – as it was at the time of its advent – should be directed to the solution of timely problems. A vision presented to us by our scholars and intellectuals is much needed today to navigate the new path. However, no benefit can be derived from this vision except in an atmosphere of intellectual freedom without terrorisation or coercion, where open and honest scientific discussions can take place without insults or accusations of heresy and *takfir*. Banning or censoring free, bold opinions to please one group or the other will put a stop to the pursuit of solutions, and our society will stagnate in a position that does not satisfy friend or foe.

19 Girolamo Savonarola (1452–1498) was an Italian Dominican friar, preacher and reformer active in Florence. He became popular and famous for denouncing clerical corruption, and the despotic rule of the Medici in Florence, as well as the exploitation of the poor. After the Florentines expelled the ruling Medici, he established a religious democratic republic in Florence with himself at its head. However, an alliance between Pope Alexander VI in Rome and Duke Ludovico of Milan, as well as internal opposition resulted in his defeat in 1489, when he was arrested, tortured, tried and burned to death.

10
The Awaited Mahdi in Contemporary Times

Certain attitudes which are the natural product of Bedouin life imposed themselves on the urban and rural peoples of the countries conquered by the Muslim armies, despite going against the basic attitudes and natures of the agricultural communities or urban populations. This victory of Arab Bedouin ideologies was the result of two key factors:

First: Islam – after the conquests – quickly turned from just being a religion to being a culture and a way of life, a methodology and a basic attitude towards existence, which swept the Islamic state (or states) from Andalusia to the west of China. Contributing to its dissemination was the large number of inter-marriages and the movement of Muslim individuals throughout the *Dār al-Islām* for Ḥajj, trade or work, to visit, or to learn *ḥadīth* and the sciences, or to participate in the conquests and invasions. Hence, the Muslim Empire became a melting pot in which all the various elements were mingled and fused together, including the Arab Bedouins and the Bedouins of North Africa.

Second: certain factors prevailed among all Islamic nations; the most important one being the political circumstances, thus reinforcing certain attitudes which were in common with those of the Bedouins, even if the latter were not its direct source.

Take, for example, the tendency to believe in fate and destiny. It is easy to discern the roots and causes of this attitude among the Bedouins. The lives of the Bedouins were completely dependent on water and pasture – rain signified survival and drought annihilation. Yet a Bedouin had no control over either of these things. Moreover, while travelling in the desert with his camels and cattle looking for pastures, he could get lost and go around in circles or be attacked by other tribes seeking to pillage his possessions. In a matter of moments, he would go from being healthy and wealthy to losing all he owned in this world, including food and water-skins, and he would find himself nearing death and starvation.

Al-Mutanabbī writes:

> Come evening he rolled out silk for them in greeting
> But next morning he covered them in dust sheeting

From the above, we can also understand a Bedouin writing verses such as:

> In the blink of an eye,
> God changes one state to another.[1]

But how should we understand such a verse, or a proverb such as: "*fī yadik wa yuqsam li ghayrik*",[2] when it is uttered by an Egyptian or Iraqi peasant? How can we explain the thought process and attitude behind it, when this peasant is confident that the seeds he has sowed in one season will produce a crop that will be harvested the following season, while planning ahead by building dams and the like to alleviate the dangers that may threaten it?

The contact with Bedouins is not the only reason for such a fatalistic attitude. It can also be attributed to the authoritarian rule that prevailed in all Islamic countries, which resulted in a situation for the urban and rural populace similar to that of the Bedouins in the desert: a formidable force that renders them completely helpless. Therefore, even non-Bedouins adopted attitudes similar to those of the Bedouins. The pages of our history books are replete with stories about people who were suddenly taken from the safety of their bed at night to be dragged in front of the governor or caliph and sentenced to death. The condemned, while facing the sword of his executioner, might

1 These verses were ascribed to an anonymous poet and quoted in the 304th night in the book *A Thousand and One Nights*.

2 Literally the proverb means: "You may have something in your hand, but then fate decrees that it goes to someone else." It has a similar meaning to the English proverbs: "Many a slip between the cup and the lip" or "Don't count your chickens before they hatch." It implies that even when a good outcome or conclusion seems certain, things can still change or go wrong.

then quote a Qur'anic verse, causing the governor's tears to flow, or he might crack a joke or make a comic comment causing the caliph to laugh, "stomp his feet and then fall on his back in laughter".[3] As a result, the man would be released and invited to the governor or caliph's council. He might even be rewarded with a house, an Arabian horse or a couple of slave girls. Conversely, can we forget Ibn al-Muqaffa^c who penned his *Risalat al-Ṣaḥāba* (*Epistle on the Caliph's Entourage*), giving advice to the ^cAbbāsid Caliph al-Manṣūr,[4] in anticipation, perhaps, of praise or inclusion in the caliph's inner circle, or to be granted wealth? Instead, he was dragged to the caliph only to have his limbs chopped off one after another, and grilled in front of him until he died!

On the subject of the "Awaited Imam", two divergent positions emerged in the Muslim world: the first was a negative, servile position, resulting from the frequent failures of revolutionary movements and the relentless persecution claiming the lives of thousands upon thousands. This created a sense of helplessness and resignation, a tendency to dispense with the idea that humans can bring about change, and instead to rely on God to bring change in the right time by sending the Mahdi, who will settle all matters to the best outcome and redeem the world.

The second position was revolutionary. Its adherents believe that "*Allah does not change the condition of a people until they change their own condition*"[5] and that a believer should first work on himself, and only then will God help him succeed in his endeavours. Therefore, struggling for the sake of change

3 Several anecdotes citing such a scene are recorded in *Kitāb al Aghānī* by al-Iṣfahānī; in *al-^cIqd al-Farīd* by Ibn ^cAbd Rabbih (246–328 AH/860–940 AD), who was a Andalusian writer, anthologist and poet; as well as in *Nawādir al-Aṣma^cī* by ^cAbd al-Malik b. Quraib al-Aṣma^cī (121–216 AH/740–831 AD), who was an Arab scholar, grammarian, philologist, anthologist and one of the earliest Arabic lexicographers. The caliph in the anecdotes differed from one anecdote to another. This uncontrolled laughter was attributed to Harūn al-Rashīd, al-Ma^ɔmūn, al-Mutawakkil, al-Mu^ctaṣṣim and al-Mu^ctaḍ interchangeably.

4 Abū Muhammad ^cAbd Allāh Rūzbih ibn Dādūya, known as Ibn al-Muqaffa' (106–142 AH/724–759 AD), was originally called Rōzbih pūr-i Dādōē and was a Persian translator, thinker and author, writing predominantly in Arabic, best known for his work *Kalīla wa Dimna*, which is similar to *Aesop's Fables*, as well as *Kitāb ādāb al-kabīr* (*The Major Work on Secretarial Etiquette*). In his *Risalat al-Ṣaḥāba,* he addresses the specific problems facing the new ^cAbbāsid ruler, who remains unnamed yet is identifiable as Abū Ja^cfar al-Manṣūr.

5 This is based on Q. 13:11: "*For his sake there are angels following one another, before him and behind him, who guard him by Allah's commandment; surely Allah does not change the condition of a people until they change their own condition; and when Allah intends evil to a people, there is no averting it, and besides Him they have no protector.*"

against existing unjust conditions is but a prelude to the emergence of the "Awaited Imam".

In any case, what we find particularly intriguing is that the idea of the "Awaited Imam" still persists to this very day. Moreover, it is one of the most prominent features of political thought among Muslims, as well as among those Christians who were affected by this "Islamic" view as a result of centuries of co-existence with Muslims. It is popular even among those whose enthusiasm for the religion has waned and those who have completely abandoned their religion.

This idea is based on the fact that the death or ousting of a ruler, and sometimes even the fall of a cabinet, invariably produces a feeling among the people that a great change is imminent, and that, "in the blink of an eye, God changes one state to another", things will improve, and the world will be filled with light and justice, just as it was filled with darkness and oppression. Yet when the new ruler assumes the reins of power, darkness is not dispelled, injustice is not corrected, and oppression does not stop. The hope is then postponed until a third ruler, the next "Awaited Imam", comes. Hope is then revived again, and again it is crushed, only to be revived again and crushed with the fourth, the fifth and so on and so forth.

Undoubtedly, the magnitude of these wholly unrealistic and illogical expectations attached to each new ruler by their subjects constitutes a substantial injustice to the new ruler. In fact, the tyranny and excessive centralisation of the systems of governance in many Islamic countries are responsible for the misconception among the people that all aspects of their lives are subject to the will of the ruler, and, accordingly, that a change of government must lead to a change in all their affairs. Often people forget that the ruler inherits from his predecessor a legacy burdened with debt, and that many of the problems may not be related to the government. The new ruler emerges and he is "like one riding a lion, everyone envies and fears him, yet he fears the beast he is riding".[6] All eyes are on this new ruler and everyone is waiting to see what he will charm out of his hat with a swift movement of his wand. God knows that the hat is often as empty as the heart of Mūsa's (Moses) mother,[7] and that the wand may have been retrieved from a dustbin on the road. When nothing comes out of

6 This is a passage quoted from Ibn al-Muqaffa's book *Kalīla wa Dimna.*

7 This metaphor is based on Q. 28:10: "*And the heart of Moses' mother became empty [of all else] and she would have betrayed him if We had not fortified her heart, that she might be of the believers.*"

the hat, surprised whispers ensue, followed by murmurs of resentment, then cries of anger.

The ruler is therefore not to blame, unless he contributed to the raised hopes and expectations among his subjects through remarks and promises he made in the early days of his reign. Unfortunately, new rulers often do just that. However, they can be excused for that, too. Even though the ruler might appear to have great power and might, he often finds himself driven to committing acts and making statements he can hardly believe in himself, and might even deny and reject. However, faced with the expectations and suggestive power of the masses, he may find himself swept by a current that washes him away, even if to an onlooker he might appear to be leading the masses and paving the way. The authoritarian governments in the East have made it easier for this to happen to any ruler, and for any ruler to start his rule uttering statements such as "I will eradicate this and that", "I will do so and so", "such and such an era has ended and it is a new dawn for this and that", "we have inaugurated the 'Corrective Revolution'," [8] "we have reinstated the rule of law", "the world will be filled with the light of justice, just as it was filled with injustice when my predecessor ruled".

There are two other characteristics that we inherited from the Arab Bedouins that made it easier for the ruler to make such unrealistic promises and utter exaggerations beyond measure:

The first characteristic: faith in the magical power of the word. The word has, for us, the same enchanting function known to the Arabs in *Jahiliyya*, when the poet used to string his words into poems before the outbreak of any battle between his tribe and its enemies. In his poem, he would praise and celebrate the victory of his people as if they actually were victorious. He would describe the disgrace and humiliation inflicted on the enemy, as if talking about something that had taken place in the past. In all of this, the poet was assuming the position of a magician with his spells and mysterious murmurs, just as superstitious people today stick needles into a doll resembling the image of their enemy, as if this action would instantly cause harm to that person. Similarly, to this day, our people subconsciously believe that when their rulers talk about prosperity, this will satiate them, as if their

8 The "Corrective Revolution" was launched on 15 May 1971 by President Anwar Sadat. It was a reform programme and a change in policy, purging the government, institutions and security forces from Nasserists.

bellies were filled to the brim. If the rulers rant about future victories, they believe that the enemy was thrown into the sea a long time ago.[9] Such things have a pleasant, calming effect, until the next day comes with even greater poverty and hunger, and it is our fate to drown in the sea.

The second characteristic: focusing on today only, at the expense of tomorrow; may tomorrow bring what it brings ("but today let me live",[10] "whoever had his lunch and worried about his dinner is from among the disbelievers" and "who knows what tomorrow may bring?").[11]

It was narrated that once upon a time a sultan demanded of Juha[12] that he teach a donkey to talk for his amusement within a year, and paid him a huge amount of money. If he failed, he would be put to death. When he was asked why he had accepted, he answered: "A year is a long time. Either the Sultan will die, or the donkey will die, or I will die."

It has already been mentioned that the Bedouin in *Jahiliyya* was unable to predict what will happen tomorrow, nor whether he will be covered with sheeting of silk or of dust. Today, a German or Swiss could plan his annual vacation on the island of Mallorca during the second half of June in five years' time. Meanwhile, the servants of God in our countries "*never say of*

---

9 The phrase "throwing the Jews into the sea" has been used by Arab politicians and leaders repeatedly. To name a few examples: Hassan al-Banna, founder of the Muslim Brotherhood, was quoted by the *New York Times* in 1948 saying "If the Jewish state becomes a fact, and this is realised by the Arab peoples, they will drive the Jews who live in their midst into the sea"; Gamal Abdel-Nasser addressed the Palestine Club in Alexandria in 1953 saying: "At our meetings and in our speeches, we said we were going to throw the Jews into the sea, and felt reassured after every speech. Then we all went back home"; Dr Fadhil Jamali, the Iraqi Representative to the United Nations, speaking to the Arab League in 1955 said: "The highest official in the League said that with 300 soldiers or North African Volunteers we could throw the Jews into the sea. The war started and His Excellency then said that with 3,000 North African Volunteers we could throw them into the sea."

10 This sentence is taken from the refrain of one of the songs by the iconic Umm Kulthum called "amal ḥayātī" ("The Hope of my Life"), which says in full: "Take all my love away . . . but today . . . but today . . . let me live."

11 All these are based on proverbs or sayings.

12 Juha is a fictitious, whimsical, mischievous character in Arab folktales and anecdotes. His tales are narrated through the ages and from many cultures. There are Arabic, Albanian, Armenian, Berber, Bosnian, Bulgarian, Chinese, Daghestani, Greek, Judeo-Arabic, Kurdish, Maltese, Macedonian, Persian, Serbian, Sicilian, Syrian, Tajik, Turkish, Uighur and Uzbek sources for his tales. He is also known as Nasreddin, Si Je'ha, Giufa, Ieha, Iugale, Gahan, Nastradin, Nastradi, Hojas, Jiha, Juha, Khodja, Mala, Apendi, Afandi and Effendi depending on the region and culture, yet the tales are almost identical.

anything 'I will certainly do it tomorrow,' without adding: 'If Allah wills'!"[13] Who knows, maybe a snitch will denounce us to the authorities so we will lose our job; maybe we will board a bus to a place for a picnic, where a brawl will break out that will land us at the police station with some political detainees, so we will all be sent to a detention camp; or maybe a new high-rise building, built from dust after the owner paid the appropriate bribes to the authority for issuing a building permit, will collapse with all of us in it.

In short, the rulers of our countries can make any promises, any pledges or vows they desire. They can forge any statistics and change the numbers; they can portray the economic conditions as rosy, such that they could not possibly be any better. They could inform us that we now lend money to the International Monetary Fund, when in the era of their predecessors – God forbid – we used to borrow from it. The gullible among us may think that these rulers are audacious, and that the truth will eventually have to come out. But how wrong we would be!

While that ruler is making these empty promises, he is thinking: "No one can guess what will happen tomorrow . . . Is it not possible that the United States will bestow billions of dollars on us tomorrow, so that the balance of payments will even out? Is not it possible that tomorrow we will discover oil fields bigger and more yielding than those of Kuwait? What else could the phrase 'what was not taken into account' mean? Isn't the Almighty God capable of changing any situation? Isn't it conceivable that before the truth comes out and people know that the International Monetary Fund has not received a loan from us, I may die or be assassinated? Then the problem of transparency and accountability will become my successor's problem and not mine!"

This is exactly the situation our people find themselves in every now and then: the ruler who promised them certain victory died suddenly of a heart attack before victory was achieved. *Malesh*[14] and never mind. The ruler

13 This is based on Q. 18.23–24: Q. 18.23: *"Never say of anything 'I will certainly do it tomorrow',"* Q. 18.24: *"without adding: 'If Allah wills!' And if you forget to say this, then call your Lord to mind and say: 'I hope that my Lord shall guide me and bring me ever closer than this to the Right Way'."*

14 *Malesh* is a colloquial Egyptian exclamation with a wealth of mischievous sub-texts, which is usually, for lack of a concise counterpart in English, translated as "No matter!" or "never mind!" It is often used sympathetically, in the sense of "that's tough", or "never you mind" or "there, there". But it also frequently serves as a somewhat cryptic apology, along the lines of "sorry" used as a concept offering regret and saving face at the same time when things do not run smoothly. It can also be used as noun to denote indifference and slackness.

who promised them great prosperity and welfare in such and such year was unfortunately assassinated before that year came. *Malesh* and never mind. The populace survive those rulers and are left bewildered, with open mouths, wondering: how was that ruler surprised by a heart attack? How dare he die before prosperity ensued? Whom can we hold accountable for these promises? The new ruler? He did not make those promises and he is not related to his predecessor. On the contrary, he has come to correct the wrongs, and to admit to his people that the economic situation is dire. His predecessor's policy may to blame, however, how do we get his predecessor back?

However, praise be to God, the new rulers in our Islamic countries often do come with new, realistic economic plans. Henceforth – we convince ourselves – all the facts will be presented to the people. The rulers will not fool anyone or cover up any defects. The overall structure of our economy is – praise be to God – generally healthy, as some foreign experts have asserted. With hard work, intensive production, and by pursuing a policy of "developmental rationalisation" instead of the previous policy of "rationalised development"[15] that proved to be unsuccessful, we can achieve miracles. We can finally achieve the elusive prosperity and welfare for all segments of the population. Next year . . . or the next . . . or in four years . . . within four years, either the sultan will die, or the donkey will die, or I will die.

So once again the path is a new one. The populace should obey and see what the outcome will be. If in the past they tried four different ways that only led to ruin, there is no harm in trying a fifth one. God willing, maybe, He will do what is good for us. We said that the first ruler was the "Awaited Imam", but he was not, and neither were the second, the third or the fourth. However, this is not proof that the fifth ruler is not the "Awaited Imam". Let us follow him, for he may fill the world with light and justice.

I believe that this very point is the crux of the problem and the real danger. One of Pavlov's[16] experiments showed that if you put dog food in a white box among different coloured boxes, the dog will examine all boxes until he finds his treat in the white one. The next day he will first head to the white box. However, if the food was put in the red box this time, the dog will

15 Obviously "developmental rationalisation" and "rationalised development" are made-up policies and a play on words.

16 Ivan Petrovich Pavlov (1849–1936) was a Russian physicist, mathematician, scientist and physiologist known primarily for his work in classical conditioning and involuntary reflex actions.

examine all boxes until he finds his treat in the red box. On the third day the dog will start with the red one. If on that day the food was deposited in the yellow box, the dog will examine them all until he finds it in the yellow box. If you pick a fourth colour on the fourth day, the dog will start, from the fifth day onward, to check all the boxes in no particular order, even if the food is placed every day, henceforward and forever, in the black box.

It seems that the theory applies to people like it applies to dogs. The populace, which keeps shifting its faith and aspirations from one ruler to the other, believing him to be the "Awaited Mahdi" or shifting its hope for reform from one government to another, believing it to be the *one* good government, only to have its hope in these rulers or governments crushed again and again, and who repeatedly discovers that following one leader after another or one government after the next, is futile and only leads to one calamity after another, will inevitably lose confidence in everything around them completely. They will not know what and whom to believe, what may actually happen and what never will, and whom to praise or condemn. It is then that they will either resemble a mad, decrepit person or a feather in the wind. Then one day another person will come – I am not saying that he is the "Awaited Mahdi", but someone who has a reasonable idea for reform. He will motion the people to embark on a course of reform, however, they will stare at him stupidly without understanding what is being said. For a moment it might seem like the populace is about to make some kind of movement, then it changes its mind, yawns, turns its face away, and continues to just sit there, lethargic and motionless.

11

A Plea for Religious Reform[1]

May God help me to thank you for writing what you wrote. May He show you the correct path and help you show it to others. May He make you and me able to carry the weight of knowledge and make us from among those who say the truth, live by it, preserve it and seek to deliver it to its people, preferring it above all else and suffering for its sake.

I have known you since we were young. I have studied your morals and your nature. I have assessed you and determined your worth. Your conviviality has increased my desire for your friendship, and the length of our companionship has increased my appreciation for you. Therefore, it is not surprising that I was unhappy when I sensed the anger in your recent letter concerning my articles about religion, or rather, the methodology I have used in these articles. However, I am claiming that your anger is not my fault; and that this claim is not a crime.

I know that you are the type of person who forgives mistakes and seeks to reform the person who has committed them. I also know that when you see something that is right, you comprehend it, promote and nurture it. I have heard you repeatedly quoting one of al-Shāfiᶜī's sayings, may God be pleased with him, "I have never debated with anyone wishing him to be

1 *Translators' Note*: this chapter takes the form of a reply to a – real or imaginary – letter received from a friend of the author's in response to the publication of the previous chapters as articles. In it, the author replies to accusations and offers some explanations for his motives and ideas for reform. It is written in the flowery language commonly used by early Islamic orators and in official communications.

wrong. I have never spoken to anyone caring about whether God chooses to show the truth through his tongue or mine." Therefore, I ask you to permit me to pen some lines as a reply and defence, and to explain to you a truth which I have learned through experience and trials, not by merely studying and looking into books.

I would like you to know that my defence is not the result of pride and a reluctance to acknowledge an error made. I may make mistakes while writing, just like a father might make a mistake while bringing up his son. I am not like the debaters of our time, whose faces turn red with rage when they are refuted and when the truth comes from their opponents rather than them. If I am able to present my arguments well, then this is a small feat next to your kindness, as you were the driving force for my argument and the reason for its inception. Therefore the greater reward and the stronger motive are yours.

The Mummy's Wrappings

You say – may God bless you and grant you His mercy – that you have sensed in my articles some apprehension and reluctance to fully disclose the full truth, and a tendency to use politeness and circumvention which, if they serve the purposes of politicians and diplomats, are certainly not qualities a religious reformer should possess. Then you whispered into my ear that a number of my positions and views, known to you through the many conversations that took place privately between us, seem changed, as if wearing a thousand masks, when they were finally published. These views, which I have chosen to make public to the believers, appear to be covered in wrappings like a mummy. They appear to be taking one step forward and one back, as if they were seeking to reveal and conceal themselves at the same time, showing their faces and obscuring them. You said – may God protect you – that my presentation of these views, even if it does not qualify as lying and deceit, lacks the complete honesty adhered to by someone following his calling, as well as the flames that burn in the writings of the revolutionary reformer.

I have allowed myself here to turn your whispers into a shout, and to announce what you have confided in me. I hope that I was not wrong when I interpreted your whisper as an attempt on your part to preserve my reputation so that it does not get tarnished, in consideration of our friendship and the bonds of brotherhood. This is an interpretation that puts the decision into my hands on whether or not I choose to keep your words secret or make them public. I am grateful to you for your extreme care and concern. However, I choose to make it public, trusting in my good intentions, and firmly believing that I am not one to promote lies or seek favour through falsehoods. God help us and save us of these two ills, and may He grant us the happiness gained from serving him and obtaining His satisfaction.

You wrote saying that the value of deconstruction sometimes exceeds the value of construction, and that scepticism is as important and useful as faith. For how can one accept the truth as a doctrine when one's mind and heart are still filled with much falsehood? You said there is no way to cleanse the people except by clearing popular religion from all the superfluous illusions and superstitions and by purifying the faith from all that which has marred and defiled it. Wisdom is like a bride who wants her house empty. The heart, once emptied of the repugnant, can be filled with the praiseworthy. If the soil is cleaned of the weeds, plants, herbs and flowers can grow, but if the weeds are not rooted out, nothing else will sprout. You said that if someone was willing to undertake the task of guiding people to the truth, he first of all needs to start to address these impurities in their faith and eradicate them. One cannot construct a building without first clearing the plot and removing all the refuse from it. If someone should exclaim that the removal of such false doctrines adopted and loved by the public because they gave them solace, comfort and happiness is a cruel act, then we should reply that this is tough love out of care for their welfare and compassion, and may God forgive us for causing them such pain. You asked which of the two is more important and should be given the utmost care: raising suspicion or instilling certainty, clearing the site or building the edifice?

Illusions of the Public

In your letter, you proceeded to list many examples of illusions of the public: such as the sanctification of the *awliyāʾ* in contradiction to the doctrine of the unity and oneness of God; the adherence to traditions that were falsely attributed to the Prophet; labelling each evolution that aims at coping with the needs of the times an innovation and heresy; calling mystical and other non-mystical doctrines and groups as Islamic; or interpreting the Qur'an in such an audacious way that leads only to one conclusion, namely, that the Qur'an does not mean what it says, but says what they mean! You said that this nonsense and other absurdities require a tireless and dedicated cleansing effort. You also said that it also requires the elite of pious thinkers to come together, and to make great efforts that know neither fatigue nor boredom, in addition to fearless honesty and strict rigorousness, unrestrained by neither mercy nor courtesy.

You have presented all this with an eloquence that any articulate person would be loath to ignore. Your letter included a vast amount of knowledge that no scholar would hesitate to draw from. The sharpness of your words is a characteristic that does not insult, as long as its motive is loyalty to the religion. Moreover, it has resulted from anger at those fantasies, myths and legends that you mentioned and which are the largest obstacles that have hampered and continue to hamper the Muslim nations from achieving progress and from understanding their present. They also cripple them and prevent them from catching up with other civilised nations. You then widened the scope and intensity of this harshness, and I felt that I was touched by its flames. For you described me, and others like me, as disgraced, both in this world and the Hereafter. You called us the compromisers, and those occupying *al-manzila bayna al-manzilatayn*.[2] You called us many other such adjectives, the kindest of which are neglectful, stalling, guarded and fearful. You accused us of wanting to speak out, saying what we know, and then being forced by fear to supress it. You said that in our writings we debate the fools, and that those who are wise usually lose their mind when discussing with fools. The most appropriate description is one of al-Buḥturī's[3] verses:

> I carve the rhymes out of each syllable
> so what if to the cows it is unintelligible

You concluded your letter saying that knowledge prohibits us from keeping it to ourselves, and encourages us to disclose it to the people. In addition,

---

2 *Al-manzilah bayna al-manzilatayn* (lit. the position between the two positions, meaning the intermediate position). It was the fourth of the five principal doctrines of the Muᶜtazalis. These five principal doctrines constituted their basic tenets. It means that they will not label anybody as believer or unbeliever, as God is the only one who can judge a person. Hence, a *fāsiq* (i.e., someone who commits one of the "greater sins") is neither considered a *muʾmin* (believer) nor a *kāfir* (infidel or disbeliever). *Fisq* then is an intermediary state between belief and disbelief. Muᶜtazalis adopted this position as a middle ground between the Kharijites and Murjiᶜites.

3 Al-Walīd b. ᶜUbayd Allāh al-Buḥturī (205–284 AH/820–897 AD) was a famous Arab poet during the ᶜAbbāsid era.

just as any ignorant person should not resign himself to his ignorance, a learned person should not hide his knowledge. You have quoted the Prophet saying: "*When God granted the scholars knowledge he enjoined on them a vow, just as he did with the prophets, to share this knowledge and not to hide it.*" If there are some scholars who secretly mock the public's illusions, they are partly to blame for the spread of these superstitions if they remain silent. How can silence be useful when its uses do not leave the scholar's head? How can silence be useful when God sent his prophets with an oral message and not with silence? You wondered: if the scholar remains silent in pursuit of safety, and the ignorant remain unaware, when will the truth be known?

Straightening What is Skewed

Your letter, which I have summarised here, violently shook me, and the words dropped out of my pen in response. If you believe that summarising your arguments in this concise form weakens them and their meaning, then please accept my apology and grant me your forgiveness. If you consider my short reply a deviation from the goal, then I am to blame. Either way, acknowledgement is due to you, because this dialogue would not have been possible without your initiative.

I begin by saying that although I do not consider myself to have reached the level of scholars, I am not one of those who remain silent and who keep what I know to myself. Never have I chosen safety. If I were one to conceal things seeking my own safety, then I would not be in the state of hardship I am in today, and I would not be facing the pressures I am under due to my writings, despite the strength of my arguments and the proofs I supply. Rest assured then that the truth remains the *Qibla*[4] of my heart. The trials that God willed me to face have removed the dim mist that covered my eyes. The confusion of a teenager and the wonder of a fool have given way to the understanding of an adult and the perspective of the prudent. I realised that the truth in the intellectual's heart, while he sits at home thinking, can turn into a falsehood when he decides to take it to the market, and to spread it among the public, to straighten that which is skewed and to expose the absurd superstitions.

4 The *Qibla* (lit. direction) is the direction Muslims face during prayers. It is fixed as the direction of the Ka'ba in Mecca.

Allow me to try to dispel the ambiguity of this last phrase, as it is not easy to understand its intent, except for the one who took it upon himself to pursue this aim. You say in your letter that I am more concerned with educating than I am with promoting the truth. However, I claim that the gradual and progressive education of the public is the only way to purify their beliefs, and to take them closer to the desired goal. Confronting them at once with the pure, unadulterated truth, with all the impurities removed, would render education incapable of helping them reach that truth. It is then that we have the right to hold the caller accountable for his methodology and for neglecting to ask himself before he embarked on spreading his message: was it more appropriate for me to remain isolated in my home and to keep what truth my wisdom and my mind have guided me to, leaving the public mired in their illusions, or was it my duty to bring the public step by step closer to this truth, taking their naiveté and gullibility into account, acknowledging their preference for physical objects, and knowing the difficulty of perceiving the honest truth from among such impurities?

Addressing the Prophet in Q. 3:159, God said: ". . . *and had you been rough, hard hearted, they would certainly have dispersed from around you . . .*"[5] It has also been narrated that the Prophet said: "*This religion is solid, so proceed into it gently, a budding plant neither cuts the ground nor does noon last.*" The Prophet himself was the best and most perfect example of patience and endurance. He was the most knowledgeable about human nature and the most compassionate when tenderly taking the believers' hands as he moved them from phase to phase. He was the most knowledgeable about the requirements of wisdom and diplomacy, always committed to the ultimate goal he envisioned. He was more aware than anyone, before or since, that politics, civility and diplomacy are required to spread the faith. He was also very much aware that instilling a new belief requires a large degree of compassion and leniency. He never shocked the feelings of the people of *Jahilliya*. The Qur'an did not descend all at once for him to inform the idolaters about it, nor did he hold back from appeasing the hypocrites and those weak of faith and hearts by charity and giving. He knew full well

5 The full verse reads Q. 3:159: "*Thus it is due to mercy from Allah that you deal with them gently, and had you been rough, hard hearted, they would certainly have dispersed from around you; pardon them therefore and ask pardon for them, and take counsel with them in the affair; so when you have decided, then place your trust in Allah; surely Allah loves those who trust.*"

that there was no contradiction between complete knowledge and showing consideration for the nature of human beings around him. He knew that progression and a gradual divulging of the truth to achieve guidance and enlightenment are not necessarily limitations on the truth, nor do they obscure it. He also knew that in this world full of ignorance, sin and other shortcomings in the human psyche, there has to be a middle way between the pursuit of justice and truth and the possibility of enduring imperfections, as well as a blending of knowledge and wisdom. We have heard of Christ's advice to his disciples to be shrewd as snakes,[6] and not to throw pearls before the swine.[7] I have no doubt that history has never known a prophet who divulged the entirety of his message to the masses of people and told them all what he knows at once.

Al-khāṣṣa wa-l-ᶜāmma *(the Elite and the Common People)*[8]

All the prophets taught their people what they could accept, comprehend and apply as long as they exerted some effort, employed their thinking ability and exercised a degree of self-restraint on their desires. However, there are also matters that can be grasped only by special minds chosen by God. These matters are shrouded in symbols and enveloped in secrets. There is a thick veil between them and the general public. They are matters that the general public is not in a position to benefit from or to follow. Forcing these matters onto them will have dire consequences of unknown limits. So, know – may God guide you – that there is some knowledge that the general public from among the believers should not be privy to. Some knowledge should be shunned, just as some or what is *ḥalāl* (permissible) should be shunned.

God Almighty said in His Holy Book: "*And do not give away your property which Allah has made for you a (means of) support to the weak of*

6 Matthew 10:16: "Look, I am sending you out like sheep among wolves; therefore be as shrewd as snakes and as innocent as doves."

7 Matthew 7:6: "Do not give dogs what is holy; do not throw your pearls before swine. If you do, they may trample them under their feet, and then turn and tear you to pieces."

8 While *al-ᶜāmma* always denoted the common people or the general public, *al-khāṣṣa* denoted the elite. However, the elite meant by that word changed in various eras, depending on the time and place, to mean the sultans, emirs, notables, high-ranking officials, judges and/or religious leaders privileged with knowledge.

understanding . . .",[9] alerting to the preservation of knowledge from those who may spoil and harm it. It is also an alert against the injustice of giving something to the undeserving, which is equal to depriving the deserving. The Prophet said: "*We the prophets were commanded to place people in their rightful positions and to talk to them according to their understanding.*" He also said: "*Anyone, who talks to people in a language they cannot comprehend, will cause a fitna (strife) to some of them.*" ᶜAlī b. Abū Ṭālib, pointing to his chest, said: "Here I hold stores and treasures of knowledge. I wish I could find somebody to share them with me. The hearts of the believers are graves holding secrets, which should not be divulged to the world, to each and every one." Al-Shāfiᶜī was once asked about an issue and he remained silent. He was then asked: "Won't you answer, may God have mercy on you?" He replied: "When I evaluate the value of my silence over that of my reply."

I would like to remind you that the tree that yields produces thick branches, and the plant that surrenders to the wind by bending with it survives. You may be a man who would rather break than bend and who refuses to see that the end may justify the means. You deem every obfuscation worthy of denunciation, even if it may eventually lead to the greater good. As for me, I believe that when the *nawāfil* (optional prayers) hurt the obligatory ones, it becomes necessary to reject them. I believe that a partial injustice is acceptable when it leads to greater justice. Don't you see that gold cannot be used by the people until it has been mixed with other metals? While religion is the ultimate truth, I claim that the broad masses are not able to accept it unless it takes on a more simplified version, accessible to their comprehension, indeed, unless it includes some impurities and superstitions. You might agree with me when I liken the truth of religion to some chemical elements that are in the gaseous form when pure, but if we want to preserve them or use them for medical purposes, it is necessary to mix them with other elements in order to turn them into a solid form, to prevent their dispersion into the air. Or I may liken the truth in religion to water, which cannot be kept except in a vessel. You and others like you,

9 Q. 4:5: "*And do not give away your property which Allah has made for you a (means of) support to the weak of understanding, and maintain them out of (the profits of) it, and clothe them and speak to them words of honest advice.*"

who are keen on promoting an honest unadulterated truth, are akin to the man who breaks the vessel to reach the water.

A man can overdo wisdom, just as he can overdo folly, virtue and sin. Many a good person had his call rejected for ignoring the lived reality. In fact, the lived reality, that you will not be able to deny, is that God has created people in various forms and with different abilities, and "*has made some of them to excel over others*".[10] Most of the human beings are those who "dirty the water, raise the prices and obstruct the roads".[11] The majority are dim-witted and focused on purely material concerns. In the past, al-Ḥasan al-Baṣrī said: "If all the people had minds, the world would be ruined." Their hard work in the various industries and the cultivation of the land will always be indispensable in order to satisfy the needs of the people. This painstaking physical work does not only deprive them of the opportunities to study, contemplate and reflect on the truth, it also causes a stagnation of the mind. It is the reason for a diminished intelligence, given what we know about the firm antagonism between mind and body. All of these – or the great majority of them – will continue to have an urgent need for a religious interpretation of this life, an acceptable, simplified solution to the puzzle of the universe, a simplified set of rules to guide their behaviour, and an ideology to offer them comfort in the abyss of misery, strength in the midst of conflict and solace in the face of death.

The Wooden Leg

The religious interpretation of this life must be simple, to be easily absorbed by those with weary minds and limited horizons. It is inevitable that these weary minds interject into this interpretation some impurities and false superstitions that they inherited generation after generation. The general

10 This is a portion of Q. 4:34: "*Men are the maintainers of women because Allah has made some of them to excel over others and because they spend out of their property; the good women are therefore obedient, guarding the unseen as Allah has guarded; and (as to) those on whose part you fear desertion, admonish them, and leave them alone in the sleeping-places and beat them; then if they obey you, do not seek a way against them; surely Allah is High, Great.*"

11 A saying attributed to Ṣaᶜṣaᶜah b. Suhān (d. 44 AH/666 AD), who when asked by Caliph Muᶜāwiya b. Abū Sufyān to describe people to him, replied: "God created people in different forms and with different abilities. Some of them were created to worship, others to engage in trade, yet others to preach and others to fight and save, but most are *rajraja* (scum or filth) dirtying the water, raising the prices and obstructing the roads."

public raises these false assumptions to a rank above good deeds and noble feelings, and finds it is easier to send a plea in supplication to the *awliyāʾ* than to seek help from a neighbour, and easier to cast a curse upon an unjust ruler than to resist such a mighty potentate. However, it is an indisputable fact that all this is a necessary evil, and an indispensable white lie. As long as this is the state of the majority of human beings, it is certain that they will not accept the religion unless they add all sorts of impurities, which they want, onto it. And woe and misfortune will afflict humanity if the majority decides to dispense with religion as a whole, once your attempt to purify it and dispel the superstitions is successful. The legless man benefits greatly from using a wooden leg to help him move around and seek out a living.

However, I hasten to deny your accusation that I am a pessimist. I have not abandoned the hope that humanity might, in time, near or far, and thanks to the dissemination of education and an enlightened careful call, and to the expanded use of machines which will reduce the burden of agricultural and industrial work, reach a degree of maturity that enables them to accept a religion devoid of superstition and nonsense, and even free of symbols and secrets. Only then will those fantasies that are fit for humanity only in its infancy stage, abandon mankind like a nanny bidding farewell to a child in her care that has grown and is ready to depart to school.

This is what I understood from your exhortations and your advice. I hope to have been successful in presenting what I believe will find your acceptance and understanding. May God help you to find the truth and open your heart to embrace it. May He inspire you to put justice above all else in your affairs, and to remain steadfast in your words and actions. May He open your eyes to fairness, and keep you from wrongdoing. May He allow you to be like the person meant by the sage who said: "Nobody has engaged in debate with the desire to realise the truth without ultimately changing his opinion!"

> *These examples, We set forth for men, and none understand them but the learned.*[12]
> *Ṣadaq Allah al-ᶜAzīm*[13]

---

12 Q. 29:43.

13 *Ṣadaq Allah al-ᶜAzīm* (lit. "God Almighty speaks the truth"). It is normally said at the end of any Qur'anic recitation except in prayer. It was counted amongst the etiquette of Qur'anic recitation.

Index

al-ᶜAbbās b. ᶜAbd al-Muṭṭalib, 46
ᶜAbbāsids, 8, 46, 79, 85, 86–7, 110, 124, 137n20, 151, 154–5, 162
ᶜAbd Allah b. Lahīᶜa, 32, 83n31
ᶜAbd Allah b. Masᶜūd (Abū ᶜAbd al-Raḥmān), 67–8, 79–80
ᶜAbd Allah b. ᶜUmar b. al-Khaṭṭāb, 81
ᶜAbd Allah b. Masᶜūd (*aḥādīth* fabricator) see al-Tamīmī al-Baṣrī, Ghayyāth b. Ibrāhīm
ᶜAbd Allah b. al-Zubayr, 77, 80
ᶜAbd al-Malak b. Marwān, Caliph, 77, 78
ᶜAbduh, Shaykh Muḥammad, 1, 8, 29, 174
Ābān b. ᶜUthmān b. ᶜAff ān, 43
Abū ᶜAbd al-Raḥmān (Companion) *see* ᶜAbd Allah b. Masᶜūd
Abū Bakr, Caliph, 125, 148n2
Abū Bakr 'Abd Allāh b. Abī Quḥāfah, (Abū Bakr al-Ṣiddīq), 18, 68n34, 80
Abu Hanifa (Numan b. Thabit al-Kufi), 85n40, 86, 89, 94, 96, 97–8, 165
Abū Hurayra al-Dawsī al-Yamānī, 81, 86
Abū Jahl *see* ᶜAmr b. Hishām
Abū Lahab, 61, 62, 63, 67, 70, 72
Abū-l-Dardāʾ, 100
Abū-l-Dhar al-Ghaff ārī, 100, 101
Abū Nuwās al-Ḥasan b. Hānī al-Ḥakamī, 91–2, 105
Abū Qābūs *see* al-Nuᶜmān b. al-Mundhir, Nuᶜmān III
Abu Rafi, 132
Abū Sufyān, 46, 70–1, 80
Abū Sulaymān, Khālid b. al-Walīd b. al-Mughīrah, 18–19
Abū Ṭālib, 64, 70, 77
Abū Turāb, 139, 140
Abū Yūsuf, (judge), 75n5, 96–7, 98, 165, 166–7
Abyssinia, 69
al-ᶜAdawiyya al-Qaysiyya, Rābiᶜa, 110n29
al-Afghanī, Sayyid Jamāl al-Dīn, 28, 174
aḥādīth (prophetic traditions), 2, 3, 29n17, 41, 73–98
  bawdiness and frivolity in, 91–3
  centenarians, 90–1
  compilations, 93–5
  and constitutional law, 17
  fabrication of, 37, 76–81, 86, 87–90, 93, 95–6, 98, 108
  impact of, 95
  isnād (chain of narration), 81–5, 88, 89, 91–2, 93–5
  about prophecies, 85–6
  storytellers', 87–90
  see also Sunna
ahl al-bayt (Prophet's household), 76, 104n7, 118
Aḥmad b. Muḥammad b. Ḥanbal *see* al-Shaybānī, Abū ᶜAbd Allāh
Aḥmad Shafīq Midḥat Pasha, 28
al-Ahram (magazine), 4, 5n10
ᶜAʾisha (3rd wife of the Prophet), 73
ᶜĀʾisha bint Ṭalḥa b. ᶜUbayd Allah, 186n16
al-Albānī, Muḥammad Nā ṣ ir al-Dīn, 29n17
al-Aᶜmash, Sulaymān b. Mahrān, 84
alcohol *see* drinking and drunkenness
al-Dīn al-Subkī, Tāj, 159
Aleppo, 137

Alfieri, Count Vittorio, 174
Algeria
  al-Ṭarīqah al-Tijānīyah (Sufi order), 116
  Islamic Salvation Front, 21
  see also Cherchell
ᶜAlī (son of the Prophet), 149, 150
Ali, Syed Ameer, 49
ᶜAli b. Abū Ṭālib, 46, 68, 76, 79, 90, 131, 132, 138, 146–7, 206
ᶜAlī b. Sulaymān, 85–6
ᶜAlīds, 79, 110
Amin, Ahmad, 1–3
  Hayati (My Life), 160–1
Amin, Hussein Ahmad
  criticism of, 4, 5
  education, 1
  influences, 8
  life, 1–2
  works, 1, 2, 4, 9, 10
ᶜAmr b. Hishām (Abū Jahl), 67n28
ᶜAmr b. Maymūn al-ᶜAwdī, 80
Anas b. Mālik, 96, 136
Andrae, Tor Julius Efraim, 55–6
angels, 129; *see also* Jibrīl
animals: sacrifice, 120n64, 121n65, 141–2; *see also* cats; dogs; donkeys
apostates, 145
al-Arab (magazine), 4
Arab League, 194n9
al-Arabi (magazine), 4, 5n10
Arabic language, 62, 168
Arabs
  expansion, 73–4
  Islamisation of, 135, 136
  study of sciences, 44
Arberry, Arthur John, 56–7
Arwā *see* Umm Jamīl bint Ḥarb
al-Asᶜad, Mundhir, 5n10
al-Asadī, Mūsa b. ᶜUqba, 43
asceticism, 100–1, 109
Ashᶜab b. Jubayr (al-Tammaᶜ), 92
al-ᶜAskarī, Muḥammad b. al-Ḥasan, 152
Asmāʾ bint ᶜUmays b. Maᶜād, 131–2
al-Aṣmaᶜī, ᶜAbd al-Malik b. Quraib, 191n3
Averroes, 180
Avicenna, 130n8
awliyāʾ (Sufi "saint"), 125–44
  definition, 132
  Egypt, 140–2
  karāmāt (miracles), 122, 132–5
  ranking of, 104–5
  sanctification of, 128–32, 201, 208
al-Aws (Banū Aws) tribe, 50n20, 72

al-Badawi, al-Sayyid, 140, 142–3
al-Bakkāʾī1 al-Kūfī, Abū Muḥammad Ziyād b. ᶜAbd Allah b. al-Ṭufayl al-ᶜĀmirī, 45
al-Banna, Hassan, 194n9
Banū ᶜAbd Shams clan, 67n30
Banū Aws tribe, 50n20, 72
Banū Hāshim, seige of, 67n31
Banū Hāshim clan, 64, 69, 70, 76
Banū Jumah clan, 67n29
Banū Makhzūm clan, 67n28
Banū al-Muṭṭalib clan, 70
Banū al-Naḍīr tribe, 45
Banū Nawfal clan, 72
Banū Qayla tribe, 72
Banū Qurayza tribe, 45, 50, 50n20
Banū Thaqīf clan, 72
Banū Umayya clan, 71, 77
Barqūq, Sultan, 143n38
Bashār b. Burd, 87–8
Basra, 86, 147
Bastet (goddess) *see* Bubastis
Battle of Badr, 63, 67nn28, 29, 30, 31
Battle of Muʾtah, 67n32
Battle of Tabūk, 91
Battle of Yamāmah, 68n34
Battle of Yarmūk, 136
al-Bazzāz al-Baghdādī, Abū Ḥamza, 110
Bedouins, 147, 185, 189–90, 194
El-Behairy, Islam, 10
Belhadj, Ali, 21n23

Bell, Richard, 55–6, 57
Bible: New Testament, 51; Matthew, 15n6, 103n3, 205n6, 7
Bible: Old Testament: Deuteronomy, 3, 50n20, 76; Judges, 15n5, 88
biography writing, 41–2
al-Bīrūnī, Abū Rayḥān Muḥammad b. Aḥmad, 126, 139
al-Bisṭāmī, Abū Yazīd Ṭayfūr b. ᶜĪsā b. Surūshān, 105, 105n9, 106nn16, 17
Blair, Tony, 22
blasphemy, 127
Blunt, Wilfrid Scawen, 174
books: "yellow books", 168
Al-Bouti, Mohamed Said Ramadan, 5n10
Bozorgmehr (Persian philosopher), 83
Bubastis (Bastet) (Egyptian goddess), 140
Buhl, Frants, 55–6
al-Buḥturī, al-Walīd b. ᶜUbayd Allāh, 202
al-Bukhārī, Abū'Abd Allāh, Muḥammad b. Ismāʿīl, 93
  Ṣaḥīḥ Muslim, 93n63, 94
Burji dynasty, 143n38
al-Bursī al-Ḥillī, Rajab b. Muḥammad b. Rajab, 118
Burton, Sir Richard Francis, 30
Bush, George W., 22

Cairo, 24, 142, 138
caliphs, 149
  Rightfully Guided Caliphs, 18, 43n3, 76n14
Carlyle, Thomas, 53–4, 59
Carr, E. H.: *What is History?,* 41–2
Catholic Church, 107
cats, 121, 140–1
censorship, 188
Centenarians, 90–1
children, 144n39, 159, 162
Christianity
  Africa, 51
  Arabian peninsula, 101
  collapse of confidence in, 26
  conversion to, 100, 128
  excommunication, 34
  influence on Sufism, 113
  Lord's Prayer, 109
  portrayal of Islam, 51–2
  religious co-existence, 33, 124
Christians
  authority figures, 110
  and "Awaited Imam", 192
  al-Buruni on, 126
  confrontations with Islam, 23–4, 44
  conversion to Islam, 153, 160
  isolationist, 32
  see also Catholic Church; Coptic Orthodox Church; Jehovah's Witnesses; Lutherans
clergy
  decline, 159–75
  hypocrisy, 31–2
  influence, 163
  see also imams
Clot, Antoine Barthelemy (Clot Bey), 30
Companions of the Prophet *see Ṣaḥāba*
Coptic Orthodox Church, 142n31
Copts, 86, 140
"Corrective Revolution", 193n8
Crusades, 24

al-Ḍaḥḥāk b. Muzāḥim, 67n27
Damascus, 118, 137, 138
Dante Alighieri: *The Divine Comedy,* 52
Dār al-Islām (Abode of Islam) movement, 146
"Dark Ages", 26
Daᶜwah, 123, 124, 145, 149, 181
democracy, 16–22
Dermenghem, Émile, 55
dervishes, 117
devil, 121
Dhul-Nūn al-Miṣrī, 105, 110, 134, 159
al-Disūqī, al-Sayyid Ibrāhīm, 142n33
al-Diyārbakrī1, Ḥusayn b. Muḥammad b. al-Ḥasan, 131–2

dogs, 9, 81, 129, 196–7
al-Doha (magazine), 4
donkeys, 140
Dozy, Reinhart, 149n5
drinking and drunkenness, 87, 100, 167
drugs *see* hashish
Druze, 156–7
Durant, Will, 180

education, 167–8; *see also* Islamic Studies; *kuttab*; *madrassas*; universities
Egypt
  al-Ṭarīqah al-Rifāᶜīyah (Sufi order), 117n49
  *awliyā*ᵓ, 140–2
  education, 167–8
  Islamic conquest of, 86
  marriage laws, 180n8
  reform, 28
  religious intolerance, 10
  "*Shaykh al-Shuyūkh*" ("Supreme Shaykh") system, 116
  Sufism, 101
  trees, 45, 138
  and Western civilisation, 30
  zar ritual, 120
  see also Cairo
Egyptians, ancient, 140–1
Eid al-Adha ("Festival of the Sacrifice"), 142n34
ethics, 124
European civilisation *see* Western civilisation

Fahd b.ʿAbd al-Azīz Āl Saʿūd, King of Saudi Arabia, 21
al-Fākihī, 186n16
*fanā*ᵓ (annihilation within God), 111, 112, 122
al-Fārisī, Salmān, 46
al-Fāsī, Yūsuf b. Muḥammad b. Yūsuf, 119
fasting, 87
fate, 189–90
fatwa (pl. *fatāwa),* 17, 143, 164, 166
festivals, 135–6, 142n34, 143
Fez, 86
fezzes, 160–1
fiqh see jurisprudence
fiqqi (derogatory term), 170, 175
fisq (state of belief), 202n2
fitna (strife), 161
Francis of Assisi, St, 36
Franks, 24
free will, 66, 153
Fundamentalists, 9, 19

Gabriel, angel *see* Jibrīl
Gabrielli, Francesco, 55
Gaudefroy-Demombynes, Maurice, 56
al-Ghazālī, Abū Ḥāmid Muḥammad b. Muḥammad, 5, 104, 112–13, 120, 130
ghulāt (extremists), 104n7, 110, 111, 112
Gibb, Hamilton, 56
Gibbon, Edward, 53, 54
Gnosis, 105n13
"God", idea of, 125, 152
Goldziher, Ignác (Yitzhaq Yehud), 55–6

Haddāwa (Sufi order), 121
al-Ḥadīd, Bab, 139
al-Ḥāfiz al-Bursī *see* al-Bursī al-Ḥillī, Rajab b. Muḥammad b. Rajab
Ḥafṣ b. Ghayyāth, 84
Hajj (pilgrimage), 62n2, 77–8, 144
al-Ḥajjāj, Muslim, 32n27
al-Ḥakīm (Sufi) *see* al-Warrāq al-Tirmidhī, Abū Bakr Muḥammad b. ᶜUmar
al-Hakim, Tawfiq, 175
al-Ḥallāj, al-Ḥusayn b. Manṣūr, 106, 106nn15, 18, 19, 20, 110, 112, 120
al-Ḥamawī, Yāqūt, 137
Ḥanafīs, 165
Ḥanbalīs, 113, 131, 154
Harīdī, Shaykh: tomb, 141, 142

al-Ḥārith al-Muḥāsibī, 108
al-Ri^c^āya li-ḥuqūq Allah, 107
Harsavardhana (Indian king), 91n54
Hārun al-Rashīd, 165, 166–7, 191n3
al-Ḥasan al-Baṣrī, 101, 110
al-Ḥasan b. ^c^Alī, 101, 150
hashish, 121
Hawwa, Sa'id, 20
Haykal, Muhammad Husayn: *The Life of Muhammad,* 50–1, 175
Hellenism, 33
Herbelot de Molainville, Bartélemy d', 106
heresy, 7, 9, 33, 108, 109, 149, 175
hermits, 144n39
al-Hilal (magazine), 4
Hishām b. ^c^Abd Allah, 96
history
early Muslim historians' concept of, 42
honesty in, 187–8
writing, 41
Hobsbawm, Eric: *The Age of Extremes,* 13
Howeidi, Fahmy, 5n10
Ḥudhayfa b. al-Yamān, 80, 85
hudūd (sing. *ḥadd*) (punishments), 166–7, 187
al-Hujwirī, Ali, 112
Kashf al-maḥjūb, 134
ḥulūl (union with God), 109, 112
humanism, 8, 10
al-Ḥunafā^ʾ^ *(Hanif)* (monotheists), 71, 100
Husayn, Taha, 2
al-Ḥusayn b. ^c^Alī, 136, 137, 138
Hussein, Yusry, 4

Ibn ^c^Abd al-Barr, 94
Ibn ^c^Abd Rabbih, 191n3
Ibn Aqil, 165
Ibn al-^c^Arabī al-Andalusī, Shaykh Muḥyī al-Dīn, 113–14, 118
Ibn ^c^Awf, ^c^Abd al-Rahman, 76
Ibn al-Ghayṭala, 64
Ibn al-Ḥanafiyyah, Muḥammad, 151
Ibn al-Jawzī, Abu^c^l-Faraj, 81, 160
Talbīs Iblīs (*The Devil's Deception*), 164
Ibn Ḥanbal, Aḥmad, 32n26, 96, 108, 156, 160, 164
Ibn Hishām, 45, 46, 48, 51, 63
Ibn Isḥāq, 43, 46, 85, 132
Sīra, 46, 48, 51
Ibn Khaldūn, 94, 130–1, 150n7
Ibn Mashīsh al-^c^Alamī, ^c^Abd al-Salām, 121
Ibn Munadhir *see* Muḥammed b. Munadhir
Ibn al-Munkadir, 159
Ibn al-Muqaffa^c^, 191, 192n6
Ibn Qayyim al-Jawziyyah, 122
Ibn Qutayba, 75
Ibn Rushd *see* Averroes
Ibn Sa^c^d, 43
al-Ṭabaqāt al-Kubra, 46, 48, 64, 68, 70
Ibn al-Sammāk, 84
Ibn Sīnā *see* Avicenna, 130
Ibn Taghrībirdī, 186n16
Ibn Taymiyyah, 113, 122, 164, 184n14
Ibn Ṭufayl, 180
Ibrāhīm, Prophet, 71n35
icons, 126, 128–9
idols, 65, 71, 100, 126, 127, 128–9, 185
ijtihād (independent legal reasoning), 4, 9
Ikhwān al-Ṣafā (Brethren of Purity; Brethren of Sincerity), 182
imams, 146, 149n5, 150, 155
immigrants 81
India
centenarians, 91
interpretation of Islam, 128
reform, 28
shrines, 138
inheritence, 79
inquisition *see Miḥna*
intercessors *see* mediators

International Monetary Fund, 13, 195
Iqbal, Sir Muhammad, 187
Iran
  ahl al-ḥaqq (Sufi group), 121
  Shi'ites, 116
  see also Persia
Iraq
  al-Ṭarīqah al-Qādirīyah (Sufi order), 116–17
  Sufism, 101, 102
  Yazidis, 121
  see also Basra
Iraqi School, 119
irhāṣ (wondrous event), 133
Irving, Washington, 59
al-Iṣfahānī, Abū-l-Faraj, 186n16, 191n3
Islam
  conversion to, 101, 103, 129, 144, 153, 160
  influences on, 5, 123–4
  and modernity, 38–9, 178–81
  mysticism in, 103
  opponents of, 23–4
  political, 5–6, 10, 189
  principles of, 177–88
  spread of, 153
"Islamic bloc", 38–9
Islamic State, 95, 101–2
Islamic Studies, 54
isolationists, 32–5
Israelites, 25

al-Jabartī, ᶜAbd al-Raḥmān, 24, 142n32, 170–1, 172–3
Jabrites, 152
Jaᵓfar b. Abū Ṭālib, 131n11
al-Jāḥiz, 8, 182
Jamaat-e-Islami, 19n17
Jamali, Dr Fadhil, 194n9
Jehovah's Witnesses, 33
Jerusalem, 41, 78, 85
Jesus Christ, 15, 44, 45, 108, 129, 154
Jews
  authority figures, 110
  Banū al-Naḍīr tribe, 45
  Banū Qurayza tribe, 50n20
  al-Bīrūnī on, 126
  co-existence, 124
  conversion to Islam, 160
  isolationists, 32
  Pharisees, 124
  proverb concerning, 194n9
  religious polemics with Muslims, 44
  see also Judaism
Jibrīl (Gabriel), 109
jihad, 28, 108, 116, 149
al-Jīlānī, ᶜAbd al-Qādir, 116–17
jilbāb, 180n7
al-Jirjānī, al-Sharīf, 132
jizya (tax), 144n39
Judaism, 33, 129; *see also* Jews
judges, 162
Juha (fictitious character), 194
jurisprudence, 5, 86, 163
jurisprudents, 96, 98
jurists
  and *awliyā*, 130–1
  and al-Badawī, 143
  and caliphs, 155–6, 164–7
  and education, 163
  and *ijtihād*, 96, 98
  and logic, 103
  storytellers compared with, 89
  and Sufism, 105–6, 108, 111
  Sunni, 103, 104, 131
  and tradition, 3, 74, 75–6, 77, 83, 85, 86–7, 97
  worldliness of, 102, 167–8, 172

al-Kalābādhī, Abū Bakr Muḥammad b. Isḥāq, 111
"*karāmāt*" (extraordinary abilities), 122
Kawākibī, ᶜAbd al-Raḥmān, 173
Khaḍra, Shayka, 138

Khālid b. al-Walīd, 16, 18, 136, 148
Khan, Sir Syed Ahmad, 28
Kharijites, 78, 146–9, 150
al-Khaṣṣāf, Abū-Bakr Aḥmad b. ᶜUmar b. Muhayr al-Shaybānī 75
al-Khaṭīb al-Baghdādī, 97n68, 159
al-Khayzurān (Hārūn al-Rashīd's mother), 137
al-Khazraj tribe (Banū Qayla), 72
al-Khazzāz al-Baghdādī, Abū-l-Qāsim al-Junayd b. Muḥammad, 111
Khorasan, 120, 159
Khorasani School, 119
Khawārij, 95, 104, 108
Khyber fort, 132
al-Kindī, Imraᵓul-Qays b. Ḥujr, 83n31
Kishk, Mohamed Galal, 5n10
al-Kūfī, ᶜĀṣim b. Abū-l-Nujūd, 66n26
al-Kufi, Numan b. Thabit *see* Abu Hanifa
Kulthūm b. ᶜAmr al-Aṭābī, 88
Kurds, 121
kuttāb (pl. *kattātīb*) (place of instruction), 162

Lammens, Henri, 55
Lane-Poole, Stanley Edward, 55–6
al-Lāt (goddess), 64n18
law, Indian, 49n18
law, Islamic, 17, 73–4
  abrogation, 94
  aḥādīth foundation of, 96
  applications, 8
  changeability of, 5
  constitutional, 17
  Sharīᶜa, 5, 7, 9, 16–17, 18, 20, 22n28, 102, 103–4, 106, 109, 111, 120, 145–6, 155, 163, 187
  and Sufism, 103
  see also ijtihād; jurisprudence
law, Jewish *see* Talmud; Torah
Le Bon, Charles-Marie Gustave, 59
Levant, 156–7
literature: European, 180–1
love: divine, 109
Lucas, Paul, 141
Lutherans, 123

al-Maᶜarrī, Abū-l-ᶜAlāᵓ, 145
Madani, Abbassi, 21, 21n23
madrassas, 162
al-Magalla al-Thaqafiyya (magazine), 4
Magi, 160
magic, 54, 117n49, 193
Mahdi, 118, 152, 191–7
al-Mahdi, Caliph, 87
al-Mahdi, Shaykh, 171
Maimonides, 3
Majādhī (sing. *majdhūb),* 121
Makḥūl al-Hadhlī, 78
al-Makkī, Muḥammad b. ᶜAlī Abū Ṭālib, 111
Mālik b. Anas b. Mālik ("Imam Malik"), 16, 75n5, 86
Mālik b. Dīnār al-Baṣrī, Abū Yaḥya, 134
al-Malik al-Zāhir Abū Saᶜīd Muḥammad al-ᶜAlāᵓī, Sultan, 143n38
Mālikī Madhhab, 16n8, 86
Mamluks, 124
al-Maᵓmūn, Caliph, 102n2, 155–6, 163, 191n3
Manar al-Islam (magazine), 4
Manāt (goddess), 64n18
al-Manfalūṭī, Muṣṭafa Luṭfī, 178n1
Manicheans, 126
al-Manṣūr, Abu Jafar, Caliph, 135–6, 191
Mansur, Anis, 4
al-Maqrīzī, 138–9
Margoliouth, David Samuel, 55–6
marriage, 99, 118, 180n8; *see also* polygamy
al-Marwah hill, 62n2
Marwān b. al-Ḥakam (Marwān I), 76
al-Marwazī, Abū Ḥāmid, 104
Mary, Mother of God, 129, 133

Ma^cshūq, Shaykh, 137
Maspero, Gaston Camille Charles, 140
Massignon, Louis, 117, 124
materialism, 29
Maududi, Abul A'la, 19
ma^cūna (divine aid), 133
al-Mawṣilī, Isḥāq, 91–2
Maymūna bint al-Ḥārith, 46n13
Mecca
  Black Stone, 131
  merchants, 68–70, 71–2, 152
  pilgrims, 142n34
  Prophet in, 91
  Sufism, 101
  Sūra, 62, 63, 64
mediators, 126–8
Medina, 63, 72, 101, 185
Mehmed V, Sultan, 17
merchants, 152, 159
Miḥna (inquisition), 102, 156, 163–4
militarism, 26–7
miracles, 44–5, 48, 129–30, 131, 133
monasteries, 137
monasticism, 99, 101, 109
monks, 129, 144n39
monotheists *see al-Ḥunafā'*
Montaigne, Michel de, 23
morality, 32, 85, 120, 124
Morocco, 28, 116; *see also* Fez
Mōsheh ben Maymōn: *Guide for the Perplexed* (*dalālat al-ḥā'irīn*), 3
mosques, 77, 78, 161, 162–3
Mount Jawshan, 137
Mu^cāwiya II, Caliph, 76n14
Mu^cāwiya b. Abū Sufyān, Caliph, 136, 207n11
Mubarak, Ali Pasha, 138, 142
Muhammad, Prophet, 3, 23, 99–100, 109, 204–5, 206
  and Abū Lahab, 64
  ascension of al-Safa hill, 61–2
  biographies, 6–7, 37, 43–59
  birthday, 122
  birthplace, 137
  death, 73
  divine message, 74
  family *see ahl al-bayt*
  infallibility, 4–5, 74
  "*khātam al-anbiyā'*" (Seal of the Prophets), 117
  love of cats, 141
  and marriage of widows, 128
  and miracles, 44–5, 48, 129–30, 131
  and al-Muṭ^cim b. ^cAdiy, 72
  personal effects, 136
  Qu'ran collections, 125
  sayings attributed to, 76, 80, 82–3
  succession, 150
  Sufi stories about, 108
  Sufis' union with, 121–2
  traditions ascribed to, 153n12
  and word of God, 109
Muhammad Ali (ruler of Egypt), 167–8, 170–2
Muḥammed b. Munadhir (Ibn Munadhir), 91–2
Muir, Sir William, 50–1, 54, 55, 56
Mukhtār al-Thaqafī rebellion, 151
Müller, Friedrich Max, 106
murīd (student, committed one), 110
murshid (spiritual guide), 110
Muslim b. al-Hajjāj (Imam Muslim), 93
Muslim Brotherhood, 5, 33–4, 194n9
Muslim Empire, 189
Muslims
  converts to Christianity, 100
  emigration to Abyssinia, 69, 100
  isolationist, 32
  non-Arab, 44, 46, 149, 154–5
  and religious doubt, 25
  and terrorism, 14
  and Western civilisation, 27–31
al-Mu^ctaḍ, Caliph, 191n3
al-Mutanabbī, Abū-l-Ṭayyib 'Aḥmad b. al-Ḥusayn, 36, 185, 190
mutashayi^cūn, 46

al-Mu^c^taṣṣim, Caliph, 155, 163, 191n3
al-Mutawakkil ^c^ala Allah, Caliph, 110, 151, 156, 191n3
Mu^c^tazilites, 8, 108, 131, 153–6, 202n2
al-Muṭ^c^im b. ^c^Adiy, 72

al-Nābighah al-Dhubiyānī, 14
al-Nablusī, ^c^Abd al-Ghanī b. Ismā^c^īl, 136
nadhr (*nazr*) (pl. *nudhūr* or *nuzūr*) ("offering" or "spiritual vow"), 139n25
al-Naḍr b. al-Ḥārith, b. ^c^Abd Manāf, 67n31
Naguib, Muhammad, Major General, 19
al-Nakhshabī, Abū-l-Turāb, 139
Naoot, Fatima, 10
al-Nasā'ī, Abū ^c^Abd al-Raḥmān Aḥmad b. ^c^Alī b. Shu^c^ayb b. Baḥr b. Sinān, 75
Nasr, Mohamed Abdullah, 10
Nasser, Gamal Abdel, 19n18, 194n9
al-Nawā, Zāri^c^, 139
al-Nawawī, Abū Zakaria Yaḥya Ibn Sharaf, 94
nazr see *nadhr*
Nile Flood Festival, 143
Noldeke, Theodor, 55–6
Numa Pompilius, 125
al-Nu^c^mān b. al-Mundhir, Nu^c^mān III (Abū Qābūs), 14
al-Nūrī, Abū-l-Ḥusayn Aḥmad b. Muḥammad, 110

October (magazine), 4
oil, 58
Orientalists, 30n19, 48, 50n22, 53, 54–8
Ottoman Empire, 23, 53, 117n50

paganism, 33, 71, 128, 135–6
Pakistan, 19n17
Palestine, 101
palm trees, 45
Pavlov, Ivan Petrovich, 196
People of the Tree, 137n20
Perceval, Jean-Jacques-Antoine Caussin de, 54
Persepolis, 135–6
Persia, 26, 154–5
  mythology, 46, 136
  Nowuz festival, 135–6
  reform, 28
  Shi'ism, 150
Petrus Venerabilis (Peter of Montboissier), 52
Pharisees, 33
philosophers, European, 177–8
piety, 161–2
pigeon racing, 86
pilgrimages, 138, 140; *see also* Hajj
plants: rituals, 141; *see also* trees
Pococke, Richard, 141
poetry, 105
polemics, 165
polygamy, 49
polytheism, 106
Portugal, 119
poverty, 101, 109
prayers, 109, 115n44, 206
preaching *see Da^c^wah*
predetermination, 152, 153
prophets, 133, 205
proselytising *see Da^c^wah*
proverbs, 31, 83, 84, 148n3, 179, 184, 190, 194nn9, 10
public transport, 179–80
punishments, 185; *see also ḥudūd*
Pythagoras, 125

Qadarites, 152
al-Qaeda, 7
al-Qahistānī, Muḥammad b. Muḥammad b. ^c^Abd Allah Nūrbakhsh, 118
al-Qaṣṣāb, Abū-l-^c^Abbas Aḥmad b. Muḥammad, 135
al- Qaṣṣāṣ, Abū Ka^c^b, 88
al-Qastallānī, 132
Qaṭarī b. al-Fujā^c^a, 148

al-Qazwīnī, Abū'Abd Allāh Muḥammad b. Yazīd b. Māja al-Rab'ī (Ibn Māja): *Sunan Ibn Māja*, 82n26
Qibla, 203n4
Qur'an, 48, 73, 109
Chapter 12, 108
Chapter 110, 63
Chapter 111, 61–4
Chapter 112, 84
collection, 125
createdness, 102n2, 146, 154, 155–6
deletions, 79–80
false interpretations, 37, 63–4
French translation, 52
learning, 162n4
legal traditions, 4
Persian translation, 46n11
and science, 49
truth of, 58
Q. 2:48, 129
Q. 2:106, 186
Q. 2:115, 107
Q. 2:172, 99
Q. 2:185, 99
Q. 2:216, 153
Q. 2.106, 154
Q. 3:37, 133
Q. 3:104, 161
Q. 3:110, 62
Q. 3:116, 63
Q. 3:159, 204
Q. 3.159, 17
Q. 4:3, 49n16
Q. 4:34, 206–7
Q. 4:59, 161n1, 205–6
Q. 4:125, 71n35
Q. 4:129, 49n16
Q. 4:133, 177
Q. 4.59, 31n25
Q. 5:27–31, 139n25
Q. 5:119, 107
Q. 5:38, 49n17
Q. 5:44, 33–4, 34n32
Q. 5:83, 107
Q. 5:90, 139n24
Q. 6:50, 86, 130
Q. 6:52, 107
Q. 6:109, 130
Q. 7:32, 99
Q. 7:188, 130
Q. 8:17, 107, 108
Q. 8:19, 63
Q. 9:25, 63
Q. 9:31, 110, 129
Q. 9:100, 119
Q. 10:18, 129
Q. 10:62, 133
Q. 10:63, 133
Q. 12:26, 53n25
Q. 13:7, 130
Q. 13:11, 191n5
Q. 13.11, 25n11
Q. 15:83, 62
Q. 15:84, 62
Q. 16:1, 62
Q. 16:103, 59n58
Q. 17:90, 130
Q: 17:91, 130
Q: 17:92, 130
Q: 17:93, 130
Q. 17.5, 25n10
Q. 18:23, 195n13
Q. 18:24, 115n44, 195n13
Q. 18:49, 171n20
Q. 19:36, 139n25
Q. 19:81, 139n23
Q. 19:82, 139n23
Q. 20:2, 99
Q. 22:78, 99
Q. 23:60, 107
Q. 24:31, 186n16
Q. 25:16, 129
Q. 25:17, 129
Q. 25:28, 80

Q. 26:206, 62
Q. 26:207, 63
Q. 26:214, 61–2
Q. 27:40, 133
Q. 28:10, 192n7
Q. 29:43, 208
Q. 32:16, 109
Q. 33:32, 186n16
Q. 33:33, 186n16
Q. 33:34, 186n16
Q. 33:41, 115n44
Q. 33:53, 186n16
Q. 33:54, 186n16
Q. 33:55, 186n16
Q. 33.59, 185–6
Q. 34:46, 107
Q. 39:53, 63
Q. 40:82, 63
Q. 42.38, 17–18
Q. 45:10, 63
Q. 46:26, 63
Q. 50:16, 104, 107, 125n3
Q. 51:44, 167n15
Q. 51:50, 107
Q. 53:4, 74n3
Q. 54:49, 108
Q. 58:17, 63
Q. 59:5, 45
Q. 63.8, 24
Q. 109.6, 22n27
Q. 111:1, 61, 62, 63
Q. 111:2, 61, 62, 70
Q. 111:3, 61
Q. 111:4, 61, 70
Q. 111:5, 61
see also sūra
Quraysh clan, 64, 67nn28, 29, 67n31, 68–72, 186n16
al-Qushayrī al-Naysābūrī, ᶜAbd al-Karīm b. Hūzān Abū-l-Qāsim, 112
Qutb, Sayyid, 19
In the Shade of the Qur'an, 19–20

rabbis, 110, 129
racial discrimination, 49
al-Rāḍī, Caliph, 167
radicalisation, 10
Radwan, Fathi, 4
Raleigh, Sir Walter, 54
Rasputin, Grigori Yefimovich, 120n62
Ratan b. ᶜAbd Allah (centenarian), 91
reform, 122, 193n8, 197, 199–208
reformers, 28
religion, 30
as a cover, 35
definition of, 125
impact of, 128
political use of, 161
popular, 143–4
rethinking, 36–8
truth of, 206–7
West and, 26–7
see also Christianity; Islam; paganism
religious scholars *see* clergy
Renan, Joseph Ernest, 140
"*riḍā*" (pleasure or satisfaction), 119–20
al-Rifāᶜī, Aḥmad, 117, 118
rites and rituals, 104, 144, 156
Rodinson, Maxime, 55
Roman Empire, 14, 33
roosters, 128
al-Rūmī, Jaᶜfar, 91
al-Rūmī, Mawlānā Jalāl al-Dīn, 117
Ruqaya (daughter of the Prophet), 68
Russia, 173, 179

sacred texts, 125–6; see also Bible; Qur'an
sacrifices, 120n64, 139
Saᶜd b. Abī Waqqās, 24
Saᶜd b. Muᶜādh, 50
al-Ṣādiq, Jaᶜfar, 139
al-Ṣafā, Ikhwān, 182
al-Ṣafā hill, 62

al-Saff āḥ, Abū-l-ᶜAbbās ᶜAbd Allah, 46n12
Ṣaḥāba (Companions of the Prophet), 43, 45, 67, 68, 68n34, 74, 80–1, 99, 115, 132
bayᶜat al-riḍwān (Pledge of the Tree), 137
biographical dictionaries, 47
false *see* centenarians
Sajāḥ bint al-Ḥārith b. Suwayd b. ᶜAqfān, 148n3
Salafism, 113n38
Sale, George, 54
Samson (Biblical character), 15
Sarbatak *see* Harsavardhana
Ṣaᶜṣaᶜah b. Suhān, 207n11
Savonarola, Girolamo, 188
Schopenhauer, Arthur, 124
sciences, 44, 49
sects, 145–57
secularism, 3, 8, 26, 30–1, 168–70, 175
Selim, Shaykh Abdel Moneim, 5n10
sermons, 165
al-Shaᶜbī, ᶜAmir b. Sharāḥīl, 89
al-Shāfiᶜī, Abū ᶜAbdullāh, Muhammad b. Idrīs, 75, 145, 199–200, 206
Shahrbānū, Princess, 150n8
Shalabi, Shaykh Adel Jalil, 5n10
Sham al-Nessim festival, 143
al-Sha'rawi, Shaykh Muhammad Metwali, 20–1
Sharīᶜa see under law, Islamic
Shaṭā (Egypt), 141
Shaṭā, Shaykh, 138
Shawqi, Ahmed, 49n15
al-Shaybānī, Abū ᶜAbd Allāh, 85, 88, 89, 96–7
al-Sayr al-Kabīr, 75
Sheba, Queen of, 133
Shi'ites
and Abū Ṭālib's conversion to Islam, 77
imama (doctrine), 149–51
mutashayiᶜūn, 46
and persecution of Sufis, 116
Twelver, 151–2
see also ghulāt; *mutashayiᶜūn*
shrines, 137–40
Shūra, 18–21, 22
slaves and slavery, 49, 144n39, 187
snake worship, 141–2
social justice, 49
social progress, 181–4
Solomon *see* Sulaymān
Sphinx, 141
Sprenger, Aloys, 54
storytellers, 87–90
succession, 145
Sudan, 118
Sufism, 101–24
awliyāʾ (saints), 104–5
baraka (blessings), 116, 167
Christian influence on, 113
decline, 118–22
foreign influences, 106
ghulāt (extremists), 104n7, 110, 111, 112
as an Islamic practice, 122–4
jurists' war on, 108
orders, 114–18, 121
and poverty, 109
and reform, 107
responses to, 109–11
second phase, 111–14
"Supreme Shaykh", 116
spread of, 101, 102–4
texts, 111–12
women, 117–18
Sufyanids, 76n14
Sukayna bint al-Husayn (the Prophet's great-granddaughter), 186n16
al-Sulamī, Abū ᶜAbd-al-Raḥmān, 112
Sulaymān (Solomon), 133
al-Ṣūlī, Abū Bakr Muḥammad b. Yaḥya: *al-Awrāq*, 167
Sunna (Prophetic Tradition), 7, 16–22, 74–6

Sunnis, 79, 87, 90, 118, 156; *see also under* jurists
sūra, 43–51, 100
  books of, 46–8
  customs and values, 44–5
  effects on West, 48–9
  factual misrepresentation in, 45–6, 67–8
  tenses in, 61–4, 66–7
  Twentieth Century, 49–51
Syria: Sufism, 101, 117n49; *see also* Aleppo; Damascus

al-Ṭabarī, 42, 43, 90
  Tārīkh, 46
tābiᶜūn (followers), 74
taboos, 6
al-Ṭaḥāwī, Aḥmad, 171
al-Ta'if, 72
takfīr ("excommunication"), 7, 34
al-Takfir wa-l-Hijra (Egyptian militant group), 33–4
Takht-e-Jamshid *see* Persepolis
Talmud, 82
Tamīm tribe, 147–8
al-Tamīmī al-Baṣrī, Ghayyāth b. Ibrāhīm (Abū ᶜAbd al-Raḥmān), 87
Tanta (Egypt), 140
al-Tantawi, Shaykh, 138
al-Tanūkhī, Abū ᶜAlī al-Muḥassin, 166
taqiyya (dissimulation), 22
Tatars, 124
al-Tawḥīdī, Abū Ḥayyān, 83, 182
taxation, 144n39
technical knowledge, 26
terrorism, 6, 7, 13–16, 21
al-Thaqafī, al-Mukhtār b. Abū ᶜUbaydah, 151
al-Thawrī, Abū ᶜAbd Allah Sufyān b. Saᶜīd b. Masrūq, 165
Thebes, 141–2
theology, 164
thieves, 49
al-Tijānī, Shaykh Aḥmad, 116n47, 118
al-Tirmidhī, Abū Bakr Muḥammad b. ᶜUmar al-Warrāq (al-Ḥakīm), 134
Torah: Book of Deuteronomy, 3, 50n20, 76
Toynbee, Arnold, 178
traditionists, 85
Treaty of Ḥudaybiyya, 137n20
trees, 45, 138
Tunisia, 116, 121
al-Tunsī, Khayr al-Dīn, 28
turbans, 160
al-Turk, Niqula b.Yusuf, 24n2
Turkey
  reform, 28
  persecution of Sufis, 116
  see also Ottoman Empire
Turks, 124
al-Ṭūsī, Abū Naṣr al-Sarrāj, 111
Tyre, 137

ᶜUbayd Allah b. Jaḥsh, 100
'ulama (sing. *'alim*) (scholars), 163
ᶜUmar b. Abū Rabīᶜa, 12, 105
ᶜUmar b. al-Khaṭṭāb, 18–19, 24, 68n34, 71n35, 73, 79, 80, 109, 125, 131
ᶜUmar Makram, 170, 171, 172, 173
Umayyads, 3, 46, 77–9, 86–7, 102, 148, 150, 151, 153, 161, 162
Umayyah b. Khalaf b. Safwān, 67n29
Umm Jamīl bint Ḥarb (Arwā), 66–7
Umm Kulthūm (daughter of the Prophet), 68, 194n10
Ummayya b. Abū-l-Ṣalt, 71n35
Umrah (pilgrimage), 62n2
United States, 13, 21, 179
universities, 180
ᶜUqba b. Abū Muᶜayiṭ, 67n30
ᶜUrwa b. al-Zubayr b. al-Awwām, 43
Usāma b. Munqidh, Prince (al-Muᵓayyad), 24
ᶜUtayba (son of Abū Lahab), 68

ᶜUtba (son of Abū Lahab), 68
ᶜUthmān b. ᶜAff ān, Caliph, 67–8, 79, 80, 162
ᶜUthmān b. al-Ḥuwayrith, 100
ᶜUthmān b. al-Khaṭṭāb, 90
ᶜUthmān b. Maẓᶜūn, 100
al-ᶜUzzā (goddess), 64n18

Vali, Haji Bektash, 118n53

Wahhabis, 108, 113, 116, 131
al-Wāqidī, 43, 46, 48, 50, 136
Waraqa b. Nawfal, 100
al-Warrāq al-Tirmidhī, Abū Bakr Muḥammad b. ᶜUmar (al-Ḥakīm), 134–5
wars, 50, 51, 148
al-Wāthiq, Caliph, 155, 163
Watt, William Montgomery, 57–8
Weil, Gustav, 54
Wellhausen, Julius, 55–6
Western civilisation, 23–4, 25–31, 177–8, 182
  effect on *Sira* writing, 48–9
  Egypt, 167–8
  as a model for Islam, 38, 39, 188
women
  behaviour, 32, 179
  emancipation, 179
  linked to fools, 139
  and marriage, 180n8
  rites and rituals, 120n64, 138, 140
  status, 48, 49, 82
  Sufi, 117–18, 159
  taxation, 144n39
  veil wearing, 121n66, 178, 185, 186n16
  widows, 128
World Bank, 13
Wustenfeld, Heinrich Ferdinand, 54

Yaḥya b. Maᶜīn, 88
Yaḥya b. ᶜUqb, 139
Yazdegerd III, Emperor, 150
Yazīd I, Caliph, 77n16
Yazīd b. Hārūn, 96
Yazīd b. Mu'awiya, Caliph, 121
Yazidis, 121
al-Yāzijī, Ibrāhīm, 178n2
Yemen, 101, 156

Zāhirīs, 108
al-Zarqānī, Muḥammad b. ᶜAbd al-Bāqī, 17
Zayd b. al-Ḥāritha, 67
Zayd b. ᶜAmr b. Nufayl, 71n35, 100
Zayd b. Thābit, 68
Zaydis, 156
Zaynab bint Jaḥsh, 67n32
Ziyād b. ᶜAbd Allah, 82
Zoroastrians, 25n9
al-Zuhrī, Muḥammad b. Muslim b. ᶜUbayd Allah b. Shihāb, 43, 77–8
Zuqāq al-Mazār, 139

EU representative:
Easy Access System Europe
Mustamäe tee 50, 10621 Tallinn, Estonia
Gpsr.requests@easproject.com

www.ingramcontent.com/pod-product-compliance
Lightning Source LLC
Chambersburg PA
CBHW071839230426
43671CB00012B/2009
* 9 7 8 1 4 7 4 4 3 7 0 8 0 *